COUNTERINSURGENCY

COUNTERINSURGENCY

DAVID J. KILCULLEN

OXFORD

UNIVERSITY PRESS

2010

OXFORD
UNIVERSITY PRESS

Oxford University Press, Inc., publishes works that further
Oxford University's objective of excellence
in research, scholarship, and education.

Oxford   New York
Auckland   Cape Town   Dar es Salaam   Hong Kong   Karachi
Kuala Lumpur   Madrid   Melbourne   Mexico City   Nairobi
New Delhi   Shanghai   Taipei   Toronto

With offices in
Argentina   Austria   Brazil   Chile   Czech Republic   France   Greece
Guatemala   Hungary   Italy   Japan   Poland   Portugal   Singapore
South Korea   Switzerland   Thailand   Turkey   Ukraine   Vietnam

Published in North America by Oxford University Press, Inc.
198 Madison Avenue, New York, New York 10016

Published in the United Kingdom in 2010
by C. Hurst & Co. (Publishers) Ltd.

www.oup.com

Oxford is a registered trademark of Oxford University Press.

Library of Congress Cataloging-in-Publication Data
Kilcullen, David.
    Counterinsurgency / by David Kilcullen.
        p.   cm.
Includes bibliographical references and indexes.
ISBN 978-0-19-973748-2; 978-0-19-973749-9 (pbk.)
1. Counterinsurgency.   2. Military policy.   3. Terrorism—Prevention.
4. United States—Military policy.   I. Title.
    U241.K55 2010
    355.02'18—dc22   2010001496

9   8   7   6   5   4   3   2   1

Printed in the United States of America
on acid-free paper

For Dave Dilegge and Bill Nagle, founders and editors of *Small Wars Journal*. They gave the counterguerrilla underground a home, at a time when misguided leaders banned even the word "insurgency," though busily losing to one. Scholars, warriors, and agitators, Dave and Bill laid the foundation for battlefield success: our generation owes them a debt of gratitude.

CONTENTS

PREFACE

This book is intended for counterinsurgents—civilian and military students and practitioners of counterinsurgency—and for the general reader interested in understanding today's conflict environment, of which insurgency forms an enduring part. It presents a selection of my work, written mainly in the field during the conflicts in Afghanistan, Iraq, and elsewhere, and presented here for the first time as a unified body of thought. Some papers appear here for the first time. Others, previously published, have been newly annotated or revised. I have included within the chapters "author's notes" with information updated as of December 2009.

This is a snapshot of wartime thinking, part of a much larger body of work. It developed on the fly, in breaks between periods of intense operational or diplomatic effort, or as opportunity presented itself in the field. Rather than retrospectively tidy things up, I have tried to reflect honestly the way my views, like those of all of us in the new counterinsurgency era, evolved as we adapted to a fast-moving situation. But where time or events have disproved a theory, or where in hindsight an insight seems to me superficial or dated, I have said so.

Insurgency is the most widespread form of warfare today. Indeed, though military establishments persist in regarding it as "irregular" or "unconventional," guerrilla war has been the commonest of conflicts throughout history, occurring in one variety or another in almost all known societies.[1] In the modern era, the Correlates of War Project,[2] a scholarly database maintained since 1963, identifies 464 wars that occurred between 1816 and the end of the twentieth century, of which only 79 (17 percent) were "conventional" interstate conflicts between the regular armed forces of nation-states, while 385 (just under 83 percent of recorded conflicts) were civil wars or insurgencies.[3]

Insurgency, therefore, is irregular not in the sense that it is uncommon—it is exactly the opposite—but in the literal sense that it is "against the rules." And since these rules are set by nation-states and their military establishments, this form of war is, always has been, and is likely to remain the preferred choice for nonstate armed groups and others who have nothing to gain from playing by rules established to favor their adversaries.

For soldiers, diplomats, development professionals, policy-makers, scholars, and informed citizens in Western democracies, therefore, understanding the preferred way of war of our likely adversaries—mastering its techniques, pitfalls, and lessons—is, and will remain for the foreseeable future, a vital activity.

This book is far from a definitive study on this ancient subject about which so much has already been written. It is merely an incomplete selection of tentative, still-developing thoughts, from a practitioner's perspective, on the guerrilla wars we are currently fighting. I hope that other practitioners and students will find in it much to agree and to disagree with, and that it will thereby form part of a continuing critical debate.

Finally, the views expressed in this book are the author's personal judgments. They do not represent the policy of any organization, government, or other institution.

COUNTERINSURGENCY

Introduction

Understanding Insurgency and Counterinsurgency

An "insurgency," according to the current U.S. military field manual on the subject, is "an organized movement aimed at the overthrow of a constituted government through the use of subversion and armed conflict.... Stated another way, an insurgency is an organized, protracted politico-military struggle designed to weaken the control and legitimacy of an established government, occupying power, or other political authority while increasing insurgent control."[1] The same field manual defines "counterinsurgency" as the "military, paramilitary, political, economic, psychological, and civic actions taken by a government to defeat insurgency."[2] "Counterinsurgency," therefore, is an umbrella term that describes the complete range of measures that governments take to defeat insurgencies. These measures may be political, administrative, military, economic, psychological, or informational, and are almost always used in combination.

Importantly, the precise approach any particular government takes to defeat an insurgency depends very much on the character of that government, making counterinsurgency, at its heart, a form of opposed or contested governance, albeit a hideously violent one. Insurgencies, like cancers, exist in thousands of forms, and there are dozens of techniques to treat them, hundreds of different populations in which they occur, and several major schools of thought on how best to deal with them. The idea that there is one single "silver bullet" panacea for insurgency is therefore as unrealistic as the idea of a universal cure for cancer.

Indeed, if you cut the qualifying adjectives out of the field manual's definition of counterinsurgency, you are left only with "actions taken by a government to defeat insurgency." This truncated definition shows that there is no template, no single set of techniques, for countering insurgencies. Counterinsurgency is, simply, whatever governments do to defeat rebellions. Thus, the character of any particular conflict is impossible to understand without reference to three defining factors: the nature of the insurgency being countered, the nature of the government being supported, and the environment—especially the human environment—in which the conflict takes place.

THE STRUGGLE TO ADAPT

In all war, but particularly in counterinsurgency, this environment is in flux. All sides engage in an extremely rapid, complex, and continuous process of competitive adaptation. Insurgents and terrorists evolve rapidly in response to countermeasures, so that what works once may not work again, and insights that are valid for one area or one period may not apply elsewhere. In many insurgency environments, rapid, large-scale social change may also be occurring: mass population movement, ethnic or sectarian "cleansing," flight of refugees and displaced persons, social revolution, or even genocide may be occurring alongside the guerrilla conflict itself. Thus, the imperative is to understand each environment, in real time, in detail, in its own terms, in ways that would be understood by the locals—and not by analogy with some other conflict, some earlier war, or some universal template or standardized rule-set.

This means that the whole art of counterinsurgency is to develop specific measures, tailored to the environment, to suppress a particular insurgency and strengthen the resilience of a particular threatened society and government. And these measures must be developed quickly enough to deal with an insurgency that is itself evolving, in time to maintain the confidence of a domestic and international public. Thus counterinsurgency is at heart an adaptation battle: a struggle to rapidly develop and learn new techniques and apply them in a fast-moving, high-threat environment, bringing them to bear before the enemy can evolve in response, and rapidly changing them as the environment shifts.

This makes organizational learning and adaptation critical success factors. David Morris, a writer and former Marine, had this to say about institutional knowledge and organizational learning during the war in Iraq:

> On the wall of the quarters I shared with a Marine lieutenant in Ramadi there was a large metal wipeboard and every morning before I went out into the city on patrol I would study it. The lieutenant had inherited it from the previous occupant and covering its every square inch was the collected wisdom of the Occupation, written in a fragmented, aphoristic style.... It was mid-2006 now and a lot of the truisms on the board either were outdated or had been reversed by events. Lessons had been learned, some too late.... I thought about all the aphorisms written on the board. In theory, each lesson represented a life. In order to know that driving on dirt roads in Ramadi was dangerous, you had to have an IED (improvised explosive device) go off in your face. Before you started draping camouflage netting over the gunner's turret atop a Humvee, you had to lose a gunner to a sniper. In order to learn the lesson, you had to lose somebody.[3]

Indeed, if this book has a central theme, it is that our knowledge of counterinsurgency is never static, always evolving. This is partly because we can never know more than a tiny amount about the complex environment in which we operate, partly because of the observer effect whereby our attempts to understand and deal with that environment inevitably alter it, and partly because the environment changes so rapidly that even if we *could* know it fully, our knowledge would be a mere snapshot that would be immediately out of date.

The Two Fundamentals: Local Solutions, Respect for Noncombatants

Despite the ground-level complexity, at a higher level of abstraction, some fundamentals do seem to apply throughout this type of warfare. These fundamentals are few—I count only two—and they are very simple to express but extremely difficult to act upon. The first is to understand in detail what drives the conflict in any given area or with any given population group. This implies the need to constantly update that understanding as the environment shifts, to develop solid partnerships with reliable local allies, to design, in concert with those allies, locally tailored measures to target the drivers that sustain the conflict and thus to break the cycle of violence.

The second is to act with respect for local people, putting the well-being of noncombatant civilians ahead of any other consideration, even— in fact, especially—ahead of killing the enemy. Convincing threatened populations that we are the winning side, developing genuine partnerships with them, demonstrating that we can protect them from the guerrillas and that their best interests are served by cooperating with us is the critical path in counterinsurgency, because insurgents cannot operate without the support—active, passive, or enforced—of the local population.

Even if we are killing the insurgents effectively, if our approach also frightens and harms the local population, or makes people feel unsafe, then there is next to no chance that we will gain their support. If we want people to partner with us, put their weapons down, and return to unarmed political dialogue rather than work out their issues through violence, then we must make them feel safe enough to do so, and we must convince them they have more to gain by talking than by fighting. Consequently, violence against noncombatant civilians by security forces, whether intentional or accidental, is almost always entirely counterproductive. Besides being simply the right thing to do, protecting and defending local noncombatant civilians is a critical component of making them feel safe, and is thus one of the keys to operational success.

But make no mistake: counterinsurgency is war, and war is inherently violent. Killing the enemy is, and always will be, a key part of guerrilla warfare. Some insurgents at the irreconcilable extremes simply cannot be co-opted or won over; they must be hunted down, killed, or captured, and this is necessarily a ruthless process conducted with the utmost energy that the laws of war permit. In Iraq and Afghanistan since 9/11, we have experienced major success against terrorists and insurgent groups through a rapid twenty-four-hour cycle of intelligence-led strikes, described as "counternetwork operations," that focuses on the middle tier of planners, facilitators, and operators rather on the most senior leaders. This cycle, known as "Find, Fix, Finish, Exploit, Assess" (F3EA) has proven highly successful in taking networks apart, and convincing senior enemy figures that they simply cannot achieve their objectives by continued fighting.[4] This approach fuses operations and intelligence and, though costly and resource intensive, can generate a lethal momentum that causes insurgent networks to collapse catastrophically.

But successful counterinsurgents also discriminate with extreme precision between reconcilables and irreconcilables, combatants and noncombatants. They kill only those active, irreconcilable combatants who must be killed or captured, and where possible they avoid making more insurgents in the process. They protect those people (often the majority) who simply want to survive the conflict, and they make it as easy as possible to leave or oppose the insurgency, and as hard as possible to stay in or support it. Scrupulously moral conduct, alongside political legitimacy and respect for the rule of law, are thus operational imperatives: they enable victory, and in their absence no amount of killing—not even genocidal brutality, as in the case of Nazi antipartisan warfare, described below—can avert defeat.

Counterinsurgency Mirrors the State

Some armchair chicken hawks (none with experience of actual warfare in any form, let alone against real guerrillas) have argued that, contrary to recent evidence, you can indeed kill your way out of an insurgency, and have even suggested that an intensely brutal and violent approach is the quickest and best way to suppress an insurgency. Two favorite examples are the Romans and the Nazis, who supposedly ignored the "politically correct" notions of modern counterinsurgency and applied mass brutality with great success.

Unfortunately for this way of thinking, the facts simply do not support it. As the historian Ben Shepherd has shown in his recent study of Wehrmacht security divisions on the Eastern Front, German commanders faced resistance warfare and partisan warfare along with a widespread popular uprising in large parts of the occupied East. Many commanders recognized the need to protect, win over, and cooperate with the population and to treat them with respect and consideration in order to reduce support for the insurgents. As Shepherd demonstrates through an exhaustive study of regimental and division-level operations by the 221st Security Division of Army Group Center, "numerous Eastern Army figures already [in 1941] saw the potential for support in a tentatively pro-German population. They also saw the need for a more sensible, measured prosecution of occupation and security policy in order to exploit it."[5] This led some units all of the time, and most units some of the time, to engage in population-security, hearts-and-minds, and civic-action operations that would be familiar to any modern counterinsurgent. Colonel Reinhard Gehlen wrote that "if the population rejects the partisans and lends its full support to the struggle against them, no partisan problem will exist"[6]—a classic statement of population-centric counterinsurgency theory.

According to most historical studies, far from helping win the antipartisan campaign, brutality and violence against local populations was a key reason for the German defeat. Although local commanders had a sound understanding of the operational techniques of counterinsurgency, their efforts were constantly undermined at the level of policy and strategy by the exploitative, rapacious, and genocidal nature of the Nazi state. Not only did the extermination policies pursued by SS battalions and special troops continuously undermine the efforts of local commanders to cultivate relationships with the population but also, as Shepherd shows, "the effectiveness of all these efforts was blunted by the fact that they never posed a fundamental challenge to ruthless economic interests [which led the Germans to despoil the East, leaving the population starving and destroying the economy] or to racist preconceptions of the population [which contributed to mass murder of noncombatants]...the ruthless, ideological, and exploitative dynamic of Nazi occupation policy in the east, then, proved an implacable obstacle" to effective counterinsurgency.[7] In Walter Laqueur's words, "the partisan leaders...would have found it much more difficult to attract recruits had the Germans treated the population decently, but this would have been quite incompatible...with the character of the Nazi leaders, their doctrine, and their aims."[8]

Some might argue that Nazi measures were, on the contrary, highly effective in achieving short-term operational aims, whatever their immoral basis and whatever the ultimate outcome of the war, which the Germans lost of course in large part through the failure of their conquest and occupation of the East. For example, Mark Mazower's recent study of German imperium in the East, *Hitler's Empire: How the Nazis Ruled Europe*, emphasizes the long-term influence of German occupation policies, and the fact that many occupied populations mounted little resistance until the Germans were clearly beaten, only then turning against the withdrawing Wehrmacht.[9] Still, it seems clear that whatever its commanders' technical skill in counterguerrilla operations, the Nazi state never seriously sought to gain the support of occupied populations, nor could it do so without changing its own fundamental nature. Robert M. Citino, a distinguished military historian of the German army and author of *The German Way of War* (2005) and *Death of the Wehrmacht* (2007), concurs with this judgment.[10]

The Romans, also, are a more complicated case than caricature would suggest. Roman commanders were indeed capable of ruthless violence against enemy populations, and they were extremely harsh toward mutineers and rebels, to deter others. Roman commanders used violence in a targeted and politically calculated way, however, to support broader objectives, and the peaceful inclusion of conquered peoples into the empire, wherever possible, was a key objective. Roman law; Roman roads; administrative systems, taxation and revenue systems; a set of carefully constructed measures to Latinize subject peoples; and the extensive use of local allies and auxiliaries were all favorite Roman techniques, emphasizing the nonmilitary and nonlethal elements of the empire's security system. Importantly, as well as being largely nonlethal, this system for much of its existence was a system of inclusive security, whereby opponents could gain entry to Roman prosperity and order by adopting certain behavioral norms and subscribing to Roman authority.

Thus, not only is the "kill them all" approach to counterinsurgency demonstrably counterproductive, but it turns out that the examples often favorably cited by its advocates—examples of the Romans and the Nazis—do not hold up under close scrutiny. All successful counterinsurgents have been willing and able to kill the enemy, often with great ruthlessness. But all have clearly distinguished that enemy from the population in which it hides, have applied violence as precisely and carefully as possible, have acted scrupulously within the law, and have emphasized measures to protect and win over the population.

The reason for this is simple, and it derives from two very distinctive features of insurgent movements: that they rely on local populations, and that while guerrillas are fluid, populations are fixed.

The center of gravity of an insurgent movement—the source of power from which it derives its morale, its physical strength, its freedom of action, and its will to act—is its connectivity with the local population in a given area.[11] Insurgents tend to ride and manipulate a social wave

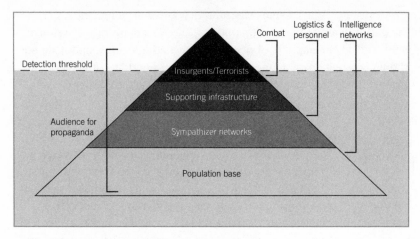

FIG I.1   Surface and Subsurface Elements of an Insurgency

of grievances, often legitimate ones, and they draw their fighting power from their connection to a mass base. This mass base is largely undetectable to counterinsurgents, since it lies below the surface and engages in no armed activity (see fig. I.1).

Insurgents need the people to act in certain ways (sympathy, acquiescence, silence, reaction to provocation, or fully active support) in order to survive and further their strategy. Unless the population acts in these ways, insurgent networks tend to wither because they cannot move freely within the population, gather resources (money, recruits), or conduct their operations. Insurgents do not necessarily need the active support of the population: they can get by on intimidation and passive acquiescence for a time, as long as they have an external (perhaps global) source of support and as long as the government does not cut off their access to the population. But without access to a mass base, an insurgent movement suffocates, so cutting the insurgent off from the population is a critical task in counterinsurgency.

Doing this by attacking the insurgents directly, however, is fraught with difficulty because guerrilla forces are fluid. As Roger Trinquier points out, "we attack an enemy who is invisible, fluid, uncatchable."[12] Unlike conventional military forces, which are tied to fixed installations, lines of communication, and key points (cities, vulnerable economic assets or utilities, government offices, and so on) that must be defended, a guerrilla force has no permanent installations it needs to defend, and can always run away to fight another day. T. E. Lawrence expressed this neatly from the insurgent's point of view:

> [The area threatened by the Arab Revolt was] perhaps 140,000 square miles. How would the Turks defend all that—no doubt by a trench line across the bottom, if the Arabs were an army attacking with banners displayed...but suppose they were an influence, a thing invulnerable, intangible, without front or back, drifting about like a gas? Armies were like plants, immobile as a whole, firm-rooted, nourished through long stems to the head. The Arabs might be a vapour, blowing where they listed.... The Turks would need 600,000 men to meet the combined ill wills of all the local Arab people. They had 100,000 men available. It seemed that the assets in this sphere were with the Arabs, and climate, railways, deserts, technical weapons could also be attached to their interests.[13]

Like any opponent in any war, an insurgent enemy needs to be pinned against an immovable object and "fixed" in order to be destroyed. As both Lawrence and Trinquier point out, insurgent enemies are extraordinarily difficult to fix because of their lack of reliance on fixed positions or strongpoints. This means that enemy-focused strategy, which seeks to attack the guerrilla forces directly, risks dissipating effort in chasing insurgent groups all over the countryside, an activity that can be extremely demanding and requires enormous numbers of troops and other resources. Counterinsurgents who adopt this approach risk chasing their tails and so exhausting themselves, while doing enormous damage to the noncombatant civilian population, alienating the people and thus further strengthening their support for insurgency. This, indeed, is precisely the trap we fell into in Iraq in 2003–4, and in Afghanistan until much more recently. Being fluid, the insurgents could control their loss rate and therefore could never be eradicated by purely enemy-centric means: they could just go to ground and wait us out.

But even though insurgents have no permanent *physical* strongpoints, no physical "decisive terrain" in military terms, they do have a fixed point they must defend: their need to maintain connectivity with the population. This is not a physical piece of real estate, but in functional—or rather, *political*—terms, it fulfils the same purpose as decisive terrain, and it therefore provides an immovable object against which we can maneuver to pin the enemy. Because the insurgent network needs the population to act in certain ways in order to survive, we can asphyxiate the network by cutting the insurgents off from the people. And they cannot simply "go quiet" to avoid that threat. They must either emerge into the open, where we can destroy them using superior numbers and firepower, or stay quiet, accept permanent marginalization from their former population base, and suffocate. This puts the insurgents on the horns of a lethal dilemma.

And the population, unlike insurgents who are extremely difficult to find, is both fixed and easily identifiable, because people are tied to their homes, businesses, farms, tribal areas, relatives, traditional landholdings, and so on. This opens up an alternative method of operating, because protecting the population and cutting its connectivity with the insurgent movement is doable, even though destroying the enemy is not. We can drive the insurgents away from the population, and then introduce local security forces, protective measures, governance reforms, and economic and political development, all designed to break the connection between the insurgents and the population, undermine the insurgents' mass base, and thereby "hardwire" the enemy out of the environment—excluding them permanently and preventing their return.

Again, in practice, this population-centric approach often involves as much fighting, if not more, than an enemy-centric approach, because putting in place effective population protection forces the enemy to come to us, so that we fight the guerrillas on our terms, not on theirs. Ironically, an effective population-centric strategy usually results in far greater losses to the enemy—in terms of insurgents killed, wounded, captured, surrendered, or defected—than does a superficially more aggressive enemy-centric approach.

Counterinsurgency Mirrors the State

The broader point, however, is that counterinsurgency mirrors the state: any state's approach to counterinsurgency depends to a large extent on the nature of that state, and the word "counterinsurgency" can mean entirely different things depending on the character of the government involved. Oppressive governments tend to enact brutal measures against rebellions, and military dictatorships tend to favor paternalistic or reactionary martial law policies, while liberal-democratic states tend to be quick—often too quick—to hand over control to locally elected civilians in a bid to return to "normalcy." To see this, one need only compare the extremely brutal approach taken by Syria's president Hafez al-Assad in crushing the Hama rebellion in 1980 or by Saddam Hussein in massacring Kurdish civilians at Halabja in 1989 with British policy in Northern Ireland—characterized by civil primacy, a focus on policing, intelligence and special operations forces, and restrained military operations under a rule-of-law framework derived from temporary emergency regulations. Different states counter insurgencies differently, and just as in any other area of government policy, the nature of a state determines to a large extent the methods it chooses.

It also follows that there is a difference between the behaviors a given government is likely to adopt when countering an insurgency in its own territory ("domestic" counterinsurgency) and the behaviors that government may adopt while intervening in another country, or in one of its own overseas territories or colonies ("expeditionary" or third-country counterinsurgency). As the counterinsurgency expert Erin Simpson has shown, the theory that democracies are less effective than autocracies in maintaining long-term counterinsurgency efforts is unsupported by the facts. Rather, the evidence she cites suggests that both democracies and autocracies do poorly when operating overseas, while both do better when operating in home territory.[14]

There seem to be two main reasons for this. First, the challenge of understanding someone else's country, securing it, and building viable local allies is vastly greater than operating on home ground in one's own country. Compare the difficulty for, say, the New York Police Department in policing New York City with the difficulties Iraqis would face were Iraq to invade the United States and attempt the same thing. Quite apart from the logistical and political challenges of expeditionary warfare, or the adaptation challenge for soldiers suddenly engaged in unfamiliar policing tasks, the sheer difficulty in understanding such an alien environment, and convincing enough locals to support the effort, poses immense problems—even before adding any organized opposition into the mix. Coalition forces faced the same daunting problems in securing Baghdad that Iraqis would have faced in New York, along with a determined and ruthless adversary in the complex Iraqi insurgent network, as well as the political and operational problems of coalition warfare. No wonder we had a few problems.

Second, counterinsurgency, like all forms of war, is fought with an eye on postconflict power structures, with each side seeking to maximize its long-term interests as the country emerges from violence. As the British strategist and general J. F. C. Fuller remarked, channeling Saint Augustine, the object of war is not victory but a better peace[15]—"better" in the sense of being more secure, prosperous, or advantageous for any given side. All sides in the conflict are fighting not just to win but to own the peace, and in counterinsurgency, an expeditionary force fights at a critical disadvantage because everybody—allies and opponents alike—knows it will leave once the fighting ends, making it by definition an unreliable long-term or postconflict ally. This gives the insurgents a "longevity advantage"; unlike expeditionary counterinsurgents, they are local and indigenous, they *will* be present after the war ends, and once again everybody knows this. The insurgents can threaten the local population with lethal consequences for cooperating with the counterinsurgents, and unless an external intervener makes extremely strenuous efforts to establish viable long-term alliances with legitimate indigenous partners—who, like the insurgents, will remain once the war ends—then it is extremely difficult to overcome this inherent insurgent advantage.

Further, in a third-country counterinsurgency there are at least two states, and at least two governments, involved: the government of the host nation in whose territory the campaign is being conducted and the intervening government providing assistance (sought or unsought) to that government. And since, as we have seen, counterinsurgency mirrors the state, in building or reinforcing a host nation-state to fight an insurgency, it therefore becomes essential for counterinsurgency strategists to ask themselves certain key questions about the nature of the local state. These include:

What kind of state are we trying to build or assist?

How compatible is the local government's character with our own?

What kinds of states have proven viable in the past, in this country and with this population?

What evidence is there that the kind of state we are trying to build will be viable here?

The fact that we, as an international community, failed to effectively ask or answer these questions at the beginning of our interventions in Iraq or Afghanistan may explain many of our subsequent problems. As these wars have continued over much of the past decade, however, civilian and military practitioners in the field have learned or relearned a great deal about effective counterinsurgency. My hope is that this brief selection of work on counterinsurgency will help that learning process.

PART 1

A GROUND-LEVEL PERSPECTIVE

Introduction to the Expanded and Annotated "Twenty-eight Articles"

The chapter that follows began as a response to the frustration of front-line soldiers, junior officers, and noncommissioned officers with the wars they were fighting in Iraq and Afghanistan, along with my own frustration at our need to clearly explain what we wanted our civilian and military teams to do, in a complex environment on the ground.

The chapter is best understood in the context of the period when it was written in early 2006, a time of rapid change within the U.S. military, the foreign service, the intelligence community, the U.S. Agency for International Development, and other departments—like the departments of Homeland Security, Justice, and Agriculture—which were struggling to adapt to the new conditions.

THE NEW COUNTERINSURGENCY MANUAL

The most important initiative of this period was the writing of the new Army and Marine Corps counterinsurgency manual, *Counterinsurgency* (FM 3–24) which was put together by a writing team led by West Point history professor Conrad Crane, under the direction of Army general David Petraeus and Marine Corps general James Mattis.

As an Army and Marine Corps collaborative effort, this manual's writing process was unprecedented at that time. Rigorous review involving practitioners, academics, diplomats, aid officials, intelligence officers, human rights experts, lawyers, and journalists was inflicted on the manual. Its scope—philosophy, politics, strategy, history, minor tactics, administration—was panoramic.

Some sections read more like a meditation on counterinsurgency than a how-to handbook. This was the first U.S. military manual with an annotated bibliography. It was downloaded more than six hundred thousand times within twenty-four hours of appearing on the Internet.

I was in Baghdad when I finished reading the first draft of the manual. It was February 2006, the week after the Samarra mosque bombing transformed the war. For many Coalition civilians in Baghdad the fighting seemed distant then, somehow "offstage": lots of people were getting killed, but you rarely experienced an incident firsthand and, apart from the occasional mortar attack, if you tried very, very hard you could pretend things were almost normal. Oily black car-bomb smoke drifted over Baghdad, and we moved between the capital and other towns by Blackhawk. Scarcely a police or army checkpoint was visible as the flat-roofed villages scrolled beneath our boots out the wide-open helicopter doors, each roof with its satellite dish tuned to al-Jazeera or al-Arabiya. The clock was ticking then, in the last hours before the storm of sectarian violence that tore the country apart through the rest of 2006 and into 2007.

In late March, back in my cluttered second-floor room in the Counterterrorism Office at the State Department, I was approached by Marine Corps captain Scott Cuomo on behalf of a small group of Marine Corps and Army officers who were engaged in writing the *Small-Unit Operations Guide*, a companion piece to the new field manual, designed to give junior commanders a set of tactics, techniques, and procedures for counterinsurgency.

Scott, who was an instructor at The Basic School at the enormous Marine Corps base at Quantico, Virginia, was a talented and experienced officer who graduated from the Naval Academy in 2001 and, like his whole generation of the Army and Marine Corps, was thrown straight into the war, commanding an infantry platoon in Iraq from the end of 2002 until 2005. (At the time of writing he is commanding Fox Company, Second Battalion, Second Marines in Helmand Province in Afghanistan.) On this day he had struggled through ninety minutes of rainy rush-hour traffic to Foggy Bottom to get to my office, to express the general frustration shared by a lot of his peers: "The Field Manual tells us what to achieve, but not what to do. It lays out the theory, but we need practical advice at company level. Can you help us think it through?"

BOTTOM-UP TACTICAL INNOVATION

It is important to remember that by this time, more than four years into the war in Afghanistan and three years into Iraq, tactical commanders like Scott were already much more experienced in the realities of counterinsurgency warfare than most senior officers, or academic counterinsurgency "experts." The junior commanders had fought through that first, chaotic period in Iraq and Afghanistan, living through the difficult time in 2003–4 when field operators realized clearly that they were in a counterinsurgency fight, but for political reasons (a desire not to legitimize the enemy) and through institutional inertia, the Defense Department refused to recognize this. Senior commanders would not even use the words "insurgency" or "counterinsurgency."

Many junior officers realized early that the way they had been trained to fight was not going to work in this environment, and that their institutions and the older generation of leaders did not have the answers they needed. So they had begun—on their own initiative—looking to past doctrine and experience of counterinsurgency to fill the gap. But to these field operators, many of the prescriptions laid out in classical counterinsurgency literature, or in interim doctrinal publications such as the October 2004 interim field manual *Counterinsurgency Operations* seemed unrealistic, outdated, or hard to apply in places like Fallujah, Ramadi, or the Bermel Valley.[1]

Senior officers—everybody from the rank of Major upward at this time—had grown up on a diet of Cold War exercises with a focus on "conventional" (i.e., state-on-state, force-on-force) warfare against the Soviets, leavened by the extremely brief and successful hundred-hour ground campaign during the first Gulf War of 1990–91. Some had gained extremely valuable experience in peace operations in Somalia, the Balkans, East Timor, Liberia, and Sierra Leone during the 1990s. As Dr. Janine Davidson shows in her definitive study of military organizational learning in the 1990s, *Lifting the Fog of Peace: How Americans Learned to Fight Modern War*,[2] commanders applied this knowledge to their new environment in Iraq and Afghanistan with excellent effect in some cases. But as she convincingly demonstrates, these were ad hoc adaptations, unsupported—indeed, sometimes actively undermined—by existing institutions and senior officials, and applied in a patchy, inconsistent manner that was largely determined by the outlook and experience of individual commanders and units.

But the military as an institution had also learned how to learn, and this turned out to be critically important. The Army had established training facilities like the National Training Center and the Joint Readiness Training Centers where units were tested in dynamic, unforgiving, two-sided exercises, and had created processes like the Lessons Learned system and the After-Action Review, which encouraged radically honest criticism and self-criticism. As *The Fog of Peace* shows, even before the outbreak of war in Afghanistan and Iraq, this had done a huge amount to give Soldiers and Marines the tools to learn from their experiences and adapt quickly when the time came.

Doctrine—the body of institutional knowledge captured in military field manuals—was and is a critical part of this toolkit. To the casual observer, field manuals can seem like straightforward descriptions of what happens in battle, along with authoritative guidance on how military forces operate. But their primary organizational function is actually as adaptation and acculturation tools. Doctrine is not only an idealized description of how things are done but also an attempt to inculcate habits of mind and action that change organizational culture and behavior. It is an institutional rudder that helps turn the enormous bureaucracies it informs. As such—and this gives field manuals their fascination for literary, cultural, and political analysts—field manuals say less about how a given military force *actually* behaves than about how it *wants* to behave, and the direction in which its leaders (or a faction within its officer corps) are pushing it.

This matters because, as discussed already, in counterinsurgency success depends on adaptability in the face of a rapidly evolving insurgent threat and a changing environment. Armies that successfully "read" this environment and adapt—using tools like field manuals—are more apt to succeed.[3] Of course, this is not unique to counterinsurgency. *The Dynamics of Doctrine*, Timothy Lupfer's study of German tactical adaptation on the Western Front, written in the early 1980s, emphasizes the role of manuals and training notes in helping armies adapt under the intense pressure of combat.[4] And it is intense: during a tour in command of training efforts in Iraq in 2004, General Petraeus likened building the Iraqi army to constructing an aircraft in flight—while being shot at.

THE COUNTERINSURGENCY MOVEMENT: COMING TO GRIPS WITH A DEEPENING WAR

Thus, in early 2006, the U.S. military was going through a concentrated period of adaptation and change. A group of intelligent and combat-experienced junior officers was working quietly to change the way that military organizations thought and operated.[5] At the same time, a slightly older generation was applying insights its members had gained before the war to the new conditions.[6] Some of these officers were informally allied with enlightened senior commanders, and some worked in concert with a small group of committed civilian experts inside and outside the government. The RAND Corporation established an Insurgency Board that brought together external researchers, along with RAND analysts, to examine the new environment through the lens of RAND's work on counterinsurgency since the 1950s.[7] In some ways, RAND acted as an institutional memory bank for the new counterinsurgency movement, in part because some veteran researchers, Steve Hosmer among them, had been present at the creation—in the 1950s, when RAND had played a crucial early role in developing classical counterinsurgency theory.

Online journals—in particular *Small Wars Journal*, run by Dave Dilegge and Bill Nagle—had long been advocates of the guerrilla warfare renaissance and had run something of an underground network for the community, connecting key players, quietly prompting change, and providing a forum for discussion, debate and the exchange of ideas. Now their energy and commitment began to pay off, as the military establishment's system of professional journals, and in-house publications began to engage with the problem. As the journals engaged, the debate widened and intensified, and the new ideas began to circulate within the military. Petraeus and Mattis, as commanders of their services' combined training centers, exercised a certain amount of influence over these journals and actively promoted the debate.

The debate in the journals showed how much the military's culture had changed from the so-called zero-defect mentality of the 1970s, moving further toward a new spirit of open criticism and self-criticism.[8] The clearest illustration of this was an article entitled "Changing the Army for Counterinsurgency Operations," by British army brigadier Nigel Aylwin-Foster, which was published in the November–December 2005 issue of the *Military Review* and was heavily critical of the U.S. Army's performance in Iraq.[9] The article became the subject of intense debate. The tone of the response was set by senior leaders, with Petraeus inviting Aylwin-Foster to speak at the review workshop for the new field manual, and General Peter Schoonmaker, Chief of Staff of the Army, circulating the article to all senior commanders and urging them to consider its implications and take corrective action where needed.[10] The commander of U.S. Army Training and Doctrine Command, General William S. Wallace, published a letter thanking Aylwin-Foster "for his contribution to our profession's intellectual discourse," encouraging wide discussion and debate of the critique, and arguing that "the Army prides itself on its ability to critically assess our performance and seek out areas where we can improve."[11] This openness to constructive criticism, and willingness to adapt rapidly to improve field performance, was a hallmark of a military institution that was fully committed to the wars it was fighting, and was increasingly ready to change in order to win them. The same could not be said of all the Allies in Iraq or Afghanistan, but it was increasingly true of the United States, which was beginning to master counterinsurgency, and was ultimately to far outpace other armies who traditionally considered themselves adept at counter-guerrilla work.

In the same time period, Colonel Bill Darley, editor of *Military Review* and another committed long-term advocate of the new approach, organized a counterinsurgency writing competition and published a special edition in the form of a counterinsurgency reader (followed in subsequent years by a second counterinsurgency reader and then an interagency reader). *Parameters* and *Proceedings*, the journals of the Army and Navy war colleges, respectively, published numerous articles on counterinsurgency, as did the *Joint Force Quarterly*, the *Marine Corps Gazette*, and the individual branch journals (*Infantry*, *Armor*, etc.).

All of this brought the counterinsurgency debate fully into the light and allowed commanders in the field to access interim doctrine before the new manual was formally published. Junior officers also established secure web forums to enable them to discuss their concerns without necessarily bringing "big Army" into the process. Companycommand .com and platoonleader.org were two early examples, and both were very important bottom-up efforts, led and run by field officers on their own initiative.

Steve Metz at the U.S. Army War College, Gordon McCormick at the Naval Postgraduate School, Tom Marks at the National Defense University, Frank Hoffman at the Marine Corps University, and many other academics at military and civilian educational institutions also played a key role, as did Professor Eliot Cohen of the Johns Hopkins School of Advanced International Studies, who convened an informal movement of like-minded experts. At times, this network acted like an insurgency within the bureaucracy, arguing its case and pushing for change in the face of outright opposition. In the wider government context, later in 2006, leaders like John Hillen, assistant secretary for political-military affairs at the State Department, Jeb Nadaner, deputy assistant secretary of defense for stabilization operations, and Elisabeth Kvitashvili, director of conflict management and mitigation at the U.S. Agency for International Development, worked energetically to bring their organizations together, as did Janine Davidson, director for stability operations capabilities at the Pentagon. In the event, the learning mechanisms Davidson identified—the cultural openness to be honestly self-critical and the processes to turn that self-criticism into purposeful action to improve—gave the bureaucratic insurgents a means to change their institutions.

Back in the spring of 2006 the problem was that even as this process of organizational change was gathering momentum, the war was also changing. Indeed, it was hotting up dramatically. The winter of 2005–6 saw a major escalation of violence in Iraq and a spreading and intensifying Taliban insurgency in Afghanistan. In Pakistan, both the Afghan and Pakistani Taliban struck cooperative peace deals with the Pakistani army, giving them control of large swathes of the frontier and spiking infiltration into Afghanistan to unprecedented levels. In the Horn of Africa, the Somali Transitional Federal Government was ousted from Mogadishu by the Union of Islamic Courts, and Al Qa'ida cells continued to spread in coastal East Africa. The enemy was on the move. It would take another year to finalize the new doctrine, but civil and military leaders in the field needed help right now.

The writing team under Con Crane circulated the draft of their new manual as widely as possible to get it out to the field, even in interim form. In Iraq, General George Casey, assisted by his personal counterinsurgency adviser, Kalev Sepp, established a counterinsurgency campaign plan, created a counterinsurgency academy outside Baghdad, and began reorienting the coalition force in Iraq to the new approach. In Afghanistan, the effort was hampered by a profusion of multinational command systems, lack of higher level attention, and reluctance on the part of some troop-contributing nations to grasp that the conflict had evolved from a reconstruction mission into a full-blown counterinsurgency.

WRITING "TWENTY-EIGHT ARTICLES"

Against this background of a deepening war and intellectual ferment across the government, I had just come back from a stint in Iraq working counterterrorism and counterinsurgency issues for Ambassador Hank

Crumpton, coordinator for counterterrorism at the State Department. Scott Cuomo's request for a concise description of what company-grade commanders needed to understand and do in counterinsurgency struck a chord with me. I had been going over my field notes from Iraq, trying to codify and organize my observations, and had a body of participant observations, interview notes, and quantitative data on which to draw, as well as my own previous command experience in earlier campaigns. But I would probably not have written "Twenty-Eight Articles" in its final form, or perhaps at all, had not a senior Pentagon official stood me up.

My bureau at State had a close (though not always harmonious) working relationship with several offices in the Pentagon, including the office of the Assistant Secretary of Defense for Special Operations and Low-Intensity Conflict. The same day Scott came to see me, I had been invited to a meeting on regional counterterrorism efforts with my opposite number, a deputy assistant secretary of defense in that office. At the last moment—just fifteen minutes out, when I was already in the Pentagon parking lot—his scheduler called to cancel the meeting. It was very late on a cold, rainy afternoon, so rather than go back to the office, I sat down in a quiet corner of the Starbucks coffee shop at Pentagon City, pulled out my little black Moleskine field notebook, and began to write the summary Scott had asked for. After I had boiled down dozens of observations, grouping them into key thoughts and organizing them in a chronological sequence, I was left with twenty-eight main points.

This coincidence put me in mind of the famous "Twenty-Seven Articles," T. E. Lawrence's article in the *Arab Bulletin* of August 1917, a document with which both I and my readers were very familiar—it was widely read within the counterinsurgency community and was being circulated among company and platoon commanders in the field in its electronic version. "Twenty-Seven Articles" is a concise, conversational, clearly written piece of advice for members of the Arab Bureau (Britain's wartime intelligence and "unconventional warfare" organization for the Palestine and Mediterranean theatres, based in Cairo) working with tribal irregulars under Prince Feisal of Mecca in an insurgency against the Ottoman Empire.[12] Lawrence, of course, wrote of insurgency and the art of military combat advising rather than of counterinsurgency per se. But I felt that if I organized my article along similar lines, and passed it to my peers in the field as a companion piece with Lawrence's already-circulating article, it would resonate with them and they would readily grasp the allusion. By the early hours of the next morning, over my laptop at home (and assisted by a bottle of Laphroaig) I had the initial draft completed, and sent it out by e-mail for peer review.

This process of peer review is critically important because of the nature of field observation in counterinsurgency warfare. Anyone who has ever participated in close combat or debriefed troops after a fire-fight knows the conundrum that hampers understanding of battle: If you weren't there, you probably don't know what happened. If you *were* there, you probably can't remember clearly. Close combat in complex terrain, as in counterinsurgency, is so confused and moves so fast that even people a few dozen meters away often do not know exactly what is happening. Meanwhile, those who *are* on the spot are subject to the psychology of crisis. Like victims of a car accident, their perceptions are heavily influenced by the expectation of imminent death or injury and the enormous shock of combat. For this reason, everyone remembers a particular engagement differently. This is nothing new—consider David Howarth's description of the battle of Waterloo: "Afterwards, nobody in the infantry…had a clear consecutive memory of what happened. They only remembered isolated moments, glimpses through the battle smoke, sudden piercing expressions of sound or smell or sight: the rest was a daze of fear, excitement or horror."[13]

This makes personal observation an unreliable basis for analysis. Nevertheless, researchers in this environment have no choice but to rely on qualitative firsthand field research based on participant observation, backed up by quantitative data when available. Unfortunately, quantitative data such as those in the Significant Activities databases (SIGACTS; the military's official record of every combat incident in a campaign) tend to be highly corrupt, because of the difficulties in reporting incidents and fitting the multiplicity of possible incident types into a small number of database categories.

When I served in Iraq in 2007 as General Petraeus's senior counter-insurgency adviser, for example, I would often go out with units in the field to observe and advise. I would always bring with me a sheaf of the latest SIGACT reporting from that unit, would try to get alongside the actual individual, officer or NCO, who had reported a particular inci-dent, and would show him the incident report as it appeared in the data-base. With every unit, and in some cases with every single report, the person who first reported the incident could no longer recognize it as it appeared in the database. This data corruption and the reductiveness of the SIGACT system tended to frustrate rigorous statistical analysis, prompting an emphasis on professional judgment and "blink" knowledge. Selection bias (U.S. units in the toughest areas, requiring most assistance, tended to receive the greatest attention) and the risk, stress, and effort inherent in data collection also tended to cloud judgment and skew emphasis.

All of this makes peer review critical for counterinsurgency research. I listed the main contributors to this review in the acknowledgments note at the end. Many of them were and are key members of the counterinsurgency community, and all brought extremely valuable insights to the process and proposed changes to what I had initially written. Thus, the final version that follows represents the collective judgment of the entire middle tier of the counterinsurgency movement, not solely my own views.

NO TEMPLATE

Within forty-eight hours of my sending the article out for review, however, the e-mail containing the document had gone "viral" around the U.S. government, the U.S. military, and Allied forces, a real indication of the speed with which the informal counterinsurgent underground could pass information to commanders out in the field. Over the next week, I received dozens of e-mails from people who were using the document in Iraq and Afghanistan, often including valuable suggestions for changes. Within a couple of months, Darley had published the article in *Military Review*, it had also been published in the *Marine Corps Gazette*, and Crane's team adapted it as an appendix to *Counterinsurgency* (FM 3–24). In part this was probably because the article filled a felt need, but the more important aspect was that it showed how fast information could circulate from the bottom up. The article was subsequently translated into Arabic and Spanish, and used in Afghanistan and Iraq by both Coalition and local forces. I received several e-mails from Afghan and Iraqi officers offering their commentaries and thanks.

The less positive aspect of such circulation was the tendency by many readers, despite the warning at the front of the article, to use it as a template. As I have emphasized in detail already, there are no standard templates or universal solutions in counterinsurgency. Fundamentals and principles exist, but they require judgment in application, and there is no substitute for studying the environment in detail, developing locally tailored solutions, and being prepared to adjust them in an agile way as the situation develops.

For publication here, I have preserved the original text of the article because it has been widely quoted and referred to in numerous other publications, so any substantive amendment to the main text would introduce considerable confusion. However, I have added expanded footnotes and annotations where subsequent events warrant it.

Twenty-eight Articles

Fundamentals of Company-level Counterinsurgency

1

Your company has just been warned for deployment on counterinsurgency operations in Iraq or Afghanistan. You have read David Galula, T. E. Lawrence, and Robert Thompson. You have studied FM 3–24 and now understand the history, philosophy, and theory of counterinsurgency. You have watched *Black Hawk Down* and *The Battle of Algiers*, and you know this will be the most difficult challenge of your life.

But what does all the theory mean, at the company level? How do the principles translate into action—at night, with the GPS down, the media criticizing you, the locals complaining in a language you don't understand, and an unseen enemy killing your people by ones and twos? How does counterinsurgency actually happen?

There are no universal answers, and insurgents are among the most adaptive opponents you will ever face. Countering them will demand every ounce of your intellect. But be comforted: you are not the first to feel this way. There are tactical fundamentals you can apply, to link the theory with the techniques and procedures you already know.

WHAT IS COUNTERINSURGENCY?

If you have not studied counterinsurgency theory, here it is in a nutshell: this is a competition with the insurgent for the right and the ability to win the hearts, minds, and acquiescence of the population. You are being sent in because the insurgents, at their strongest, can defeat anything weaker than you. But you have more combat power than you can or should use in most situations. Injudicious use of firepower creates blood feuds, homeless people, and societal disruption that fuels and perpetuates the insurgency. The most beneficial actions are often local politics, civic action, and beat-cop behaviors. For your side to win, the people do not have to like you, but they must respect you, accept that your actions benefit them, and trust your integrity and ability to deliver on promises, particularly regarding their security. In this battlefield, popular perceptions and rumor are more influential than the facts and more powerful than a hundred tanks.

Within this context, what follows are observations from collective experience: the distilled essence of what was learned by all of us who went before you. They are expressed as commandments, for clarity—but they are really more like folklore. Apply them judiciously and skeptically.

PREPARATION

Time is short during predeployment, but you will never have more time to think than you have now. Now is your chance to prepare yourself and your command.

1. **Know your turf.** Know the people, the topography, economy, history, religion, and culture. Know every village, road, field, population group, tribal leader, and ancient grievance. Your task is to become the world expert on your district. If you don't know precisely where you will be operating, study the general area. Read the map like a book: study it every night before sleep and redraw it from memory every morning, until you understand its patterns intuitively. Develop a mental model of your area—a framework in which to fit every new piece of knowledge you acquire. Study handover notes from predecessors; better still, get in touch with the unit in theatre and pick their brains. In an ideal world, intelligence officers and area experts would brief you. This rarely happens; and even if it does, there is no substitute for personal mastery. Understand the broader "area of influence"—this can be a wide area, particularly when insurgents draw on "global" grievances. Share out aspects of the operational area among platoon leaders and NCOs: have each individual develop

a personal specialization and brief the others. Neglecting this knowledge will kill you.

2. **Diagnose the problem.** Once you know your area and its people, you can begin to diagnose the problem. Who are the insurgents? What drives them? What makes local leaders tick? Counterinsurgency is fundamentally a competition between many groups, each seeking to mobilize the population in support of its agenda—counterinsurgency is always more than two-sided. So you must understand what motivates the people and how to mobilize them. You need to know why and how the insurgents are getting followers. This means you need to know your real enemy, not a cardboard cutout. The enemy is adaptive, is resourceful, and probably grew up in the region where you will operate. The locals have known him since he was a boy—how long have they known you? Your worst opponent is not the psychopathic terrorist of Hollywood myth, it is the charismatic follow-me warrior who would make your best platoon leader. His followers are not misled or naïve: much of his success is due to bad government policies or security forces that alienate the population. Work this problem collectively with your platoon and squad leaders. Discuss ideas, explore the problem, understand what you are facing, and seek a consensus. If this sounds unmilitary, get over it. Once you are in theatre, situations will arise too quickly for orders, or even commander's intent. Corporals and privates will have to make snap judgments with strategic impact. The only way to help them is to give them a shared understanding, then trust them to think for themselves on the day.

3. **Organize for intelligence.** In counterinsurgency, killing the enemy is easy. Finding him is often nearly impossible. Intelligence and operations are complementary. Your operations will be intelligence driven, but intelligence will come mostly from your own operations, not as a "product" prepared and served up by higher headquarters. So you must organize for intelligence. You will need a company S2* and intelligence section—including analysts. You may need platoon S2s and S3s, and you will need a reconnaissance and surveillance

---

* AUTHOR'S NOTE (2009): S2 refers to an intelligence staff officer or section in a headquarters, S3 refers to the operations staff.

(R & S) element. You will not have enough linguists—you never do—but consider carefully where best to employ them. Linguists are a battle-winning asset: but like any other scarce resource, you must have a prioritized "bump plan" in case you lose them. Often during predeployment the best use of linguists is to train your command in basic language. You will probably not get augmentation for all this: but you must still do it. Put the smartest soldiers in the S2 section and the R & S squad. You will have one less rifle squad: but the intelligence section will pay for itself in lives and effort saved.*

4. **Organize for interagency operations.** Almost everything in counterinsurgency is interagency. And everything important—from policing to intelligence to civil-military operations to trash collection—will involve your company working with civilian actors and local indigenous partners you cannot control, but whose success is essential for yours. Train the company in interagency operations—get a briefing from the State Department, aid agencies, and the local police or fire brigade. Train point men in each squad to deal with the interagency. Realize that civilians find rifles, helmets, and body armor intimidating. Learn how not to scare them. Ask others who come from that country or culture about your ideas. See it through the eyes of a civilian who knows nothing about the military. How would you react if foreigners came to your neighborhood and conducted the operations you planned? What if somebody came to your mother's house and did that? Most important, know that your operations will create temporary breathing space, but long-term development and stabilization by civilian agencies will ultimately win the war.

5. **Travel light and harden your Combat Service Support.** You will be weighed down with body armor, rations, extra ammunition, communications gear, and a thousand other things. The enemy will carry a rifle or RPG, a

---

* AUTHOR'S NOTE (2009): Since this paper was written, enormous strides have been made in forward-deploying analysts to battalion and company level, pushing intelligence capability forward to field units, creating operations/intelligence fusion cells, and training combat units in the tactics, techniques, and procedures of information collection, reporting, and analysis. Nevertheless, most commanders in the field still find they need to put more effort than initially anticipated into intelligence work at the company level. Units that emphasize intelligence-led operations at the local level and structure each cycle of operations to generate actionable intelligence for the next still tend to do much better than units that wait for information from higher headquarters.

shemagh, and a water bottle if he is lucky. Unless you ruthlessly lighten your load and enforce a culture of speed and mobility, the insurgents will consistently outrun and outmaneuver you. But in lightening your load, make sure you can always "reach back" to call for firepower or heavy support if needed. Also, remember to harden your CSS. The enemy will attack your weakest points. Most attacks on Coalition forces in Iraq in 2004 and 2005, outside preplanned combat actions like the two battles of Fallujah or Operation Iron Horse, were against CSS installations and convoys. You do the math. Ensure that your CSS assets are hardened, have communications, and are trained in combat operations. They may do more fighting than your rifle squads.

6. **Find a political/cultural adviser.** In a force optimized for counterinsurgency, you might receive a political-cultural adviser (POLAD) at company level: a diplomat or military foreign area officer, able to speak the language and navigate the intricacies of local politics. Back on Planet Earth, the corps and division commander will get a POLAD: you will not, so you must improvise. Find a political-cultural adviser from among your people—perhaps an officer, perhaps not (see article 8). Someone with people skills and a "feel" for the environment will do better than a political science graduate. Don't try to be your own cultural adviser: you must be fully aware of the political and cultural dimension, but this is a different task. Also, don't give one of your intelligence people this role. They can help, but their task is to understand the environment— the political adviser's job is to help shape it.*

7. **Train the squad leaders—then trust them.** Counterinsurgency is a squad and platoon leader's war, and often a private soldier's war.† Battles

---

* AUTHOR'S NOTE (2009): Today, new capabilities exist to help combat units understand their environment. These include Human Terrain Teams, Female Engagement Teams, bilingual/bicultural advisers, and (in some places) tribal or community engagement cells. But these specialized capabilities cannot substitute for personal understanding of local languages, cultural norms, and local grassroots politics. Units whose leaders master these issues perform best.

† AUTHOR'S NOTE (2009): This comment refers specifically to combat action, which is often fleeting and occurs at close range, so that only the local commander on the spot (almost always a junior officer or NCO) is able to influence the firefight as it unfolds. Brigade and battalion commanders have an extremely important longer term role to play in synchronizing and cueing resources that set the conditions under which those junior commanders operate. This makes the platoon and squad the key tactical units and the brigade the key maneuver unit, especially in urban areas. In mountain and winter warfare (as in parts of Afghanistan for much of the year), the key maneuver unit is usually the battalion. Despite all this, the fundamental truth remains that the man on the spot with a gun—insurgent or counterinsurgent—at the start of a firefight has the greatest influence on how that fight develops.

are won or lost in moments: whoever can bring combat power to bear in seconds, on a street corner, will win. The commander on the spot controls the fight. You must train the squad leaders to act intelligently and independently without orders. If your squad leaders are competent, you can get away with average company or platoon staffs. The reverse is not the case. Training should focus on basic skills: marksmanship, patrolling, security on the move and at the halt, basic drills. When in doubt, spend less time on company and platoon training and more time on squads and individuals. Ruthlessly replace leaders who do not make the grade. But once people are trained, and you have a shared operational "diagnosis," you must trust them. We talk about this, but few company or platoon leaders really trust their people. In counterinsurgency, you have no choice.

8. **Rank is nothing: talent is everything.** Not everyone is good at counterinsurgency. Many people don't understand the concept, and some who do can't execute it. It is difficult, and in a conventional force only a few people will master it. Anyone can learn the basics, but a few "naturals" do exist. Learn how to spot these people and put them into positions where they can make a difference. Rank matters far less than talent—a few good men under a smart junior NCO can succeed in counterinsurgency, where hundreds of well-armed soldiers under a mediocre senior officer will fail.

9. **Have a game plan.** The final preparation task is to develop a game plan: a mental picture of how you see the operation developing. You will be tempted to try and do this too early. But force yourself to wait: as your knowledge improves, you will get a better idea both of what needs to be done and of your own limitations. Like any plan, this plan will change once you hit the ground, and may need to be scrapped if there is a major shift in the environment. But you still need a plan, and the process of planning will give you a simple robust idea of what to achieve, even if the methods change. (At the very least, having a game plan allows you to know what you are deviating from.) This is sometimes called "operational design." One approach is to identify basic stages in your operation: for example, "establish dominance; build local networks; marginalize the enemy." Make sure you can easily transition between phases, both forward

and backward in case of setbacks. Just as the insurgent can adapt his activity to yours, you must have a simple enough plan to survive setbacks without collapsing. This plan is the "solution" that matches the shared "diagnosis" you developed earlier—it must be simple, and known to everyone.

THE GOLDEN HOUR

You have deployed, completed reception and staging, and (if you are lucky) attended the in-country counterinsurgency school.* Now it is time to enter your sector and start your tour.

This is the golden hour. Mistakes made now will haunt you for the rest of the tour, while early successes will set the tone for victory. You will look back on your early actions and cringe at your clumsiness. So be it: but you must act.

10. **Be there.** The first rule of deployment in counterinsurgency is to be there. You can almost never outrun the enemy in this environment. If you are not present when an incident happens, there is usually little you can do about it. So your first order of business is to establish presence. If you cannot do this throughout your sector, then do it wherever you can. This demands a residential approach—living in your sector, in close proximity to the population, rather than raiding into the area from remote, secure bases. Movement on foot, sleeping in local villages, night patrolling: all these seem more dangerous than they are. These techniques establish links with the locals, who see you as real people they can trust and do business with, not as

---

* AUTHOR'S NOTE (2009): In 2006, General Casey had just established the Iraq Counterinsurgency Training Center at Taji, north of Baghdad. The school has since expanded and done excellent work for generations of coalition troops in Iraq, training the Surge brigades in 2007 under the inspired leadership of Colonel Manny Diemer. An Iraqi army counterinsurgency school was established on the same base in 2007 on the personal initiative of a highly independent junior Special Forces officer, Captain James Patrick, and is also performing well. In Afghanistan, the International Security Assistance Force Counterinsurgency Training Center was established outside Kabul in 2007. Founded by Captain Dan Helmer, it is currently led by Colonel John Agoglia, an extremely capable and experienced counterinsurgent, a key member of the counterinsurgency underground in 2005–6, and former head of the United States Army's Peacekeeping and Stabilization Operations Institute. This center provides training for Coalition and Afghan personnel from all agencies, civilian and military. In both Afghanistan and Iraq, these centers are "finishing schools," providing a final in-country polish to the predeployment training that people receive before arriving and acting as centers of excellence and corporate knowledge for their respective theatre of operations.

aliens who descend from an armored box. [Ultimately, they make the people your partners, and those partnerships become your first line of defense.] Driving around in an armored convoy—day-tripping like a tourist in hell—degrades situational awareness, makes you a target, and is ultimately more dangerous.

11. **Avoid knee-jerk responses to first impressions.** Don't act rashly; get the facts first. The violence you see may be part of the insurgent strategy, it may be various interest groups fighting it out, or it may be people settling personal vendettas.* Or it may just be daily life: "normality" in Kandahar is not the same as in Kansas. So you need time to learn what normality looks like. The insurgent commander also wants to goad you into lashing out at the population or making a mistake. Unless you happen to be on the spot when an incident occurs, you will have only secondhand reports and may misunderstand the local context or interpretation. This fragmentation and "disaggregation" of the battlefield—particularly in urban areas—means that first impressions are often highly misleading. Of course, you cannot avoid making judgments. But if possible, check them with an older hand or a trusted local. If you can, keep one or two officers from your predecessor unit for the first part of the tour.† Try to avoid a rush to judgment.

12. **Prepare for handover from Day One.** Believe it or not, you will not resolve the insurgency on your watch. Your tour will end, and your successors will need your corporate knowledge. Start handover folders, in every platoon and specialist squad, from Day One—ideally, you would have inherited these from your predecessors, but if not you must start them. The folders should include lessons learned, details about the population, village and patrol reports, updated maps, photographs—anything that will help newcomers master the environment. Computerized databases are fine, but keep good backups

---

* AUTHOR'S NOTE (2009): remember also that you are by far the most militarily powerful armed actor in the local people's environment and they may use you to their advantage—portraying their local tribal, business, or political rivals as "insurgents" in order to mislead you into harsh actions that harm their rivals and strengthen their own position. This danger is much more acute in the early stages of a deployment, when you are still figuring out the key relationships among local people. In the words of a colleague in the Horn of Africa: "As soon as you fly into one of these places, you've taken sides—and you don't even know it yet."

† AUTHOR'S NOTE (2009): Many units now send a few officers and NCOs forward to work with their predecessor unit, in order to gain situational awareness. Other units have an offset rotation such that intelligence and civil affairs staffs rotate only half their people, and at a different time from the main combat unit. Both these approaches work well.

and ensure you have hard copy of key artifacts and documents. This is boring, tedious, and essential. Over time, you will create a corporate memory that keeps your people alive.

13. **Build trusted networks.** Once you have settled into your sector, your next task is to build trusted networks. This is the true meaning of the phrase "hearts and minds," which comprises two separate components. "Hearts" means persuading people their best interests are served by your success; "minds" means convincing them that you can protect them, and that resisting you is pointless. Note that neither concept has to do with whether people like you. Calculated self-interest, not emotion, is what counts. Over time, if you successfully build networks of trust, these will grow like roots into the population, displacing the enemy's networks, bringing him out into the open to fight you, and seizing the initiative. These networks include local allies, community leaders, local security forces, NGOs and other friendly or neutral nonstate actors in your area, and the media. Conduct village and neighborhood surveys to identify needs in the community—then follow through to meet them, build common interests, and mobilize popular support. This is your true main effort: everything else is secondary. Actions that help build trusted networks serve your cause. Actions—even killing high-profile targets—that undermine trust or disrupt your networks help the enemy.*

14. **Start easy.** If you were trained in maneuver warfare, you know about surfaces and gaps. This applies to counterinsurgency as much as any other form of maneuver. Don't try to crack the hardest nut first—don't go straight for the main insurgent stronghold, try to provoke a decisive showdown, or focus efforts on villages that support the insurgents. Instead, start from secure areas and work gradually outward. Do this by extending your influence through the locals' own networks. Go with, not against, the grain of local society: first win the confidence of

* AUTHOR'S NOTE (2009): Trust is a function of reliability. Indeed, in local languages in many parts of the world where we operate, the words for "honor" and "reliability" are similar or the same. Dependability is key—local people must believe that you will follow through and deliver on promises in a reliable manner. Over time, the predictability and order that you create through dependability makes people feel safer and encourages them to work with you. Again, emotions are secondary here—if locals like you but believe you cannot be relied on, you come to seem pathetic to them.

a few villages, and then see who they trade, intermarry, or do business with. Now win these people over. Soon enough, the showdown with the insurgents will come.* But now you have local allies, a mobilized population, and a trusted network at your back. Do it the other way around, and no one will mourn your failure.

15. **Seek early victories.** In this early phase, your aim is to stamp your dominance in your sector. Do this by seeking an early victory. This will probably not translate into a combat victory over the enemy: looking for such a victory can be overly aggressive and create collateral damage—especially since you really do not yet understand your sector. Also, such a combat victory depends on the enemy being stupid enough to present you with a clear-cut target, a rare windfall in counterinsurgency. Instead, you may achieve a victory by resolving long-standing issues† your predecessors have failed to address, or co-opting a key local leader who has resisted cooperation with our forces. Like any other form of armed propaganda, achieving even a small victory early in the tour sets the tone for what comes later, and helps seize the initiative—which you have probably lost due to

---

* AUTHOR'S NOTE (2009): indeed, the better you do in building a close relationship with the people, the more you threaten the enemy's connectivity with the population, from which insurgents draw their strength and freedom of action. This will bring the enemy to you like a magnet: they must fight to restore that linkage or be defeated, and they know it. Thus, a close relationship with the people provokes the enemy to attack both you and your local partners. This is inevitable and is actually a good thing, because it allows you to control the terms of the engagement and brings the enemy into the open where they can be found, fixed, and destroyed with minimal collateral damage. As Colonel Chris Cavoli points out, this also helps the people see the insurgents as attackers and you as their protector, so that even if the enemy initiates the firefight you win the political engagement.

† AUTHOR'S NOTE (2009): The practice of District Stabilization Analysis is an important tool in identifying opportunities for early successes. Too often in the past, we have gone into districts with the attitude "I am here to address all your grievances and fix all your problems." The problem with this is that in any given district there are dozens of problems, many of which are ancient or intractable grievances that cannot be fixed or may be beyond our current capacity. The approach of trying to find and fix problems thus tends to dissipate our effort in nonstrategic activity: we go looking for problems, find them, and spend all our effort in addressing them in a haphazard way. District Stabilization Analysis takes a different approach—by first mapping grievances and issues and then boiling them down to grievances that (1) are currently creating violence or instability; (2) are actually being exploited by the enemy; and (3) are things we can do something about, in a meaningful timeframe, with current resources. With this analysis completed, units often find that the dozens of grievances are reduced to two or three issues they can address and that will actually have an impact in reducing instability and violence. The next step is equally important: successful units do not stovepipe their efforts along lines of operation (such as security, governance, development, or essential services)—rather, they form multidisciplinary tiger teams to focus on each identified grievance and ensure that on each tiger team there is a security representative, a governance representative, a development representative, and so on. Units that are operating this way in Afghanistan and Iraq today tend to be doing much better than units that simply adopt a "see grievance, fix grievance" approach.

the inevitable hiatus entailed by the handover-takeover with your predecessor.

16. **Practice deterrent patrolling.** Establish patrolling methods that deter the enemy from attacking you. Often our patrolling approach seems designed to provoke, then defeat, enemy attacks. This is counterproductive: it leads to a raiding, day-tripping mindset or, worse, a bunker mentality. Instead, practice deterrent patrolling. There are many methods for this, including "multiple" (also known as "satellite") patrolling, where you flood an area with numerous small patrols working together. Each is too small to be a worthwhile target, and the insurgents never know where all the patrols are—making an attack on any one patrol extremely risky. Other methods include so-called blue-green patrolling, where you mount daylight overt humanitarian patrols which go covert at night and hunt specific targets. Again, the aim is to keep the enemy off-balance, and the population reassured, through constant and unpredictable activity—which, over time, deters attacks and creates a more permissive environment. A reasonable rule of thumb is that one-third to two-thirds of your force should be on patrol at any time, day or night.

17. **Be prepared for setbacks.** Setbacks are normal in counterinsurgency, as in every other form of war. You will make mistakes, lose people, or occasionally kill or detain the wrong person. You may fail in building or expanding networks. If this happens, don't lose heart. Simply drop back to the previous phase of your game plan and recover your balance. It is normal in company counterinsurgency operations for some platoons to be doing well, while others do badly. This is not necessarily evidence of failure. Give local commanders the freedom to adjust their posture to local conditions. This creates elasticity that helps you survive setbacks.

18. **Remember the global audience.** One of the biggest differences between the counterinsurgencies our fathers fought and those we face today is the omnipresence of globalized media. Most houses in Iraq have one or more satellite dishes. Web bloggers, print, radio, and television reporters and others are monitoring and commenting on your every move. When the insurgents ambush your patrols or set off a car bomb,

they do so not to destroy one more track but because they want graphic images of a burning vehicle and dead bodies for the evening news. Beware the "scripted enemy," who plays to a global audience and seeks to defeat you in the court of global public opinion. You counter this by training your people to always bear in mind the global audience, assume that everything they say or do will be publicized, and befriend the media. Get the press onside: help them get their story, and trade information with them. Good relationships with nonembedded media—especially indigenous media—dramatically increase your situational awareness, and help get your message across to the global and local audience.

19. **Engage the women, beware the children.** Most insurgent fighters are men. But in traditional societies, women are hugely influential in forming the social networks that insurgents use for support. Co-opting neutral or friendly women, through targeted social and economic programs, builds networks of enlightened self-interest that eventually undermine the insurgents. You need your own female counterinsurgents, including interagency people, to do this effectively.* Win the women, and you own the family unit. Own the family, and you take a big step forward in mobilizing the population. Conversely, though, stop your people from fraternizing with local children. Your troops are homesick; they want to drop their guard with the kids. But children are sharp-eyed, lacking in empathy, and willing to commit atrocities their elders would shrink from. The insurgents are watching: they will notice a growing friendship between one of your people and a local child and will either harm the child as punishment or use the child against you. Similarly, stop your people from throwing candies or presents to children. It attracts them to our vehicles, creates crowds the enemy

---

* AUTHOR'S NOTE (2009): The United States Marine Corps has created specialized Female Engagement Teams (FETs) for operations in Afghanistan to engage with local women in the highly segregated Pashtun society in which Marines are operating today. Some commanders have also benefited greatly from the advice and insight on local opinion and networks that women counterinsurgents bring to the table due to their unique access. The FETs and similar army teams operating under the Lioness program are extremely valuable in getting to the other 52 percent of the population with whom male counterinsurgents have a difficult time interacting. One key issue is the work rate and stress level of women operating in this role—in many cases, because of the constant need for female searchers and interviewers and the very limited number of women deployed in FETs, the women's work rate can spike dramatically beyond what was initially predicted, at the risk of exhaustion. The obvious long-term solution is to deploy more women in this role; in the interim, commanders need to watch the work rate, ensure adequate rest and recovery time for the FET, and watch for burnout.

can exploit, and leads to children being run over. Harden your heart and keep the children at arm's length.

. **Take stock regularly.** You probably already know that a "body count" tells you little, because you usually cannot know how many insurgents there were to start with, how many moved into the area, how many transferred from supporter to combatant status, or how many new fighters the conflict has created. But you still need to develop metrics early in the tour and refine them as the operation progresses. They should cover a range of social, informational, military, and economic issues. Use metrics intelligently to form an overall impression of progress—not in a mechanistic "traffic light" fashion. Typical metrics include: percentage of engagements initiated by our forces versus those initiated by insurgents; longevity of friendly local leaders in positions of authority; number and quality of tip-offs on insurgent activity that originate spontaneously from the population; economic activity at markets and shops. These mean virtually nothing as a snapshot—trends over time are the true indicators of progress in your sector.*

GROUNDHOG DAY

Now you are in "steady state." You are established in your sector, and your people are settling into that "Groundhog Day" mentality that hits every unit at some stage during every tour. It will probably take people at least the first third of the tour to become effective in the environment, if not longer. Then in the last period you will struggle against the short-timer mentality. So this middle part of the tour is the most productive—but keeping the flame alive, and bringing the local population along with you, takes immense leadership.

---

* AUTHOR'S NOTE (2009): Other measures include the presence or price of exotic vegetables and fruits in market stalls (indicating that people are engaging in trade with other parts of the country), the cost of local transportation (indicating the perception of road security), the percentage of roadside bombs reported by the local people versus found by us, the collection of taxation or operation of local courts by the host nation government versus the enemy, and the level of community participation in education, public health, and agriculture programs. Again, trends over time are what matter: the actual data on any given day are much less important. Many units in Afghanistan are now experiencing success with the Tactical Conflict Assessment and Planning Framework (TCAPF), developed to help track popular perceptions and confidence. Company commanders, especially in Afghanistan, can expect to receive TCAPF training and to spend considerable effort and time collecting TCAPF data. This can be extremely valuable in identifying and resolving local sources of instability and violence.

21. **Exploit a "single narrative."** Since counterinsurgency is a competition to mobilize popular support, it pays to know how people are mobilized. In most societies there are opinion-makers: local leaders, pillars of the community, religious figures, media personalities, and others who set trends and influence public perceptions. This influence—including the pernicious influence of the insurgents—often takes the form of a "single narrative": a simple, unifying, easily expressed story or explanation that organizes people's experience and provides a framework for understanding events. Nationalist and ethnic historical myths, or sectarian creeds, provide such a narrative. The Iraqi insurgents have one, as do Al-Qa'eda and the Taliban. To undercut their influence, you must exploit an alternative narrative—or, better yet, tap into an existing narrative that excludes the insurgents. This narrative is often worked out for you by higher headquarters—but only you have the detailed knowledge to tailor the narrative to local conditions and generate leverage from it. For example, you might use a nationalist narrative to marginalize foreign fighters in your area, or a narrative of national redemption to undermine former regime elements that have been terrorizing the population. At the company level, you do this in baby steps, by getting to know local opinion-makers, winning their trust, learning what motivates them, and building on this to find a single narrative that emphasizes the inevitability and rightness of your ultimate success. This is art, not science.

22. **Local forces should mirror the enemy, not ourselves.** By this stage, you will be working closely with local forces, training or supporting them, and building indigenous capability. The natural tendency is to build forces in our own image, with the aim of eventually handing our role over to them. This is a mistake. Instead, local indigenous forces need to mirror the enemy's capabilities and seek to supplant the insurgent's role. This does not mean they should be "irregular" in the sense of being brutal, or outside proper control. Rather, they should move, equip, and organize like the insurgents—but have access to your support and be under the firm control of their parent societies. Combined with a mobilized population and trusted networks, this allows local forces to "hardwire" the enemy out of the environment, under top-cover from you. At the company level, this means that raising, training, and employing local indigenous auxiliary forces (police and military) are

valid tasks.* This requires high-level clearance, of course, but if support is given, you should establish a company training cell. Platoons should aim to train one local squad, and then use that squad as a nucleus for a partner platoon, and company headquarters should train an indigenous leadership team. This mirrors the "growth" process of other trusted networks, and tends to emerge naturally as you win local allies—who want to take up arms in their own defense.

23. **Practice armed civil affairs.** Counterinsurgency is armed social work:† an attempt to redress basic social and political problems while being shot at. This makes civil affairs a central counterinsurgency activity, not an afterthought. It is how you restructure the environment to displace the enemy from it. In your company sector, civil affairs must focus on meeting basic needs first, and then progress up Maslow's hierarchy as each successive need is met. A series of village or neighborhood surveys, regularly updated, are an invaluable tool to help understand the population's needs and to track progress in meeting them over time. You need intimate cooperation with interagency partners here—national, international, and local. You will not be able to control these partners—many NGOs, for example, do not want to be too closely associated with

---

* AUTHOR'S NOTE (2009). In operations in Iraq in 2007 and subsequently in Afghanistan, we developed what has become known as the Four-Component Partnering Model. This was expressed in the commander's guidance of June 2007 as "Never leave home without an Iraqi." In Regional Command East in Afghanistan today, the Combined Action Program is another excellent example of this approach. In essence, the four-component model ensures that whenever and wherever we operate, at whatever size of force, four components must always be represented: Coalition military, local military, local police, and local civilian authorities. This could be as large as a Coalition brigade, local battalion, police district, and local mayor or as small as an infantry squad with a couple of local troops, a local policeman, and a representative from the local community council. Experience has shown that when we operate in this combined action manner, the performance of all four elements improves. Coalition military forces have access to language and cultural understanding and improved situational awareness through their local partners. Local military forces have access to coalition enablers—intelligence, firepower, medical support, and mobility—and have a constant example of military professionalism to emulate. Local police can no longer act corruptly or oppressively because they are continuously monitored; they can also focus on community-based policing tasks and upholding the rule of law because they are protected and supported by their military partners. And civilian officials can now access and work with the population, build credibility and connectivity by resolving local disputes, and exercise civil primacy in directing the police and local military operations when appropriate. This approach complements, but in no way replaces, the use of full-time mentors and advisers operating continuously with local police and military units through embedded training teams.

† AUTHOR'S NOTE (2009): Some critics of the application of social science to counterinsurgency have decried this statement as a perversion of the independence and "impartiality" of disciplines like anthropology and sociology. While I firmly believe that these disciplines do indeed have a valid and valuable role in counterinsurgency—efforts to improve U.S. troops' cultural understanding of local societies have saved hundreds of Iraqi and Afghan lives through the Human Terrain System program, for example—I would emphasize that this article is talking about something else: not "armed social science" but social work—community organizing, welfare, mediation, domestic assistance, economic support—under conditions of extreme threat requiring armed support.

you because they need to preserve their perceived neutrality. Instead, you need to work on a shared diagnosis of the problem, building a consensus that helps you self-synchronize. Your role is to provide protection, identify needs, facilitate civil affairs, and use improvements in social conditions as leverage to build networks and mobilize the population. Thus, there is no such thing as impartial humanitarian assistance or civil affairs in counterinsurgency. Every time you help someone, you hurt someone else—not least the insurgents. So civil and humanitarian assistance personnel will be targeted. Protecting them is a matter not only of close-in defense but also of creating a permissive operating environment by co-opting the beneficiaries of aid—local communities and leaders—to help you help them.*

24. **Small is beautiful.** Another natural tendency is to go for large-scale, mass programs. In particular, we have a tendency to template ideas that succeed in one area and transplant them into another, and we tend to take small programs that work and try to replicate them on a larger scale. Again, this is usually a mistake—often programs succeed because of specific local conditions of which we are unaware, or because their very smallness has kept them below the enemy's radar and helped them flourish unmolested. At the company level, programs that succeed in one district often also succeed in another (because the overall company sector is small), but small-scale projects rarely proceed smoothly into large programs. Keep programs small: this makes them cheap, sustainable, low-key, and (importantly) recoverable if they fail. You can add new programs—also small, cheap, and tailored to local conditions—as the situation allows.†

---

* AUTHOR'S NOTE (2009): For aid officers and other development professionals in a counterinsurgency environment, it is important to note that there is a real qualitative difference between operating in a field environment outside a war zone and operating in a counterinsurgency environment. In "normal" development work, there are spoilers and local opponents to consider, but the real "enemy" is poverty, disease, and lack of capacity. In a counterinsurgency, all these things remain important, but there is also an enemy aid officer out there, running programs in direct competition with ours. The Taliban run agricultural teams to help farmers get the most out of the poppy crop, for example, along with local law courts and taxation programs and business advice for start-up firms in the drug cultivation, gem smuggling, and timber smuggling businesses that the Taliban exploit. The presence of a competing aid program fundamentally changes the game, making everything a competitive political endeavor. This is an important point for aid agencies to consider, particularly in light of the fact that as of 2008, for the first time, more than 50 percent of total U.S. foreign assistance worldwide was being delivered in conflict or postconflict zones.

† AUTHOR'S NOTE (2009): Your aim should be to proliferate locally tailored versions of small programs that work rather than to expand those programs into big programs (which often fail). It should go without saying, but unfortunately does not, that local ownership and buy-in is critical in developing these local small programs.

25. **Fight the enemy's strategy, not his forces.** At this stage, if things are proceeding well, the insurgents will go over to the offensive. Yes, the *offensive*—because you have created a situation so dangerous to the insurgents, by threatening to displace them from the environment, that they have to attack you and the population to get back into the game. Thus it is normal, even in the most successful operations, to have spikes of offensive insurgent activity late in the campaign. This does not necessarily mean you have done something wrong (though it may: it depends on whether you have successfully mobilized the population). At this point, the tendency is to go for the jugular and seek to destroy the enemy's forces in open battle. This is rarely the best choice at company level, because provoking major combat usually plays into the enemy's hands by undermining the population's confidence. Instead, attack the enemy's strategy: if he is seeking to recapture the allegiance of a segment of the local population, then co-opt them against him. If he is trying to provoke a sectarian conflict, go over to "peace enforcement mode." The permutations are endless, but the principle is the same: fight the enemy's strategy, not his forces.

26. **Build your own solution—only attack the enemy when he gets in the way.** Try not to be distracted, or forced into a series of reactive moves, by a desire to kill or capture the insurgents. Your aim should be to implement your own solution—the "game plan" you developed early in the campaign and then refined through interaction with local partners. Your approach must be environment-centric (based on dominating the whole district and implementing a solution to its systemic problems) rather than enemy-centric. This means that, particularly late in the campaign, you may need to learn to negotiate with the enemy. Members of the population that supports you also know the enemy's leaders—they may have grown up together in the small district that is now your company sector—and valid negotiating partners sometimes emerge as the campaign progresses. Again, you need close interagency relationships to exploit opportunities to co-opt segments of the enemy. This helps you wind down the insurgency without alienating potential local allies who have relatives or friends in the insurgent movement. At this stage, a defection is better than a surrender; a surrender is better than a capture; and a capture is better than a kill.

GETTING SHORT

Time is short, and the tour is drawing to a close. The key problem now is keeping your people focused, preventing them from dropping their guard, and maintaining the rage on all the multifarious programs, projects, and operations that you have started. In this final phase, the previous articles still stand, but there is an important new one:

27. **Keep your extraction plan secret.** The temptation to talk about home becomes almost unbearable toward the end of a tour. The locals know you are leaving, and probably have a better idea than you of the generic extraction plan—remember, they have seen units come and go. But you must protect the specific details of the extraction plan, or the enemy will use this as an opportunity to score a high-profile hit, recapture the population's allegiance by scare tactics that convince them they will not be protected once you leave, or persuade them that your successor unit will be oppressive or incompetent. Keep the details secret, within a tightly controlled compartment in your headquarters. And resist the temptation to say goodbye to local allies: you can always send a postcard from home.

FOUR "WHAT IFS"

The articles above describe what *should* happen, but we all know that things go wrong. Here are some "what ifs" to consider:

What if you get moved to a different area? You prepared for Ramadi and studied Dulaim tribal structures and Sunni beliefs. Now you are going to Najaf and will be surrounded by al-Hassan and Unizzah tribes and Shia communities. But that work was not wasted. In mastering your first area, you learned techniques you can apply: how to "case" an operational area, how to decide what matters in the local societal structure. Do the same again—and this time the process is easier and faster, since you have an existing mental structure, and can focus on what is different. The same applies if you get moved frequently within a battalion or brigade area.

What if higher headquarters doesn't "get" counterinsurgency? Higher headquarters is telling you the mission is to "kill terrorists," or is pushing for high-speed armored patrols and a base camp mentality. They just do not seem to understand counterinsurgency. This is not uncommon, since company-grade officers today often have more combat experience than senior officers. In this case, just do what you can. Try not to create expectations that higher headquarters will not let you meet. Apply the adage "First do no harm." Over time, you will find ways to do what you have to do. But never lie to higher headquarters about your locations or activities: they own the indirect fires.

What if you have no resources? Yours is a low-priority sector: you have no linguists, the aid agencies have no money for projects in your area, you have a low priority for funding. You can still get things done, but you need to focus on self-reliance, keep things small and sustainable, and ruthlessly prioritize effort. Local community leaders are your allies in this: they know what matters to them more than you do. Be honest with them, discuss possible projects and options with community leaders, get them to choose what their priority is. Often they will find the translators, building supplies, or expertise that you need, and will only expect your support and protection in making their projects work. And the process of negotiation and consultation will help mobilize their support and strengthen their social cohesion. If you set your sights on what is achievable, the situation can still work.*

What if the theatre situation shifts under your feet? It is your worst nightmare: everything has gone well in your sector, but the whole theatre situation has changed and invalidates your efforts. Think of the first battle

* AUTHOR'S NOTE (2009): Too often we arrive thinking we know better than the locals and foisting on communities a series of programs they neither want nor need; then we feel offended and surprised when these programs fail. The three critical requirements for local ownership in a counterinsurgency environment are (1) some form of transparent, local, community-based council or oversight body that assists in suggesting and monitoring projects; (2) openly published accounts that local communities can access, so that they can satisfy themselves that they are being dealt with fairly without corruption; and (3) community involvement, ideally through jobs on a particular aid project, or through the participation of local businesses. The National Solidarity Program in Afghanistan is a model of this type of program. Doing things on a commercial rather than an aid basis is also usually desirable, because aid programs are a symbol of the government and the international community and often draw unwelcome insurgent attention while increasing local people's dependency on outside support and creating vulnerability to elite capture, enabling local strongmen to control and pervert programs in their own interest. This applies mainly to development and reconstruction programs, but the same principles apply to local security programs also.

of Fallujah, the al-Askariya shrine bombing, or the Sadr uprising. What do you do? Here is where having a flexible, adaptive game plan comes in. Just as the insurgents drop down to a lower posture when things go wrong, now is the time to drop back a stage, consolidate, regain your balance, and prepare to expand again when the situation allows. But see article 28: if you cede the initiative, you must regain it as soon as the situation allows, or you will eventually lose.

CONCLUSION

This, then, is the tribal wisdom, the folklore of those who went before you. Like any folklore, it needs interpretation, and it contains seemingly contradictory advice. Over time, as you apply unremitting intellectual effort to study your sector, you will learn to apply these ideas in your own way, and you will add to this store of wisdom from your own observations and experience. So only one article remains. If you remember nothing else, remember this:

28. **Whatever else you do, keep the initiative.** In counterinsurgency, the initiative is everything. If the enemy is reacting to you, you control the environment. Provided you mobilize the population, you will win. If you are reacting to the enemy—even if you are killing or capturing him in large numbers—then he is controlling the environment, and you will eventually lose. In counterinsurgency, the enemy initiates most attacks, targets you unexpectedly, and withdraws too fast for you to react. Do not be drawn into purely reactive operations: focus on the population, build your own solution, further your game plan, and fight the enemy only when he gets in the way. This gains and keeps the initiative.

Acknowledgments

Although any errors or omissions in this chapter are mine alone, many people contributed directly or indirectly to it. They included Caleb Carr, Eliot Cohen, Audrey Cronin, Hank Crumpton, Janine Davidson, Jeff Davis, T. X. Hammes, John Hillen, Frank Hoffman, Scott Kofmehl, Christopher Langton, Tom Mahnken, Tim Mulholland, John Nagl, Tom Ricks and Mike Vlahos. Rob Greenway, Bruce Hoffman, Olivier Roy, and Marc

Sageman influenced my thinking over several months. A current serving officer of the Central Intelligence Agency and two other members of the intelligence community also made major contributions but cannot be named. Finally, the many company commanders, platoon leaders, and others I have worked with in Iraq and elsewhere inspired this effort. You carry the burden of counterinsurgency today, and into the future.

Measuring Progress in Afghanistan

2

How should the International Security Assistance Force (ISAF) track progress in the Afghan campaign? How should Coalition capitals and headquarters assess performance? What should subordinate organizations assess and report, to determine whether the mission is on track?

WHY METRICS MATTER

This analytical chapter offers some thoughts on measuring progress in Afghanistan. It draws on my experience working in or on Afghanistan since 2005, on a broader understanding of metrics in counterinsurgency, on observations from fieldwork, and on input from Afghans and internationals—civilian and military—currently in the field. Given the fluidity of the war, however, this chapter is merely a snapshot of developing thinking on a highly complex set of issues.

In 2009 in Afghanistan, ISAF seems to be in an adaptation battle against a rapidly evolving insurgency that has repeatedly absorbed and adapted to past efforts to defeat it, including at least two previous troop surges and three changes of strategy. To end this insurgency and achieve peace, we may need more than just extra troops, new resources, and a new campaign plan: as General Stanley McChrystal has emphasized, we need a new operational culture. *Organizations manage what they measure, and they measure what their leaders tell them to report on.* Thus, one key way for a leadership team to shift an organization's focus is to change reporting requirements and the associated measures of performance and effectiveness.

As important, and more urgent, we need to track our progress against the ISAF campaign plan, the Afghan people's expectations, and the newly announced strategy for the war. The U.S. Congress, in particular, needs measures to track progress in the "surge" against the President Obama's self-imposed eighteen-month timetable. To be effective, these measures must track three distinct but closely related elements:

1. **Trends in the war** (i.e., how the environment, the enemy, the population, and the Afghan government are changing)

2. **ISAF's progress against the campaign plan** and the overall strategy, including validation (whether we are doing the right things) and evaluation (how well we are doing them)

3. **Performance of individuals and organizations** against best-practice norms for counterinsurgency, reconstruction, and stability operations

Metrics must also be meaningful to multiple audiences, including NATO commanders, intelligence and operations staffs, political leaders, members of the legislature in troop-contributing nations, academic analysts, journalists, and—most important—ordinary Afghans and people around the world.

We should also note that if metrics are widely published, then they become known to the enemy, who can "game" them in order to undermine public confidence and perpetuate the conflict. Thus, we must strike a balance between clarity and openness on the one hand and adaptability and security on the other.

SHARED DIAGNOSIS

Because we need to track so many things for so many people, a shared diagnosis—a vision of what the nature of the conflict is and what is driving it—is essential. Neglecting this diagnosis risks a situation where analytical staff are drowning in data—lacking a clear conception of what matters and what does not, they collect on everything, creating a mass of disparate data that makes tracking progress harder. By definition, any assessment changes as the conflict develops, but it is essential to maintain

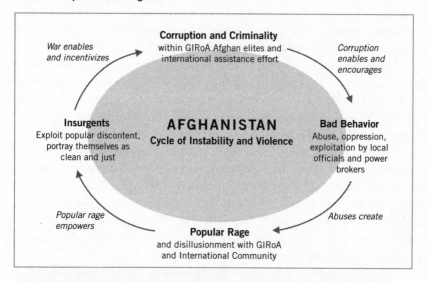

SOURCE: Afghanistan is experiencing a cycle of increasing instability and violence, with four key drivers: (1) *corruption* in the government, in the societal elites, and in the international assistance effort, which enables and encourages (2) *bad behavior by government officials and power brokers*, which in turn creates (3) *popular rage and disillusionment*, which empowers (4) the *insurgency*. The war against the insurgents in turn creates further opportunities and incentives for corruption and criminality, driving the cycle onward.

a *common set of core metrics*, as well as to maintain a *consistent methodology*, so that second-order effects and trends can be analyzed over time.

Figure 2.1 shows one such shared diagnosis. This is not the only possible analysis; other ISAF and coalition analysis products provide substantially more detail and rigor, and their analysis differs somewhat from this example. But it illustrates the type of simple diagnosis that is needed.

Note that this is a gross oversimplification, like any model of any conflict. But it needs to be this simple so that it can be understood, remembered, and carried in the head of every district stabilization officer, company commander, police mentor, development professional, diplomat, and intelligence officer.

DISTRICT STABILIZATION ANALYSIS

Most NATO headquarters are organized along "continental staff system" lines, with sections for operations, intelligence, personnel, logistics, communications, and so on. Mirroring this headquarters layout, campaign plans are organized along logical "lines of operation" (LOOs). Typically, in counterinsurgency, these include security, development, governance, rule of law, and essential services, among others.

This is not the best way to manage the Afghan campaign, because LOOs can create stovepipes: each LOO team tends to focus on its own issues, and teams may lack adequate working-level mechanisms for the combined planning and execution—that are essential for carrying out the work of stabilizing districts—reducing identified local drivers of violence and instability. This lack of such mechanisms in turn creates a tendency to dissipate effort in nonstrategic activity—everyone on the headquarters knows what the district's basic problems are, but it is nobody's day job to fix any given problem. Responsibility is fragmented across multiple groups, each of which "owns" part of a problem but lacks the authority (or the sense of ownership) to solve it. Stabilizing the district becomes everybody's job and therefore nobody's.

There is a tendency to place the burden on senior commanders, expecting them to deal with this through a "commander's intent" that is supposed to unify efforts across LOOs. The problem is that real-world commanders, no matter how brilliant, simply lack the "bandwidth" to master the intensely detailed nuances of each local problem, map these to multiple LOOs, and then coordinate across multiple agencies (many of which they do not control) to generate unified action. In practice—and understandably, since insurgents kill our people daily while unemployment and corruption do not—on a minute-by-minute basis, most military commanders prioritize kinetics (fighting the insurgents) and deal with other issues mainly through periodic (weekly or monthly) interagency reviews. In doing so, they tend to treat, or even exacerbate, the symptoms of instability while neglecting its causes.

In contrast, our field team's experience with units that deployed in the mid-2009 troop augmentation (including the Second Marine Expeditionary Brigade and the Fifth Stryker Brigade Combat Team, Second Infantry Division), and with the Office of Transitional Initiatives in Afghanistan (of the U.S. Agency for International Development), suggests that a different approach, sometimes known as *district stabilization analysis*, may be more effective.

This approach is a three-stage process of *assessment*, *triage*, and *audit*, after which the unit involved creates "integrated issue teams" to manage priority stabilization targets. In the *assessment* phase, the unit conducts an analysis to map all the grievances, issues, and problems across a particular district, aiming to identify the main drivers of violent conflict. Since this is Afghanistan, the assessment typically results in a lengthy list of problems, many of which are long-standing, intractable issues that simply cannot be fixed by outsiders.

In the *triage* phase, the unit selectively reduces this list down to a priority action list, by identifying problems that meet the following three criteria:

1. The problem is actually, currently, driving instability that creates Afghan-on-Afghan violence in the district in question;
2. The insurgents are actually, currently, exploiting the problem in order to increase the strength, reach, or public appeal of their movement within the district;
3. ISAF can make a meaningful, sustainable contribution to resolving the problem, in a viable timeframe (18 months to 2 years), within current resources.

This triage process typically results in a much-reduced list of two to three priority problems in each district, representing issues that have strategic impact and that the unit can also do something about: problems that both matter to the population and are fixable by us in a meaningful time frame and within existing resources.

In the final, *audit* phase, the unit reviews all its activities—development spending, security effort, key leader engagement, direct action against high-value targets, partnering and mentoring, intelligence collection, and so on—against these priority problems. In many cases, units doing this operational audit for the first time discover that their efforts have been dissipated in attempts to solve numerous grievances that do not matter, cannot be fixed, or would take too long or need too many resources. Often they also find that the attempt to deal with multiple grievances simultaneously has both raised and disappointed community expectations over time, creating a credibility gap in the minds of the local population. The audit process allows units to redirect effort onto identified *priority stabilization targets* and begin to rebuild local partnerships.

Redirecting this effort involves organizing for success: rather than stovepiping along LOOs, the unit can tiger-team around identified stabilization targets. This is done by forming multidisciplinary stabilization teams ("stab teams"), one for each priority issue, with one individual in charge of each team who has the personal day-to-day responsibility to track and deal with that issue.

Staff sections contribute to these stab teams just as they do in any integrated planning process—rather than having stovepiped teams for security, development, rule of law, and so on, the unit forms a team for each identified driver of conflict (e.g., a corrupt subdistrict governor, an influential local Taliban court, or a capable bomb-making cell) and allocates a representative to each issue team from the security, development, rule of law, essential services, and intelligence sections.

This is not the only workable method. For example, Canadian forces in Kandahar have recently experienced considerable success with their Key Village Approach, using specialized stab teams that focus on identified priority grievances in key local districts lying astride the main insurgent approaches to Kandahar city. Whatever technique is adopted, the critical thing is that the unit should develop a shared understanding of the key drivers of conflict in its area of responsibility, form a unified issue team to deal with each driver, and make one individual responsible for working each issue.

This is where, as the campaign develops, developing *common core metrics* to match this methodology come into their own.

COMMON CORE METRICS

Metrics in this sense are observable indicators—detectable events in the environment that indicate progress toward, or away from, identified goals. Because consistency over time is important, a small number of enduring key indicators is better than a large number of frequently changing indicators. Ideally, assessment staffs are looking for surrogate indicators that allow them to detect deeper trends in the environment that may not be directly observable. They are also looking for clusters—indicators that tend to occur together and, taken in context, can be interpreted together to generate a picture of overall trends.

Interpretation of indicators is critically important, and requires informed expert judgment. It is not enough merely to count incidents or conduct quantitative or statistical analysis—interpretation is a qualitative activity based on familiarity with the environment, and it needs to be conducted by experienced personnel who have worked in that environment for long enough to detect trends by comparison with previous conditions. These trends may not be obvious to personnel who are on short-duration tours in country, for example.

Metrics that can be deceptive, and therefore should be avoided, include:

1. **Body count.** At the start of a conventional engagement, if we are facing one hundred of the enemy, and we kill twenty, we can assume that eighty are left. In counterinsurgency, this logic does not hold: the 20 killed may have 40 relatives who are now in a blood feud with and are obligated to take revenge on the security forces who killed the 20, so the new number of the enemy is not 80 but 120. Of course, it is impossible to know whether this is or is not the case—so body counts tell us little about overall enemy strength. Moreover, body-count data are notoriously corrupt and subjective, with differing interpretations of insurgent versus civilian casualties, and are open to being "gamed" by the enemy or by corrupt security force units who might deem killed civilians posthumously to be "combatants."

2. **Military accessibility:** the ability of a security force unit to move from point A to point B within its area of responsibility. The level of weaponry, size of force, and number of combat engagements required to conduct a given move changes over time depending on the security situation, but overall this indicator is problematic because it depends on the enemy's desire and willingness to engage us. If a unit always gets into firefights in a particular area, we can assume the presence of active hostile insurgents there. But the reverse is not the case—absence of armed opposition does not indicate lack of enemy presence. The enemy may simply be choosing not to fight, for reasons ranging from lack of numbers to lack of popular support (or, conversely, a desire to protect proinsurgent local populations) to the fact that the enemy may use the district as a rest area or logistic base or may have the objective of organizing the population in that area, rather than fighting the security forces.

3. **SIGACTs,** especially those involving violence against the Coalition. These are often used as a surrogate metric for overall progress, on the assumption that more SIGACTs are bad and fewer SIGACTs are better. This is understandable but again problematic. Violence tends to be high in contested areas and low in government-controlled areas. But it is also low in enemy-controlled areas, so that a low level of

violence indicates that *someone* is fully in control of a district but does not tell us who. In 2010, we will insert approximately thirty-seven thousand extra troops into Afghanistan, on top of twenty thousand in 2009, so by definition SIGACTs will be higher, since there will be more troops engaging in combat. There will also be an observer effect—not only will more combat actually occur but also we will have more eyes out on the ground observing and reporting violence. Thus, almost certainly, violence involving the Coalition (actual and reported) will rise in the next year, but this higher violence level will not in itself tell us whether we are winning or losing.

4. **Dialog with the enemy.** Our Afghan interlocutors have discussed with us in detail their way of war, which includes regular contact with enemy leaders (via telephone, via letter, or face to face). This occurs partly because people across all factions of the insurgency and the government side are related to each other, have common district or tribal ties, and know each other well; because many families have members on both sides; and because in Afghanistan, warfare is normally accompanied by direct messaging. Unlike us, Afghans do not necessarily stop talking to the enemy when they start fighting: most conflicts end when one group switches sides or agrees to surrender. Thus, the mere fact that our local partners are in dialog with the enemy is not an indicator in and of itself of disloyalty to the government.

5. **Any single numerical metric.** Numerical indicators tend to be misleading because quantitative data is so difficult to collect and verify in Afghanistan. Numerical indicators include body counts, incident counts, SIGACTs, and numbers of Afghan police or soldiers trained. Numerical indicators are essential, but they must be carefully interpreted in the context of other quantitative data, along with a qualitative (political) assessment of conditions in a given district.

7. **Any input metric.** Input metrics are indicators based on our own level of effort, as distinct from the effects of our efforts. For example, input metrics include numbers of enemy killed, numbers of friendly forces trained, numbers of schools or clinics built, miles of road completed, and so on. These indicators tell us what we are doing but not the effect we are having. To understand that effect, we need to look at *output metrics* (how many friendly forces are still serving three

months after training, for example, or how many schools or clinics are still standing and in use after a year) or, better still, at *outcome metrics*. Outcome metrics track the actual and perceived effect of our actions on the population's safety, security, and well-being. This matters because in counterinsurgency, if we want the population to cease supporting or tolerating the enemy, we need to make them feel safe and convince them that they are better off siding with the government than with the insurgents. Note that they not only have to *be* safe. They must also *feel* safe, or they will not be motivated to choose the government side. Thus, popular perceptions are critical, and these cannot be tracked through measures of our input alone.

MORE USEFUL METRICS

Metrics with greater utility can be divided into four categories, based on the four key factors in any counterinsurgency: the population; the supported (host nation) government; the security forces (military and police); and the enemy. A selection of possible metrics includes the following.

Population-related Indicators

- **Voluntary reporting.** The number of unsolicited tip-offs from the population, in relation to insurgent activity, can indicate the level of popular confidence in the Afghan security forces and willingness to support the government. This indicator must be verified by assessing the percentage of tip-offs that prove to be accurate: a low accuracy level may indicate that the population is hedging, trying to placate the security forces with inaccurate information, or using the security forces to settle scores with local rivals by denouncing them as insurgents.

- **Percentage of reported IEDs that are actually found.** Reporting of IEDs is an important subset of the voluntary reporting metric, because accurate reporting indicates that the population is willing to act voluntarily to protect the security forces. These devices account for roughly 50 percent of ISAF casualties in Afghanistan. Yet approximately 80 percent of IEDs that are discovered (as distinct from those that explode) are spotted simply because someone, often an Afghan, sees the

IED on the side of the road and tells someone. Variations in the percentage of Afghan-originated IED reports that are accurate may therefore correlate with variations in levels of local support for ISAF and the government.

- **Price of exotic vegetables.** Afghanistan is an agricultural economy, and crop diversity varies markedly across the country. Given the free-market economics of agricultural production in Afghanistan, risk and cost factors—the opportunity cost of growing a crop, the risk of transporting it across insecure roads, the risk of selling it at market and of transporting money home again—tend to be automatically priced in to the cost of fruits and vegetables. Thus, fluctuations in overall market prices may be a surrogate metric for general popular confidence and perceived security. In particular, exotic vegetables—those grown outside a particular district that have to be transported further at greater risk in order to be sold in that district—can be a useful telltale marker.

- **Transportation prices.** Again, Afghanistan's trucking companies tend to price risk and cost—the risks of insurgent attack, IEDs, kidnapping, or robbery, and the costs of bribes, kickbacks, and other forms of corruption—into the prices they charge for transportation on the country's roads. Thus, variations over time in the price for transporting a standard load on a given route can indicate variations in the level of public perception of security, and of corruption and criminality, along that route. As with all other indicators, variations over time are more significant than the price on any particular day.

- **Progress of NGO construction projects.** Numerous NGOs are engaged in construction projects across Afghanistan, using local materials and labor. Unlike government projects (which the insurgents may attack on principle), NGO projects tend to go well when they have access to low-cost materials and an adequate labor supply and tend to suffer when costs rise due to insecurity. Thus, NGOs running multiple projects at different points across the country may have a fairly clear idea of security conditions and confidence levels, based on the degree of progress in their projects.

- **Influence of Taliban versus government courts.** Taliban mobile courts operate across much of the south and east of Afghanistan, providing dispute resolution, mediation, and sharia-based rule-of-law services to the local population and making judgments that are enforced by local Taliban vigilante cells that operate much as insurgent "police." Rule of law and local-level governance has developed into a major insurgent focus over the past two years. Public willingness to seek, accept, and abide by judgments from Taliban courts may indicate popular support for the insurgents, or it may simply reflect a default choice in the absence of an alternative— for example, in districts where there are no local government courts (most of the south) or where traditional tribal courts have been displaced. The Taliban courts' range of movement and the volume of cases being brought to them considered in comparison to the volume of cases being brought to local government courts may indicate whether the population sees the government or the insurgents as fairer, swifter, or more able to solve their problems.

- **Rate of participation in programs.** More generally, both the government and the insurgents run a range of community programs, economic programs, and political activities that seek popular participation. The rate of participation in these programs varies over time both between villages and within the same village. While it is generally difficult to gauge participation in enemy programs with great precision, participation in Afghan government or Coalition programs is easier to track and may indicate the degree to which the local community perceives the Afghan government as a legitimate actor with the ability to address its problems.

- **Tax collection.** A classical counterinsurgency metric is the rate of taxation compliance, specifically the population's rate of compliance with the government's taxation programs versus that with the insurgents' taxation system. The insurgents operate a robust, predictable taxation system across most of Afghanistan. The government does not; it collects hardly any taxes at the local level. By contrast, corrupt officials and police collect illegal tolls and taxes at checkpoints. In this situation, a three-way comparison is needed that takes into account the effects of the insurgents' taxation (where a high degree of local compliance indicates a high degree of insurgent control), of the government's taxation (where the emergence of any fair and predictable system would represent an improvement in government effectiveness), and of the illegal extortion (which indicates the level of corruption of key local officials and may correlate to popular rage and discontent).

- **Afghan-on-Afghan violence.** Unlike statistics that track violence against the Coalition, the amount of Afghan-on-Afghan violence (whether the cause is insurgent action, the actions of government officials and security forces, or criminality) is a good indicator of the level of public security. In areas where there is a high level of Afghan-on-Afghan violence, the population is very unlikely to feel safe enough to put their weapons down and join in peaceful negotiation or support for the government. Likewise, a spike in Afghan-on-Afghan violence in a particular area probably correlates to a drop in public confidence.

- **Rate of new business formation and loan repayment.** The number of new local businesses being formed each month, along with the rate of loan repayment to local moneylenders, can be an indicator of public confidence and economic growth. In Afghanistan, the rate of small business formation is typically low, while the rate of repayment is usually fairly high. Both indicators, however, fluctuate in line with availability of capital and confidence in the future of Afghanistan. These indicators also tend to vary markedly between urban and rural areas, and the contrasting numbers may serve as a measure of how public perceptions differ in the cities and larger towns compared to smaller villages. The urban-rural divide is a long-standing social cleavage in Afghanistan—one the Taliban has exploited in the past—and is worth tracking closely.

- **Rate of new starts on urban construction** (especially residential housing and markets). Especially in urban areas, this rate can be an important surrogate indicator of the level of popular confidence in the future. People who lack a sense of security and an expectation that the future will be better than the past tend to be less willing to invest in major construction projects. As with other indicators, fluctuations in the rate over time may be more telling than the absolute number in any given area at any one time.

- **Percentage of local people with secure title to their houses and land.** Land reform is a long-standing issue in many parts of Afghanistan. Land ownership was a major flashpoint in the Soviet-Afghan war and back into the nineteenth century and earlier. In many areas, corrupt power brokers exploit complicated land disputes. The Taliban have at times acted as mediators and sought to resolve these disputes justly, in order to further their influence; at other times, they have deliberately exacerbated and exploited land disputes in order to gain the allegiance of local people who are party to a dispute. A key element of public confidence and perception of stability is having secure title to land and other property. Therefore, the percentage of people in a given district who have secure title to their property can be an indication of stability, whereas a large number of unresolved or power-locked land or title disputes can indicate potential for instability and insurgent exploitation.

Host Nation Government indicators

- **Rate of assassinations and kidnappings** of local officials, tribal elders, district notables, and ordinary people. This rate can be an indicator of instability in a district. For example, a province that is experiencing frequent assassinations of local subdistrict governors, police officials, or other government representatives or a high turnover of local people in positions of authority may be experiencing a concerted insurgent push to displace or destroy a local elite. In general terms, a high rate also indicates a high degree of instability, even in the absence of overt insurgent activity. On the other hand, a low assassination or kidnapping rate does not necessarily indicate that a district is progovernment—a district that has a low assassination rate, produces low levels of voluntary reporting, and has a low violence level may simply be an enemy district that is stable under insurgent control.
- **Civilian accessibility.** As already mentioned, military accessibility is not a good indicator of insurgent activity. Civilian accessibility is a better one. If local officials are unable to travel or work in a given area or must do so with an escort, if they are frequently kidnapped or assassinated, or if the local population avoids an area, this tends to indicate insurgent or criminal presence. Even in the absence of insurgent violence directed at Coalition or Afghan security forces, "no-go areas" for civilian government officials tend to indicate a high degree of insurgent control.
- **Where local officials sleep.** A large proportion of Afghan government officials currently do not sleep in the districts for which they are responsible—district governors may sleep in the provincial capital, while some provincial governors sleep in Kabul or in their home districts in other provinces. In some cases, when a local official does not sleep in his assigned district, this may indicate a lack of security and high threat, in which case the district is likely to be heavily insurgent-contested or even insurgent-controlled. In other

cases, the official may sleep with his own kin group in a different district out of personal preference, indicating that he may be acting as an "absentee governor" or may have been appointed as an outsider to control the district, rather than representing it. In either case, the official in question is less likely to be seen as legitimate and effective by the local population. Thus, changes in this indicator may indicate changes in local perceptions of the government.

- **Officials' business interests.** It is often useful to map officials' business interests and those of their relatives and tribal kinship groups (ownership of companies, bids for Coalition or Afghan contracts, control of local production resources) against incidents of violence and unrest in districts for which they are responsible. Determining these interests can be difficult (though the local population usually knows them) but can be revealing—incidents of violence against USAID construction projects, for example, may be insurgent-inspired or may simply reflect the efforts of an official who owns a rival company to undermine a project with a view to eventually taking it over. An official whose tribe or family is a party to a land or water dispute or who has business interests in a particular piece of land may also be an illegitimate broker in the eyes of the local population, who may turn to the Taliban for relief. Likewise, officials who engage energetically in counternarcotics operations but simultaneously own substantial poppy fields in other parts of the country may simply be eliminating their rivals' crops to further their own interests. A district-based "register of officials' assets," regularly updated, can therefore be a very useful tool for interpreting incidents of violence.

- **Percentage of officials purchasing their positions.** Many local government officials in parts of Afghanistan gain their official positions through an informal (and illegal) system of patronage and nepotism, where they purchase their positions for a substantial sum, paid to a higher-level official, often a relative. This system creates incentives for corruption, since these officials must now recoup their investment through extorting money from the population and may have to pass kickbacks to their patron. They have essentially purchased a "license to exploit," and over time government positions come to be seen as opportunities to fleece the population rather than to serve Afghanistan. Obviously, this creates enormous opportunities for the insurgents to exploit. In a given district, therefore, a high percentage of officials owing their positions to the illegal purchase system tends to correlate with a high degree of corruption, and may correlate with the population having a more-than-normal willingness to collaborate with the insurgents.

- **Rate of budget execution** (how much of their allocated budget line ministries, provincial and central government officials, and local councils are actually able to spend) is a potential indicator of the degree of government effectiveness. Districts where allocated funds are being spent in a timely manner are more likely to be receiving an adequate level of government services, local officials are likely to be more capable managers, the absorptive capacity of the local economy is likely to be higher, and corruption *may* be lower. Conversely, districts that do not execute their budget effectively may be suffering from poor-quality officials, lack of economic capacity, and a lesser degree of essential services. Coalition units may also be at fault: the tendency to dump Commander's Emergency Response Program (CERP) funds on underperforming districts through block grants can generate the appearance of a short-term "quick fix" but can also have an addictive effect that causes local officials to sit on their own funds while letting the foreigners spend and may create habits of dependency that ultimately undermine the effectiveness of the local economy.

- **Capital flight.** During the period of intense uncertainty in late 2009, as Afghans anxiously awaited the U.S. decision on which strategy to select and whether or not to reinforce the effort, we saw millions of dollars leaving Afghanistan on a weekly basis, as Afghans shifted their assets outside the country in expectation of instability and possible civil war. When this type of behavior spikes, this may indicate a significant lack of confidence in the future and public uncertainty. Changes in the rate of capital movement outside the country may track closely with changes in public confidence, hence in the credibility and legitimacy of Afghan government and international community efforts in the eyes of local elites.

- **Rate of formation of antiinsurgent lashkars.** Districts that are opposed to the insurgents but also distrustful of the government tend to have a high rate of formation of *lashkars* (tribal or district fighting groups) that seek to protect the community against all comers. Thus, the formation of antiinsurgent *lashkars* in a given area may indicate that the population distrusts both the government and the insurgents and is a possible indicator of "swing voter" behavior or autarkic "a plague on all your houses" attitudes on the part of local community leaders.

- **Public safety function.** The side that performs the public safety function—protecting the population from crime and violence—tends to be seen as the more legitimate and effective. Given the high level of police corruption and abuse in some parts of Afghanistan, many of our interlocutors scoff at the idea of going to the police for protection. By contrast, the Taliban have been carefully building a reputation for swift and harsh but fair punishment of criminals and for protecting local people from abuse. The Taliban's published legal code, the layeha, binds both Taliban units and populations to a set of standards enforced by local Taliban cells. In Kandahar and some other centers, the Taliban maintain a public safety hotline (akin to a 911 call center) that local people can call in an emergency, to confirm or deny Taliban involvement in an incident, or to seek Taliban assistance. These behaviors, coupled with a moderate to high level of abuses by local officials and police, may indicate that the local population sees the insurgents as more legitimate and effective than the government in a given area.

Security Force Indicators

- **Kill ratio** (ratio between kills inflicted and kills suffered). Whereas raw body count is a poor indicator, this ratio can be a useful indicator of a unit's level of confidence, aggression, and willingness to close with the enemy. However, in assessing this metric it is essential to control for civilian casualties, escalation-of-fire incidents, and other possible indicators (discussed below) that a given unit may be engaging in brutality or abuse. Kills resulting from indirect fires (artillery or mortars) or air strikes or kills by supporting Coalition units also do not count. The only data relevant to this indicator are confirmed kills/captures directly inflicted by the unit in question on positively identified insurgents actually engaging in combat operations. As with many metrics, the absolute number of kills or captures at any given moment is less important than second-order data relating to trends over time. If a unit's kill ratio is improving, this *may* indicate greater confidence, better dominance over a given area, better intelligence, and possibly a closer relationship with local populations. But like other indicators, kill ratio must be interpreted in relation to other data before this can be known.

- **Ratio of wins to losses.** At the most general level, units that consistently win their engagements—inflicting more losses than they suffer, retaining possession of disputed ground, and protecting key population groups—are usually performing better than units that consistently lose. In practice, however, most security force units win most engagements against insurgents, so that changes in the win-to-loss ratio over time are more significant than the absolute proportion of wins to losses. Again, in calculating this ratio, it is essential to control for engagements won due to artillery/air support or Coalition force intervention, as these do not count in assessing the unit itself.

- **Ratio of kills to wounds/captures.** In a standard combat engagement, for every one enemy killed, analysts usually expect to see three to five enemy wounded or captured. This is of course simply a general guideline, but some Afghan security force units consistently kill four or five enemy to one wounded or captured. This abnormal kill-to-wound ratio bears closer investigation. It may be that the enemy always fights to the death or that Afghan units have a remarkably high level of marksmanship, though field observation and anecdotal evidence suggests neither of these is the case. It may also be that these units are relying on airpower and artillery and that this is generating this anomalous ratio. Alternatively, a kill-to-wound ratio of 4–5 to 1 (rather than the normal 1 to 3–5) may indicate that units are engaging in extrajudicial killings or deeming dead civilians posthumously to be "enemy." There is insufficient evidence at this time to be certain, but as an indicator of possible security force brutality, this needs to be closely tracked.

- **Ratio of guilty to innocent detainees** (the proportion of individuals detained who on subsequent investigation turn out to be closely, genuinely linked to the insurgency). A unit that has a low detainee guilt ratio may be arresting lots of local military-age males, but if most of these are innocent, it can be having a sharply negative effect on local support and may even be producing insurgents, as innocent detainees become radicalized in temporary detention and families become radicalized through the unwarranted seizure of their young men. Conversely, a unit that has a high detainee guilt ratio is detaining mainly individuals who are genuinely linked to the insurgency, and this is a surrogate indicator that its intelligence is of high quality, its methods are showing appropriate restraint, and it is probably gaining the confidence of the local population by developing a reputation for accuracy and effectiveness.

- **Ratio of recruitment to desertion.** In general, when an organization's recruitment rates are higher than its desertion rates, morale can be said to be functionally adequate. When desertion rates rise, along with other indicators like increased sickness rates and short-term absences without leave, organizational morale is likely to be dropping. (The rate of short-term absence without leave is not a reliable indicator in itself, however, because in countries like Afghanistan where recruits have little or no access to a banking system, they tend to go absent without leave after payday to take their pay home.)

- **Proportion of ghost employees.** Some Afghan military and police units have a proportion of "ghost employees" on their books. In most cases, these are fictional employees whose pay the unit commander claims from higher headquarters but then puts aside for his personal use. While this practice is unlikely to be stamped out any time soon, the proportion of ghost employees in a unit and the way this proportion changes over time may indicate the degree of corruption of the commanders concerned. It does not necessarily indicate poor morale. It *may* do so if unit members feel they are being exploited, but in some cases they see the practice as legitimate: in a society without robust social security or veterans' pensions, some units use ghost employees to create a pool of funds that go to the welfare of incapacitated police or soldiers and the families of those killed in action.

- **Location at start of firefight.** Every firefight in Afghanistan is played out in front of an audience and has a political and military meaning in the eyes of that audience. Afghan elders frequently call Coalition commanders at the end of an engagement in order to offer their play-by-play commentary on a firefight that has just ended. One of the key elements in how the population interprets a firefight is the location of opposing forces. For example, if security forces are located in a population center, standing with the population at the start of an engagement, and the enemy attacks down from the hills, then the population frequently seems to interpret the insurgents as the aggressors and the security forces as their protectors. Thus, even if the insurgents win the firefight, they may lose politically by pushing the population into our arms. Conversely, when security forces attack into a village or valley, even if acting on solid intelligence, the population sometimes perceives them as the aggressors and may side with the insurgents. This is especially so in night attacks, surprise attacks, or engagements in remote terrain where rural populations are traditionally suspicious of strangers. If a unit is consistently located in close proximity to protected populations at the start of firefights and consistently wins those firefights, this *may* indicate that the unit is gaining credibility and legitimacy in the eyes of the population.

- **Escalation-of-fire incidents and civilian casualties.** Units that consistently get involved in escalation-of-force incidents (where troops fire on civilians who fail to stop at roadblocks, drive too close to convoys, or otherwise appear threatening) or are responsible for significant numbers of civilian casualties *may* have an overly aggressive attitude to the local population and may be placing too little emphasis on protecting civilians. They may also be overly nervous and frightened of their environment and hence trigger-happy. Almost certainly, units that frequently kill or wound civilians lack a close relationship with the local population, lack viable local partners, and lack a good information network, making them more vulnerable to insurgent attacks.

- **Duration of operations.** Single-day operations—in which a unit sleeps every night in its fortified base and only goes out in the daylight—tend to indicate lack of confidence, lack of energy, or the existence of a tacit (or possibly even explicit) live-and-let-live deal with the insurgents. Single day, large-unit sweep operations (daylight search operations, cordon-and-knock sweeps, or short-duration raiding operations) may also be having a negative effect in their own right. A unit that consistently conducts multiday operations that last for up to several weeks and lives in its area of responsibility rather than merely visiting it tends over time to develop a closer rapport with the local population, becomes more familiar with local enemy groups, and protects its population while dominating its area more effectively.

- **Night operations.** If a given unit frequently operates by night or stays out for several nights on operations, this may indicate that the unit is dominating its area of operations, is confident in its environment, and has the upper hand. In particular, if night operations tend to be protective (e.g., ambushing potential enemy routes used to infiltrate population centers and intimidate government-aligned population groups) then they may contribute to a popular feeling of safety and normality and hence may bring the local population to the government's side. On the other hand, if night operations are aggressive (e.g., raiding, hard-knock search operations, use of air strikes and indirect fire to "deny" areas to insurgents) they may actually contribute to a feeling of insecurity on the part of the population and hence may have a destabilizing effect on the district.

- **Small-unit operations.** Units that mount a larger number of smaller unit operations (at squad, platoon, or company level, depending on the local threat profile) tend to cover a greater area within their area of responsibility, with greater thoroughness. Willingness to conduct multiple small-unit operations also indicates a greater degree of confidence and an expectation of defeating the enemy if encountered.
- **Combined action operations.** Operations involving combined action—where Coalition units intimately partner with local military, police, civilian authorities, and Coalition civilian agencies down to the small-unit level—tend to indicate improved performance by all partners in the action. Coalition forces tend to perform better because they have access to local knowledge, language skills, and situational awareness. Local military forces can access Coalition fire support assets, intelligence, mobility, medical support, and other enablers and have a constant professional exemplar in the presence of Coalition troops. Local police are relieved of the burden of direct combat with main-force insurgents and can focus on their policing role, and they are constantly monitored, reducing the risk of corrupt or abusive behavior. Local and Coalition civilian authorities and agencies are able to operate in higher-threat environments as part of a combined action team, giving them greater reach and endurance, better protection, and the ability to demonstrate responsible leadership and deliver essential services to the population.
- **Dismounted operations.** If a unit frequently operates on foot, this may be an indicator that it is more confident in its environment, has greater reach across its area of responsibility (much of which,

in Afghanistan, may be out of reach of the road system), and has a better rapport with local populations. Anecdotal evidence and data from other campaigns suggests that units that operate dismounted may also be less vulnerable to roadside IEDs, though this has yet to be confirmed in the Afghan context. Conversely, units that always operate from the supposed safety of road-bound armored vehicles may be predictable (due to always following a limited number of roads), may be easily ambushed, and may lack rapport with the population, which may see them as alien, strange, or cowardly. The roadside IED is clearly a military weapon, but it is also a political weapon the insurgents use to separate the security forces from the population. Dismounted operations can redress this separation. In practice, due to the size of Afghanistan and the lack of friendly troops, almost all operations commence with a road or air move to a jumping-off point from which units may proceed dismounted. Furthermore, the positive effects of dismounted operations may improve the relationship between the unit and the population across its whole area of responsibility, not just in the actual areas where it operates dismounted.

- **Driving behavior.** The driving style of a unit—whether drivers push civilian vehicles out of their way, whether they wait their turn in traffic, how aggressively they force civilian cars back from convoys, whether or not they illuminate passing traffic with laser sights, whether they hog the center lane of the road or drive in lane—is a good atmospheric indicator of a unit's attitude toward the population and hence of the population's likely attitude toward that unit. Units that drive rudely, alienate the population, and disrupt traffic and commerce with aggressive driving techniques usually have poor community rapport.

- **Reliance on air and artillery support.** If a unit relies too heavily on air strikes, artillery and mortar fire, and other forms of nonorganic support (i.e., assets not owned by the unit but rather called upon through higher headquarters) in most of its engagements, this may indicate lack of confidence and unwillingness to engage with the enemy or the local population. It also creates conditions that may lead to increased civilian casualties or collateral property damage, as the unit is employing area weapons that it does not control rather than organic direct-fire weapons. This tendency can be assessed by comparing the size of units engaged in a given series of combat actions with how often they call on nonorganic fires: if a unit consistently draws on indirect fire even when engaging much smaller enemy groups, it may have a confidence problem. Conversely, if the unit regularly gets into situations where its small units encounter large enemy groups and have to be rescued by indirect fire, it may be overreaching or may be overmatched in its area of operations and require reinforcement.

- **Pattern-setting and telegraphing moves to the enemy.** Units that set patterns—always moving on set routes, always leaving or entering bases from the same direction at the same time, selecting the same overwatch positions on patrol after patrol, or developing standard ambush positions or observation posts—tend to become more vulnerable to insurgent ambushes, IEDs, and attacks. Likewise, if a unit has a tendency to accidentally telegraph its moves to the enemy (e.g., by always massing helicopters in the same way before a raid) it may be more vulnerable to being outmaneuvered by the insurgents. On the other hand, deliberately telegraphing moves to the population is often appropriate in Afghanistan: even the Taliban rarely move from one valley or village to another without seeking community permission, and Coalition units can message local populations—"we are coming into your valley next month, you have ten days to expel the enemy from your villages or we will be forced to mount a clearance operation"—in order to force the enemy to move without fighting. This does not always work, but it is a technique that is familiar to Afghans because it is often used in their traditional forms of conflict, and it may have a positive effect in some circumstances.

- **Possession of the high ground at dawn.** The Afghan campaign, in addition to being a counterinsurgency, a stabilization operation, and a competition for governance, is also a classic mountain warfare campaign, especially in Regional Command North, East, and some parts of Regional Commands South, West, and Capital. Thus, the basic tenets of mountain warfare tactics apply, including control of the high ground, maintenance of wide fields of observation from key terrain, dominance of peaks overlooking key routes, ability to bring plunging fire onto identified enemy positions, and ability to move on the high ground at night. Units that consistently hold the high ground at dawn tend to demonstrate a mastery of this form of warfare, whereas units that are consistently overlooked by the enemy at first light tend to struggle in this environment.

Enemy Indicators

- **High-technology inserts.** The Taliban are generally a low-tech guerrilla force, but they do possess and deploy some high-tech capabilities: satellite phones, accurized weapons, sniper optics, and (in some parts of the country) high-tech components for IEDs. Presence of these high-tech inserts in a given insurgent group may indicate that it has access to better funding or greater support from external sponsors, and such a unit is more likely to be a full-time main force Taliban column rather than a local (so-called Tier 2) guerrilla group.
- **Insurgent medical health.** The health of insurgent detainees from a given area is also an indicator of the nature of the insurgent organization in that area. Local guerrillas tend to suffer numerous health problems, ranging from malnutrition through malaria, tuberculosis, leishmaniasis, and other parasitic diseases to diabetes, respiratory tract infections, and other chronic health problems. Their health problems tend to track those of the local population in a given area. Main force units, on the other hand, often have a better general level of health, and insurgents based in Pakistan or directly sponsored by external agencies may have received inoculations or other medical support—in both cases, the healthier an insurgent, the more likely he is to have received external assistance.
- **Presence of specialist teams and foreign advisers.** Some Taliban main-force units work with specialist teams—snipers, heavy machine-gun and mortar teams, rocket teams, specialized reconnaissance teams, intelligence teams, media-propaganda teams, and so on. Some also often include foreigners (i.e., of non-Afghan origin) and occasionally foreign advisers (usually Pakistani or Central Asian in origin). The presence of these specialized teams and especially of foreign advisers in a given district may indicate that a main-force enemy column is working in that district.
- **Insurgents' village of origin.** There difference between insurgents who originate from villages within the same district where they fight (local guerrillas) and those who fight outside their district of origin is extremely important. Local guerrillas are often part-time fighters, frequently switch sides in the conflict on the basis of local (tribal or economic) motivations, and more generally are part of the fabric of local society. If a security force unit is to

stabilize a given district it needs to defeat these local guerrillas, but it must also emphasize their reintegration, reconciliation with them, and winning them over; after all, they represent key members of the society the unit is trying to stabilize. Thus, attempts to destroy local guerrillas outright can backfire by alienating communities and can create blood feuds that perpetuate the conflict. On the other hand, insurgents who operate outside their district of origin, or even originate from outside the country can be deemed "foreign fighters" in the eyes of the community. They often lack tribal ties or rapport with the community and should be targeted with maximum lethality, as ruthlessly as is legally permissible. As a foreign body within local society, these fighters can be killed and captured intensively (as long as targeting is accurate and avoids innocent civilians) without disrupting our relationship with the locals. Indeed, local communities may actually feel safer and may partner more closely with units that ruthlessly target foreign-origin insurgents while seeking to reintegrate and reconcile with local guerrillas.

- **First-to-fire ratio** (percentage of firefights in which our side fires first). This ratio is a key indicator of which side controls the initiation of firefights and is a useful surrogate metric to determine which side possesses the tactical initiative. If our side fires first in most firefights, this likely indicates that we are ambushing the enemy (or mounting preplanned attacks) more frequently than we are being ambushed. This in turn may indicate that our side has better situational awareness and access to intelligence on enemy movements than the insurgents, and it certainly indicates that we have the initiative and the enemy may be reacting to us. Most important, the side that initiates the majority of firefights tends to control the loss rate, and this can be checked by mapping insurgent losses against which side fired first in the engagements where those losses were suffered—if the insurgents are losing most of their casualties in firefights they initiate themselves, then they are in control of their own loss rate and can simply stop picking fights if their losses become unsustainable and restart operations once they recover. If they are losing most of their casualties in engagements we initiate, then we control their loss rate and can force them below replenishment level and ultimately destroy the network in question.

- **Price of black market weapons and ammunition.** Afghanistan has a substantial black market in weapons, ammunition, explosives, and other military equipment. As in any other free market, the price of weaponry on this black market reflects supply (availability of weapons) and demand (the rate of arming or rearming among population groups and the insurgent requirements for weapons to support their operations). Thus, price fluctuations over time—especially in standard weapons such as Chinese or Romanian AKs, or in commodities such as 7.62mm short AK rounds—can indicate changes in insurgent operational tempo, an increase in community demand (due to insecurity), or a drop in supply due to improved interdiction.
- **Ratio of surrendering insurgents to those killed/captured.** A larger number of defectors, deserters, or surrenders on the part of an insurgent group may indicate a drop in that group's morale. Conversely, unwillingness to surrender—fighting until killed or captured—on the part of insurgent fighters can indicate high motivation. Analysts can seek indications of an insurgent network's morale by comparing changes over time in the insurgent kill/capture rate with changes in the insurgent surrender/desertion rate. These ratios should also be considered in relation to the insurgent recruitment and retention rate—if an insurgent group's loss rate is high but it has no difficulty obtaining local recruits, then it is likely to be experiencing a high degree of local support.
- **Midlevel insurgent casualties.** The insurgents' loss rate is also a useful indicator, especially in relation to losses in the middle tiers of the insurgent organization—the level below the senior leadership group, comprising planners, operational facilitators, technical specialists, trainers, recruiters, financiers, and lower-level operational commanders. Killing senior leaders may not actually damage the insurgency particularly, especially if senior leaders who are killed are simply replaced by younger, hungrier, more radical and more operationally experienced leaders from the next generation. Likewise, the insurgents can (and do) expect to lose a significant number of foot soldiers and to replace them relatively easily with minimum disruption. On the other hand, killing or capturing the insurgent "middle management" tier can do significant damage to the organization, while leaving senior leaders intact

and perhaps even convincing them over time that their campaign is futile, and without killing large numbers of lower-tier fighters and sympathizers who may be good candidates for reintegration. Thus the insurgent loss rate at the middle level of the network is an especially important indicator of the network's health and resilience.

TENTATIVE CONCLUSIONS

Tracking progress in counterinsurgency is notoriously difficult, and in a complex and fast-moving campaign like Afghanistan, with dozens of actors on all sides and numerous interested parties, it is even more problematic than usual. Nevertheless, in order to react effectively to changes in the enemy and the environmentor, ideally, to preempt enemy actions and gain the initiative, we must measure progress—in the war itself, against the campaign plan, and against recognized norms of best-practice counterinsurgency and stabilization operations.

This chapter has presented a selection of core metrics along with key indicators and some thoughts on assessment and conflict management methodology. Like any other set of thoughts on the campaign, these ideas draw on a long history of counterinsurgency thinking over the past several decades, as well as more recent experience in Afghanistan. They were also out of date the moment they were written down.

As in any other endeavor in counterinsurgency, the challenge for commanders and assessment staffs is to remain agile, seeking not to template previously useful metrics but to constantly develop and apply new indicators, based on a shared diagnosis of the nature of the conflict and what is driving it. These indicators must track developments in the four basic elements of the campaign: the local population, the host-nation government, the security forces, and the insurgents themselves. And they must be carefully interpreted, applying judgment and qualitative reasoning, rather than simply counted.

Introduction to "Globalization and the Development of Indonesian Counterinsurgency Tactics"

"Globalization and the Development of Indonesian Counterinsurgency," first published in the journal *Small Wars and Insurgencies* in March 2006, summarizes some of the research from my doctoral dissertation, completed in 2000 for the University of New South Wales, on insurgency and counterinsurgency in Indonesia.[1]

The full dissertation (available online) is a study of how guerrilla warfare affects individuals and groups at the village level in traditional societies, and was based on extended fieldwork case studies in Indonesia and East Timor.[2] It examines the political power-diffusion effect occasioned by both insurgency and counterinsurgency warfare, in which authority flows away from civilian leaders at the level of the central or national state, toward local armed leaders, and toward the village or tribal level. These leaders, operating at the head of locally powerful armed groups embedded within the society, tend to acquire increasing authority and influence over communities as a conflict progresses, and their authority tends to be greater in proportion to the degree of traditionalism and xenophobia of the population group in question and perceived external threat to it. The effect operates for both insurgents and counterinsurgents, with military forces engaged in counterinsurgency campaigns also tending to decentralize and to forge powerful local partnerships that detach local commanders from central civilian authority but give them great influence with local communities.

The dissertation also traced the development of Indonesian counterinsurgency technique since 1945 and identified the major strengths, weaknesses, and lessons of the unique Indonesian approach. Indonesia fought a protracted campaign against Islamic separatist insurgents—the Darul Islam movement, from which several modern terrorist groups trace their origins—beginning in the 1940s, through the 1950s, and into the early 1960s. This conflict, although it was larger, bloodier, and more widespread than the Malayan Emergency—the British anti-Communist counterinsurgency campaign in the Federation of Malaya during the same period—is not widely known outside Indonesia. This is partly because, as Sebestyen Gorka has argued, although there are literally hundreds of examples of insurgency warfare to choose from, the counterinsurgency community tends to draw its canon of case study examples from a much narrower selection, often colonial-era campaigns involving expeditionary forces from Western countries. As Gorka points out, taking too narrow a selection of examples can significantly skew any conclusions drawn from the experience of European colonial powers, postwar reconstruction, or Cold War campaigns.[3] The Indonesian case lies outside this canon, and as a domestic counterinsurgency involving entirely non-Western actors, it is well worth studying as a means to broaden the frame of reference.

In response to the threat of Islamist separatist insurgency and terrorism, the Indonesian army developed a unique approach to low-intensity warfare, defeating Darul Islam with remarkable effectiveness. The army applied the same approach in East Timor from 1975, with initial success. Ultimately, however, the technique proved unsuitable to modern conditions and eventually became entirely counterproductive, contributing to Indonesia's loss of East Timor in 1999. Another important factor was the difficulty, as already discussed, that the Indonesians faced in conducting an expeditionary counterinsurgency campaign in East Timor, as against a domestic counterinsurgency in the case of West Java.

Until I began the field research for the dissertation, the political effects of low-intensity conflict in Indonesia (including insurgency, guerrilla warfare, and terrorism) upon villages, populations, and military forces had not been studied in detail by a field researcher working on the ground with insurgent groups, security forces, extremist movements, and local populations. Although researchers like Jeffrey Record and Gerald Hickey had conducted seminal studies at the province and village level in Vietnam, and the political scientist Karl D. Jackson had studied the Darul Islam movement in the context of traditional authority in West Javanese society, an extended case study applying ethnographic field research methods to a population-based assessment of Indonesia's experience of guerrilla warfare had not been attempted.[4] I tried to fill that gap.

COUNTERINSURGENCY BEFORE 9/11

The process of conducting extended residential fieldwork in Indonesia, as a serving Australian Army officer, is worth discussing in detail in the context of organizational learning and adaptation.

The Australian Army is charged with defending an enormous island continent (the sixth largest country in the world) that has only a tiny population of twenty-five million people but covers, when its external territories are taken into account, almost one-seventh of the globe. Australia is a classic trade-dependent maritime state with major economic and political partners in the United States, Southeast and Northeast Asia, the Middle East, and Europe. This unique set of circumstances has given rise to a strategic culture of forward defense, in which the Australian Defence Force (ADF), because it is several orders of magnitude too small to conduct a passive continental defense of its immense area of responsibility, tends to operate primarily as an expeditionary power-projection force in the littoral tropical environment of Southeast Asia, and to send expeditionary forces further afield in support of alliance interests.[5]

Between 1939 and 1973, for example, the Australian Army was engaged in continuous operations—mainly jungle warfare and counterinsurgency—across the Pacific and Southeast Asia, as well as World War II, the Malayan Emergency, the Borneo Confrontation, and the Korean and Vietnam wars. Between 1987 and 2001, Australia committed land-based expeditionary forces to Fiji, Namibia, Cambodia, Western Sahara, Somalia, Rwanda, Bougainville (twice), Mozambique, Kuwait, East Timor, and the Solomon Islands.[6] Australia has no marine corps, but because of this tradition of rapid expeditionary deployment of light forces in littoral environments, often making use of airborne and amphibious forces, Australian soldiers tend to operate much like marines—one of many reasons why the Australian Army has long had a very close relationship with the U.S. Marine Corps.

Part of this outward, expeditionary focus is an emphasis on area studies, languages, and close engagement with regional military forces. Unlike some armed forces that segregate their area specialists into separate professional streams, in the Australian system, every army officer undergoes language testing before graduating from the military academy at Duntroon, and officers are expected to become proficient in regional (i.e., Southeast Asian or Pacific) languages. In the late 1980s, when I graduated from the academy, language proficiency or a higher degree in Asian studies were requirements for promotion beyond the rank of Captain, creating a career-based incentive for such study.

Besides this broader pool of baseline regional expertise, the army selected certain officers for advanced specialized training in regional languages and cultures, at the ADF School of Languages. I was one of these, completing a twelve-month Indonesian language course after completing my first two tours as a rifle platoon commander, specialist platoon commander, and company second-in-command in a light infantry battalion.

Established in 1942 to teach Japanese to Allied intelligence officers, the School of Languages was at that time a huddle of buildings on a weather-beaten promontory at Point Cook, Australia's oldest military airfield, southwest of Melbourne. The school is one of the world's great military language colleges, with a proverbially demanding native-speaker teaching staff; a curriculum that covers language, cultural, and area studies; and a student body drawn from the Intelligence, Special Forces, and military attaché communities. In 1993, when I studied there, it occupied the same run-down air force huts where my grandfather had trained as aircrew before leaving Australia to fight in New Guinea in World War II. Student pilots in PC-9 trainer aircraft buzzed us, occasionally too closely for their instructors' comfort, as they circuited the airstrip. Nearby hangars dated to 1903; on one of them a historic dent was preserved, relic of a minor air crash during training by Lieutenant, later Air Marshal Sir Richard Williams, a towering figure in the history of the air force and the first military pilot trained in Australia, who led No. 1 Squadron of the Australian Flying Corps in support of T. E. Lawrence during the Arab Revolt, later commanded a wing of the Royal Air Force, and became chief of air staff between the wars. Neither the "crash hangar" nor the other buildings seemed to have had so much as a lick of paint since my grandfather's time. Southerly winds, straight from Antarctica according to student myth (though not geographic reality), raked the school for much of the year, only partly masking the smell from the enormous sewage farm next door. Rifle ranges, student pilots, and a jetty for high-speed rescue boats kept things noisy, as well as cold and smelly; the school's most distinguished graduate once called it "the outhouses of excellence."

After graduating from Point Cook, I did further specialized training in military assistance and advisory work with indigenous irregular troops, and then commanded military advisory teams with Indonesian Special Forces and Airborne troops in West Java in 1994 and 1995. It was during this work that I made a network of close contacts in the Indonesian military and local communities in the area, first became aware of the Darul Islam insurgency, and decided to undertake a doctorate in Indonesian counterinsurgency.

Another effect of the small size of the ADF is a long-standing emphasis on joint service institutions and operations. The Australian Defence Force Academy (ADFA), where I completed the academic component of my officer training, is a University College of the University of New South Wales and, in addition to training officer cadets of all three services, offers postgraduate degrees to both civilian and military students, including doctorates. I could have applied to take time off from my military duties and attend full-time study at ADFA, but I decided instead to study in my spare time, take no time off from work, and accept no funding from the military. The defense academy agreed to take me on as an external part-time student, and throughout the six years it took me to complete my doctorate I spent only a few months at the university campus. Instead, I used my evenings and weekends, my generous annual leave, and the allowance that language-qualified officers receive for independent travel within their "target country" each year to undertake several periods of extended residential fieldwork in Indonesia. I was also lucky enough to win one of two Dunlop Asia Fellowships awarded each year by the University of Melbourne and the Asialink Foundation, a generous grant that gave me enough money to conduct fieldwork research in country without being too badly out of pocket. I spent this time studying insurgents, militias, and activists in Indonesia and Timor, often working alone in remote areas with tribal and community leaders and local people.

In the event, I managed to complete two case studies, despite being deployed on three military operations (in Cyprus, Bougainville, and East Timor) during this period. These focused on the Islamic insurgency in West Java between 1948 and 1962 and the guerrilla campaign in East Timor between 1974 and 2000. I also managed to do a limited amount of extra fieldwork in Malaysia and Papua New Guinea to produce a comparative analysis of the Malayan Emergency, the Borneo Confrontation, and the West Papua campaign.

The West Java case study was conducted between June 1995 and December 1996, in Australia, the United Kingdom, Indonesia, and the Netherlands. My initial research concentrated on primary sources in

Australian and British archives. In the field phase, I undertook fieldwork in three modules, living in small villages and interacting with local people, including security forces, local populations, and insurgents. The first module comprised oral history interviews in Jakarta, Bandung, Garut, and the surrounding rural subdistricts. The second module consisted of Indonesian-language primary source research and interviews in Jakarta and Bandung. The third module was a terrain analysis of the Garut basin. This included the first-ever ethnographic and geographic survey of areas in West Java affected by Islamic insurgency. I then conducted follow-up interviews, imagery analysis, and statistical analysis in The Hague and at the Rijksinstituut Voor Oorlogsdocumentatie (NIOD), the Netherlands institute for war documentation, in Amsterdam. I received very generous support from the military history section of the Netherlands Army general staff during this period.

The East Timor case study was conducted in 1999–2000. Research comprised primary source analysis in Australia and fieldwork in Dili, Balibo, Ermera, and the surrounding district. Fieldwork, again in a small village environment working through open-ended personal engagement with local communities, participant observations, terrain analysis, and interviews with local people, militia, the Indonesian military, Timorese guerrillas, and UN personnel. I managed to take extensive fieldnotes on terrain, culture, political structure, and military operations, using a standard ethnographic methodology based on participant observation and interviews, along with oral combat-historical analysis. This case study was, and remains, the only contemporaneous field analysis of the 1999 International Force in East Timor (INTERFET) campaign.

Overall, fieldwork formed the major component of the study, comprising more than eight months of residential field research and forty-three hundred hours of interviews in Indonesian, Sundanese, and Tetuñ, the local language of East Timor. The fieldwork data showed that low-intensity warfare in Indonesia between 1945 and 1999 did indeed demonstrate a political power-diffusion effect. This effect was triggered by the outbreak of guerrilla warfare, which itself flowed from crises generated by processes of modernization and change within Indonesian society.

These crises were also affected by events outside Indonesia, including invasion by Japan, the Cold War, the Asian financial crisis, and increasing economic and media globalization. They resulted in a breakdown or weakening of formal power structures, allowing informal power structures to dominate. This in turn allowed local elites to develop political and military power at the local level while being subject to little control from higher levels. This prompted a process of power diffusion from central and civilian leadership levels to local leaders with coercive means—most often military or insurgent leaders.

Having been triggered by guerrilla operations, however, such power diffusion was heavily influenced by contextual variables, of which the most important were geographical factors, political culture, traditional authority structures, and interaction with external events. Topographical isolation, poor infrastructure, severe terrain, scattered population groupings, and influence by traditional hierarchies tended to accelerate and exacerbate the loss of central control. Conversely, good infrastructure, large population centers, good communications, and a high degree of economic and governmental institutionalization tended to slow such diffusion. Moreover, while power might be diffusing at one level of analysis (e.g., at the level of the central nation-state) it might also be centralizing at another (e.g., into the hands of military leaders at a local subnational level).

The fieldwork also provided a detailed exposition of Indonesia's unique counterinsurgency and counterterrorist technique. This technique, developed in West Java in the 1950s, was later applied in conflicts all over Indonesia, including East Timor, Irian Jaya, and Aceh. Under the specific conditions of West Java, it was dramatically effective in ending the campaign against Darul Islam after a twelve-year stalemate. When applied later in East Timor, the technique was initially successful, but it imposed an adaptational pressure that forced the insurgents to modify their tactics and take their cause to the international community. The inability of the Indonesian military and government to adapt their technique so as to deal with the insurgency under international scrutiny ultimately cost Indonesia the province of East Timor. Indonesia's application of the same technique against sophisticated modern terrorist and extremist groups has also been problematic.

In more general terms, the study (summarized in part in the article that follows) shows the growing influence of globalized media, world public opinion, and changing international norms on the conduct of counterinsurgency. As an insight into these processes and as an example from outside the narrow canon of classical counterinsurgency, the Indonesian case is worthy of detailed examination.

Globalization and the Development of Indonesian Counterinsurgency Tactics

3

In the Javanese wet season of 1995, I commanded an Australian Army Mobile Training and Advisory Team, operating alongside Indonesian forces in the Priangan highlands of West Java. As close relationships developed with my Indonesian military and civilian counterparts and the local population, it became apparent that the area had experienced devastating conflict in the 1950s and 1960s.

This conflict was an Islamist insurgency, led by the Darul Islam movement.[1] Lasting from 1947 until 1962, it was larger and bloodier than the Malayan Emergency of the same era, directly threatened the political survival of the Republic of Indonesia, and was won—decisively—by the Indonesian government. Moreover, in 1995 the area was peaceful, relatively prosperous, and integrated into Indonesian society. Despite such a comprehensive victory, this remarkable campaign was and remains almost unknown in Western military circles.[2]

With interest piqued, I spent the next six years (between military postings and operational tours) completing a doctoral dissertation on insurgency and counterinsurgency in Indonesia. This article presents some results of that analysis, and seeks to highlight the impact of globalization on the development of Indonesian counterinsurgency tactics.[3]

METHODOLOGY

The research for my aforementioned dissertation involved two primary and three secondary case studies. The primary studies—West Java and East Timor—comprised historical research using operational and intelligence archives, complemented by geographical analysis using field exploration, terrain studies, maps, and air photographs. Each involved two to four months' fieldwork. Two secondary studies—Irian Jaya and the Borneo Confrontation—involved historical and geographical analysis and field visits but no residential fieldwork. The final study was a comparative analysis of the Malayan Emergency.

The research methodology was to commence with a literature review of published sources and then examine military and national archives. Fieldwork followed, applying interviews, participant observation, terrain analysis, and ethnographic and geographic surveys. Often, because of the variable standards of cartography in Indonesia, this entailed exploring poorly mapped terrain before settling down to residential fieldwork in local villages. Fieldwork was iterative, continuously reevaluating data in the light of later evidence, returning to the same area, or reinterviewing people several times.

There were, perforce, differences between the studies. The West Java study followed an expedition approach. Freedom of movement was excellent because of the close relationship between Australia and Indonesia at that time, and because the area was relatively peaceful. I spent extended periods visiting former guerrilla strongholds in the Priangan mountains and discussing tactics, ideology, and organizational methods with ex-insurgents—some of whom are now involved in Laskar Jihad or the revived Darul Islam and Jema'ah Islamiyah movements. In Timor, by contrast, I was an infantry company commander, with very limited time for research. Fieldwork was based on direct participant observation, interviews, and oral history. For obvious reasons, freedom of movement was limited, but I spent lengthy periods with local people in the context of patrol operations in the border region.

THE INSURGENCY IN WEST JAVA

West Java comprises a low-lying plain, interspersed with discrete, jungle-covered hill-masses.[4] In the 1950s, these mountainous areas were heavily forested and largely uninhabited; most still are. As an indication of terrain difficulty, the West Java case study area included twenty-two forested peaks over ten thousand feet in altitude, six of which were active volcanoes.[5] Conversely, the lowlands are fertile and well developed, with excellent infrastructure, intensive wet rice agriculture, and an extremely high population density of more than ninety persons per square kilometer. The population is almost entirely Sundanese with—in the 1950s—syncretic Islamic belief systems based largely on oral tradition and a village-centered hierarchical culture characterized by exchange-based patron-client relationships.[6]

The Darul Islam insurgency arose from disagreements about the nature of postwar independent Indonesia. Should Indonesia be a secular republic or an Islamic state? Should civil secular law, or Islamic sharia law apply? Should Indonesia be a federation or a unitary republic? The people of West Java were strongly Islamic, and one of their most influential leaders was Sekarmaji Marijan Kartusuwiryo, from Garut in West Java. A key group of Islamic leaders, including Kartusuwiryo, advocated that Indonesia should become an Islamic state or, failing that, a federal state in which individual provinces could adopt sharia. Sukarno argued strongly for a secular unitary Republic, with appropriate safeguards for religious freedom but recognition of Indonesia's majority-Islamic status. Ultimately, Sukarno's view prevailed, and the declaration of independence in 1945 was based on a unitary secular republic. But Kartusuwiryo was not reconciled to this outcome.

Two factors were at play—first, some Islamic leaders had opposed the Japanese, whereas many secular leaders, including Sukarno, had collaborated with them. This weakened secular leaders' credibility in the eyes of Islamic nationalists, while also making these leaders unacceptable to the Dutch, who had returned after the Japanese surrender and were attempting to re-establish their rule. Second, Kartusuwiryo considered the new Republic of Indonesia too weak to protect his people in West Java. After the 1948 Renville agreement, under which Republican forces agreed to evacuate West Java, the Republican troops left the province in order to defend Central Java more effectively.[7] Kartusuwiryo regarded this as a betrayal and declared an independent Islamic state, named Negara Islam Indonesia, in West Java. The suppression of this separatist state took fifteen years and cost more than fifteen thousand lives.

The War of Independence

Having declared independence, Kartusuwiryo's Darul Islam fought on in West Java against the Dutch after the departure of Republican forces.

Indeed, intelligence reports compiled by the Netherlands Expeditionary Forces Intelligence Service during this period show that the Dutch considered Darul Islam a much more formidable opponent than the Indonesian Republic.[8] Numerous factions were fighting the Dutch—Islamic groups, communists, socialists, and students, as well as the Republic. The Republic was by no means the largest of these "struggle organizations," as the Dutch counterinsurgency forces called them, There were also multiple states involved. For example, Aceh had never acknowledged foreign rule, and continued to assert independence. Meanwhile the BFO states (so-called after the Dutch initials for their organizing body, the Federal Consultative Assembly), a group of twelve islands in eastern and central Indonesia, fought on the Dutch side.

In West Java, a triangular contest developed between the Republic, the Dutch, and Darul Islam. The Dutch dominated the towns and urban fringes by day and attacked fixed Republican positions but had little success in penetrating the countryside. Darul Islam dominated the villages, rural areas (by night), and forested hills. Republican forces largely avoided West Java after 1948 and tended to lose heavily in their encounters with Darul Islam—in one famous incident, a Republican army unit was betrayed, poisoned, and ambushed by Darul Islam guerrillas.[9] However, in the transfer of sovereignty after the War of Independence, the Republic inherited the Dutch positions, giving the Republicans control of the towns and urban fringes by day and leaving Darul Islam to control the mountains and villages by night.

In the 1950s, the Republic made little headway against the continuing insurgency. Indonesian democracy was highly unstable, with the longest serving cabinet lasting thirteen months, and some lasting only weeks. The military and society were affected by "guerrilla-ism": the many wartime factions had yet to be integrated into a modern state.[10] The Indonesian Communist Party was a powerful force. The role of the Indonesian army (Tentara Nasional Indonesia) was uncertain, and there were several coups or near-coups.

Guerrilla Ascendancy

Darul Islam flourished under these conditions. Their principal base areas corresponded to the mountainous areas of the province, central locations from which guerrillas could raid low-lying villages, rail and road links, crops, and lowland towns. The guerrillas benefited from the topographical advantage conferred by holding a central dominating position. This allowed them to observe and raid the lowlands at will—avoiding the Indonesian army's areas of strength and maintaining operational freedom of action.

Darul Islam achieved impressive ascendancy over the government in this period. Key incidents included two attempts on the life of President Sukarno—one in Jakarta—and numerous train and road ambushes that destroyed the economic life of the province. Adding insult to injury, one of the principal Darul Islam planning conferences of this period even took place in the Preanger Hotel in downtown Bandung, the provincial capital, theoretically government controlled.[11] The main effort, however, was a campaign of terrorism and intimidation against lowland villagers. The defense minister commented: "One could say that the rebels control every jungle-covered hill visible from Bandung. TNI [Indonesian army] units have tended to operate autonomously, without central coordination. This hands the initiative to the rebels."[12]

NASUTION AND THE THEORY OF GUERRILLA WARFARE

Abdul Haris Nasution, commander of the army's Siliwangi Division in West Java during the War of Independence, was the key army leader at this period. His 1952 book *Fundamentals of Guerrilla Warfare* described in detail the methods of irregular warfare used by the Republic against the Dutch and canvassed measures for suppressing insurgencies and internal unrest.[13] Nasution argued for intimate cooperation between the military and local populations at all levels, and for psychological operations designed to win popular loyalty at the expense of insurgents. All this was to be integrated into a system Nasution called "total people's defense." Nasution's ideas drew partly on world counterinsurgency practice, but also showed clear understanding of World War II partisan and resistance movements and embodied several innovative ideas that the Indonesian army later applied in suppressing the Darul Islam insurgency.

A regional revolt by military commanders in Sumatra in 1958–59, unrelated to Darul Islam, gave Nasution an opportunity to shine as a planner and field commander. Although he ran primarily a conventional campaign, his success in suppressing this revolt gave him the necessary prestige to unite Indonesia's armed forces, which had previously been factionalized and poorly coordinated. Concomitantly, the fragile parliamentary democracy that had been in force since 1950 toppled. It was replaced, under the tutelage of Sukarno, with "Guided Democracy"—which included martial law and a greatly expanded role for the armed forces within the Indonesian social and political system.[14] Guided Democracy, in improving political unity and stability at the central and provincial levels of government, created the conditions that enabled the military to plan and execute an overall strategy to combat the Darul Islam insurgency in Java.

A New Strategy

In 1959, officers from the Siliwangi Division, including a group from the Indonesian special forces, evolved a winning strategy. The plan was devised over several months by a group of operationally experienced planners and intellectually talented commanders, with support from the highest levels of the armed forces, including personal involvement by Nasution. The campaign plan this group developed was known as Pokok Perencanaan Pemulihan Perdamaian Keamanan, loosely translated as "Planning Guidance for Perfecting Peace and Security" (P4K)—in essence, pacification.[15] The declared aim of the strategy was to "defeat the enemy's ability to maneuver, until the enemy is confined within certain discrete areas, which can then be cleared area by area."[16] To this end, a blocking force of two divisions was established on the interprovincial boundary between West and Central Java to prevent infiltration and deny the insurgents freedom of movement. West Java was then classified into zones according to security—"A" areas were those controlled by the government, "B" areas were contested areas, and "C" areas were rebel strongholds, subsequently declared "destruction areas" (*daerah perhancuran*). This system appears superficially similar to the system of "black" and "white" areas applied by General Sir Gerald Templer, the British commander in the contemporaneous Malayan Emergency, but was more probably based on Dutch methods evolved during the War of Independence.[17]

The P4K strategy was to consolidate control in A areas through a combination of civic action and psychological activities and then clear C areas in a series of large-scale cordon-and-search operations, starting with Banten in the west and gradually clearing the surrounding province of West Java, from West to East, to isolate Kartusuwiryo's home area around Garut. The B areas were to be cleared in follow-up operations, which in practice rarely eventuated, as the guerrillas after losing their mountain strongholds (the C areas) could no longer effectively strike the contested lowlands. Finally, on 4 June 1962, after a series of deep-penetration operations, a hunter team commanded by Lieutenant Suhanda, then a platoon commander in Special Forces battalion 328 (a highly competent and respected unit with which I later served as an advisor) succeeded in capturing Kartusuwiryo and his key lieutenants, and organized insurgent activity collapsed in a matter of months.[18] In only two years, the combination of political unity, better military coordination, and the new operational techniques of P4K had defeated an insurgency that had flourished for the preceding twelve years.

Tactical innovation

At the tactical level, P4K included a code of conduct based on the observance of Islamic principles along with rules of behavior designed to protect and win over the population. These rules formed part of an overall psychological campaign designed to influence perceptions among the uncommitted population by demonstrating that the insurgents were no more Islamic or devout than any other Indonesians and by contrast were corrupt and inefficient, addicted to banditry, and prone to atrocities. Portrayal of the guerrillas as "gangs" or "bandits" was part of this approach.

The P4K strategy also emphasized the establishment of local militias controlled by army cadres. The largest of these was the Village Security Organization, which provided local guard forces, security patrols, and security for critical installations. This organization and militias like it also provided sound locally based sources of information about the enemy and local population, available to local commanders and thus producing a flow of actionable intelligence.

Some recent Western practice (as in Vietnam, East Timor, and Iraq today, though notably not in Malaya or currently in Afghanistan) shows a tendency to raise regular indigenous units as nuclei for future national armed forces, expected to eventually bear the brunt of major combat operations. This is sometimes accompanied by a disregard for the value of indigenous irregular troops. By contrast, Indonesian practice has always been to use local indigenous forces as an auxiliary adjunct, operating in a partisan role alongside regular army combat forces.

A further key innovation was a cordon-and-search technique known as *pagar betis*, which freed army strike forces to attack rebel strongholds. *Pagar betis*, "fence of legs," has been a highly influential concept in Indonesian counterinsurgency.[19] In a conventional cordon and search, the first requirement is to control the local population, which requires large numbers of troops. The second key requirement is area surveillance, requiring more troops. Finally, the operation requires a large force to cordon off the target area and a strike force to enter the cordoned area to search for and destroy the enemy. Orthodox methods thus require a substantial operation to deal with only a small enemy group—the ten-to-one ratio of "classical" counterinsurgency theory.

Pagar betis, on the other hand, used militias to secure the villages. The Village Security Organization, with small army cadres, secured each village or town. A small surveillance element provided overwatch, and then—the key to the concept—civilians from each village around the perimeter of a Darul Islam–controlled hill area were taken to a designated zone where they formed a cordon, linking up with neighboring villages (see fig. 3.1). Each village had to provide a certain number of people, and the village chief could periodically substitute individuals, provided the total remained constant. Feeding the people in the cordon was the village's problem, and the army provided a small post every few hundred meters to control the cordon and prevent insurgents from escaping or cordon members deserting.

FIG 3.1   Pagar Beti's cordon-and-search technique, West Java 1950s.

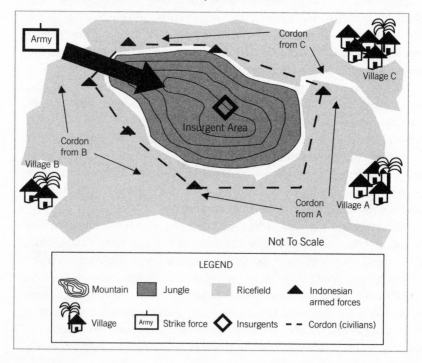

This method both minimized military manpower needed in the cordon and solved the village security problem—no village was likely to rebel when most villagers were effectively hostages in the cordon. Thus, all available troops were released to serve as the strike force. The insurgents were in an invidious position. They had to either stay and be captured or break out, potentially killing local villagers—their natural supporters—and losing popular support. From the armed forces' point of view, what might be a brigade operation using conventional methods became a two-company operation, and the troops thus released undertook civic action tasks to win over the population.

Pagar betis also reversed the topographical advantage the guerrillas had enjoyed. Because conventional forces required roads and population centers for logistic infrastructure of the armed forces, most early operations focused on the lowland areas and main road routes. This allowed Darul Islam to maintain base areas in centrally located hill-masses and conduct overnight raids into all the surrounding valleys. Because the armed forces could never muster enough troops to secure every valley, the guerrillas could raid with relative impunity wherever the security forces were not. By contrast, *pagar betis* used the whole population of the lowlands to encircle the hills, both controlling the local population and turning the Darul Islam strongholds into encircled death traps.

This technique, a genuine tactical innovation by Indonesian planners, was so effective that it allowed the army to crush the insurgency in two years, after twelve years of failure, through a series of coordinated sweeps. This success cemented *pagar betis* as a trademark counterinsurgency tactic of the Indonesian armed forces well into the 1990s.

Lessons Learned and Unlearned

The army's behavior in subsequent campaigns, and the official postoperation analyses and official histories, indicate that planners drew five key lessons from West Java.[20] The first was the enormous effectiveness of *pagar betis*, both as a population control measure and a manpower-saving cordon-and-search tactic. The introduction of well-conducted *pagar betis* operations coincided with such a dramatic reversal of the army's poor track record in countering the insurgents that it had enormous impact on most soldiers' thinking. So important was this lesson that the Indonesian army has applied this method in almost every conflict since.

Second, these planners developed a focus on destroying the insurgent forces—what one might call, borrowing a term from nuclear strategy, a "counterforce" approach, or what has more recently come to be known as an "enemy-centric" strategy. The alternative—attacking the popular support base or trying to remove the grievance leading to the insurgency—might be termed a "countervalue" or "population-centric" strategy. The latter was adopted in the Malayan Emergency but never became a key element of the Indonesian approach. Indeed, the very success of P4K carried the seeds of future problems, for it may have encouraged the army to think of counterinsurgency as an activity primarily aimed at destroying the insurgents rather than defeating their strategy.

Third, the army learned the effectiveness of "decapitating" an insurgent movement. Once Kartusuwiryo was captured, the insurgency collapsed within months. This made an enormous impression on Indonesian planners, and in every counterinsurgency campaign since, the Indonesian army has allocated significant emphasis and resources to killing or capturing insurgent leaders.

Fourth, the army became skilled in the use of local militias. Building on their experience in the War of Independence, it was natural for the army to use local auxiliaries against Darul Islam, employing village militia for static security duties and intelligence work. This has become the standard Indonesian approach to counterinsurgency; it can be seen in Aceh and Papua at present, in the approach to regional communal conflict in Maluku and Sulawesi, and of course in East Timor before 1999.

The fifth lesson was the key role of special operations. The Indonesian army's special forces played the key role in capturing Darul Islam leaders, thus ending the insurgency. Their employment as elite counterinsurgency and strike troops, within a framework of security operations by regular troops and militias, was critical to the army's success against Darul Islam and has since become the standard Indonesian approach.

Unfortunately, the Indonesian army seems to have missed or misinterpreted some key lessons. These included the critical importance of population density: *pagar betis* and the use of militias depended on the presence of enough local civilians to make up cordons and defend villages. Similarly, the landscape was highly fertile: many fields in West Java produce several rice crops a year. This meant substantial numbers of local farmers could be transferred from agriculture to cordon tasks without creating critical food shortages in the relatively short time frames (two weeks to two months) of a *pagar betis* operation.

The hierarchical structure of Darul Islam was also an important factor in its defeat. Kartusuwiryo had enormous personal charisma and authority, and the Darul Islam movement had a sophisticated governmental structure with a series of *shura* (councils) and with himself as imam at its head—so that with his capture, the insurgency collapsed. This weakness was exacerbated by the fact that Darul Islam had no unifying distinctive ideology with broad appeal to the population. Its Islamic belief system was shared with the security forces, while its actual behavior rapidly degenerated into banditry and criminal extortion. During my fieldwork in 1996, one of the commonest comments about Darul Islam I heard local people make was that they were not true Muslims. This perception was deliberately generated through the army's psychological operations[21]—which merely emphasizes that the guerrillas' appeal was based on separatism (a political critique of the Indonesian state), not on a distinctive religious ideology per se.

A final key observation which we might make in relation to the West Java case is that this counterinsurgency campaign was fought with almost no public scrutiny within Indonesia and virtually absent any interference or knowledge on the part of the world community. In the much less globalized environment of the late 1950s, it was possible to employ methods that were highly effective but relatively harsh on the local population without any substantial political or humanitarian backlash. This was very different from the situation during the second major case study presented here: East Timor.

THE INSURGENCY IN EAST TIMOR OF 1974–99

East Timor is roughly the same size as West Java, but there the similarity ends. The case study area was East Timor's northwestern border region including Balibo, Bobonaro, and Ermera districts. This area forms a dissected plateau, extremely mountainous in places and with little vegetation. A network of numerous small villages, often located on the highest hill features, originally covered the landscape; twenty-five years of conflict tended to force the population into a smaller number of larger villages and created large areas of uninhabited secondary scrubland.[22]

The Origins of the Conflict

The immediate cause of the Timor conflict was the May 1974 coup in Portugal by the Armed Forces Movement, which began withdrawing from Portugal's colonies, including Timor, almost as soon as it assumed power. Numerous political parties emerged to fill the resulting power vacuum, including the Marxist group Frente Revolucianária de Timor-Leste Independente (FRETILIN), the pro-Indonesian Associacão Popular Democratia Timorense (APODETI), and various royalist, conservative, and labor parties. After months of tension, a civil war began. After FRETILIN rapidly defeated the other parties, they united into the Anti-Communist Movement (Movimento Anti-Comunista, MAC) and sought Indonesian protection. While FRETILIN consolidated its power in East Timor, Indonesia, perceiving FRETILIN's Marxist orientation as a major security threat, began operations against it.

From September 1974 until July 1975, Indonesia conducted a subversion campaign from West Timor using radio propaganda, clandestine support for APODETI, intelligence cultivation of sympathetic and influential Timorese, and an international media campaign. The intent was to destabilize Timor, win over anti-FRETILIN political groups, and encourage the ascendancy of leaders favorable to integration with Indonesia. An early success was the defection of about three hundred members of a clan group loyal to a leader based near the border, who fled to the Indonesian province of West Timor where they received military training under Indonesian sponsorship.

During the civil war, from August to early October 1975, the Indonesian army provided clandestine support to MAC, apparently originally intending to use it as a proxy so as to avoid overt involvement. But FRETILIN's rapid defeat of MAC in the early phase of the fighting rendered this plan unworkable. Indonesian strategy now changed to direct invasion, but while forces were prepared, it was essential to keep MAC "in the game" by covertly supporting it and maintaining the perception that it was capable of effective counterattack. As MAC's defeat became apparent, local Indonesian army commanders in West Timor were increasingly drawn into crossborder fighting.[23]

In September and October 1975, Indonesian special forces cadres, at the head of locally raised militias, infiltrated and destabilized the border regions and then invaded East Timor. The Indonesian government portrayed this invasion as a MAC counterattack. The Indonesian special forces controlled the activity, forming partisan forces made up of local people. These partisans progressed slowly toward Dili, while FRETILIN attempted to cement its control over the rest of Portuguese Timor. On 28 November 1975, FRETILIN unilaterally declared independence from Portugal and formed the Democratic Republic of East Timor.

This triggered Indonesia's overt invasion of Portuguese Timor on 7 December 1975, which Indonesia had been preparing for some time, to follow up its proxy forces' poor performance. The Indonesian army quickly gained control of the bulk of East Timor's lowlands—all the major coastal towns, the border region, and the Maliana plain. FRETILIN initially controlled the remainder of the territory and some 80 percent of the population of East Timor.[24] Between January 1976 and December 1981, Indonesian army combat operations gradually restricted the area under FRETILIN control to the region around Viqueque and Mount Matebean in the central mountain range, but much of the population remained in FRETILIN-controlled areas in the interior. Besides a policy of territorial control, the army pursued a decapitation strategy aimed at killing or capturing key FRETILIN leaders. But despite the December 1978 capture of Nicolau Lobato, president of FRETILIN, by a special forces hunter team led by Lieutenant Prabowo Subianto (later a major general, commander of the special forces, and son-in-law of President Suharto)—an almost textbook repeat of the 1962 capture of Kartusuwiryo—the insurgency resolutely refused to collapse. Unlike the hierarchical, personality-centered Darul Islam insurgency, FRETILIN was a decentralized, cell-based organization with a strong unifying Marxist and nationalist ideology and thus apparently more resistant to decapitation.

Guerrilla Operations

Nevertheless, as Jose Alejandro "Xanana" Gusmao became president of FRETILIN in 1981, it was clear that time was running out for FRETILIN despite its success in delaying the Indonesian conventional drive into the interior. Accordingly, the population was urged to move out of the mountains and into the Indonesian-controlled zone, and FRETILIN began to conduct guerrilla operations from much smaller base areas.

The Indonesian army began to apply *pagar betis* techniques; it cordoned FRETILIN base areas, resettled the population into larger villages closer to main roads and the coast, and created large depopulated "free-fire zones." A series of major *pagar betis* operations around Mount Matebean created immense hardships for civilians, who were forced to participate in cordons and suffered food shortages resulting from the diversion of the agricultural workforce into cordon activities. FRETILIN attacks dropped in intensity and frequency, and the Indonesian army expected a quick victory. Instead, a stalemate developed. The army was unable to eliminate the guerrillas, while FRETILIN was unable to prevent the army from pacifying the lowlands, resettling the population, and commencing an intensive program of development and civic action designed to win over the Timorese.[25]

The Urban Insurgency

By the early 1980s, the Indonesian army had defeated FRETILIN as a conventional force; by 1989, the armed wing of FRETILIN had been marginalized and fought to a stalemate. The Timorese resistance movement responded by transforming its supporting infrastructure of sympathizers, supporters, facilitators, and enablers into a sophisticated urban subversive movement: the Clandestine Front. This, in turn, led to enhanced international support and increased effectiveness in the movement itself. By the late 1990s, FRETILIN still survived in its mountain base areas and occasionally attacked the army, but the scale and intensity of the fighting was not comparable to that of the early 1980s. Instead, FRETILIN fulfilled the symbolic functions of armed resistance and administration-in-waiting. The main effort for both the Indonesian army and the resistance was the propaganda war and the urban subversive campaign, which bore some tactical similarities to the first Palestinian intifada, which occurred around the same time.[26]

The effectiveness of this approach on the part of the resistance was enhanced through the leverage generated by an influential, vocal, and well-educated Timorese diaspora in Australia, Europe, and elsewhere, who kept the Timorese insurgency alive in world consciousness through activism in international forums and the increasingly globalized media. Over time, the Timorese diaspora, operating in concert with the Clandestine Front, generated substantial international pressure on Indonesia over its occupation of Timor. The unification of previously fragmented political elements within the diaspora (and inside Timor itself) under the umbrella organization the Timorese National Resistance Council (Consejo Nacional de Resistência Timorense) increased this leverage further.

The Indonesian army's response was to operate through covert and clandestine paramilitary and intelligence groups. On the intelligence front, recruitment of agents and informants and interception of mail, email, and telephone communications was stepped up. Maintained networks of informants were developed to generate human-source intelligence from the population, and some penetration of the Clandestine Front occurred. Overt security measures became a means of controlling the population rather than combating the insurgency: within this overt framework, the special forces, along with militias, carried out a covert campaign of coun-terterror, countersubversion, and clandestine operations.[27]

The militia groups had originated from the MAC partisans and other anti-FRETILIN groups of the 1970s but had been of little relevance dur-ing the early phases of conventional operations. By the late 1980s, how-ever, these groups had become the principal Indonesian army's tool for urban and rural counterinsurgency. There was a qualitative difference between the partisan groups of the 1970s—who had been employed in the field alongside Indonesian regular troops and acted from broad politi-cal and clan allegiance—and the militia groups of the 1990s. The latter were largely recruited and employed by the Indonesian army's special forces, who promised them personal financial benefit or awarded them personal patron-client relationships. These militia groups were formed in eleven out of the thirteen districts of East Timor, under the leadership of local prominent personalities who had benefited from the Indonesian occupation.[28]

COMPARATIVE ANALYSIS

There are similarities in principle between the two primary case studies, and equally significant differences of specific detail.

The P4K approach, as applied in West Java, involved significant hardship for the local population. This included forced participation in operations, exploitation of cordon participants as de facto hostages to guarantee the loyalty of their villages, and the use of villagers as human shields during contacts. In the prevailing environment of minimal interna-tional scrutiny at the time, the benefits of this approach outweighed any disadvantage. Indeed, these methods were not significantly harsher than the population controls and forced resettlements conducted during the same period in the Malayan Emergency.

In East Timor, however, P4K and *pagar betis* created problems. Timor's terrain did not allow the encirclement of discrete guerrilla bases. As noted, the terrain and vegetation of West Java—islands of mountain-ous jungle in a sea of rice fields—were essential prerequisites for *pagar betis*, as they allowed encirclement of the guerrillas and protection of the lowland population from them. By contrast, East Timor is a dissected plateau without discrete jungle and cleared areas and thus with little opportunity for encirclement. Moreover, the road and rail infrastruc-ture of West Java allowed the movement and supply of large numbers of troops and civilians, something that was extremely difficult in East Timor.

Moreover, the demography of the two theatres was very different. West Java comprised heavily populated, well-developed lowlands surrounding uninhabited, jungle-covered hills. Its high population density allowed very large numbers of civilians to be pressed into service without seriously disrupting the economy, and its fertility allowed large numbers of people to be employed in security tasks without risk of famine. In East Timor, the low population density made it impossible to generate as many people for cordon operations and they suffered severely because of the difficulty in resupplying food and water. Meanwhile, as noted, the people remaining in the villages suffered when the labor force needed to cultivate crops in the infertile, arid soil was depleted. The hardship the civilian population endured by was thus extreme. Whereas my fieldwork respondents in West Java reminisced in a broadly positive manner about *pagar betis* operations against Darul Islam, Timorese respondents regarded these operations as the height of the Indonesian army's brutality.[29] The Timorese population, scattered in small highland villages rather than clustered in lowland areas (as in West Java), was also frequently caught in the crossfire between guerrillas and army forces or hurt by the anti-FRETILIN blockade of the highlands.

The West Javanese insurgents were also different from those in East Timor. Because the Darul Islam fighters' allegiances were personal and religious (though they were very hierarchical), as noted, the decapitation of their leadership in June 1962 brought a rapid collapse. By contrast, FRETILIN was tightly disciplined and hierarchical, but its command and control were decentralized, and it was organized on the basis of political ideology and a Marxist cell structure, making it highly resistant to decapitation.

Another key difference was that the Darul Islam insurgents had been Muslims (whereas the East Timorese majority was Catholic). This was critical, as the largely Muslim Indonesian army forces originated from a cultural and religious base very similar to that of Darul Islam. This allowed the army to win over the local people, to understand and sympathize with their aspirations and to "out-Muslim" the Darul Islam—an important element of P4K and a key psychological operations objective of the army. In Timor, the Indonesian army forces mainly had different religious and cultural backgrounds from the insurgents and usually originated from other parts of the archipelago. This disparity allowed the Catholic Church to become a uniting force for the resistance, despite its lack of an active insurgent or subversive role, and hampered the Indonesian army's ability to appeal to cultural and religious values shared with the populace and the insurgents. Catholicism became intimately linked to Timorese self-identity and resistance to the occupation: more than 80 percent of Timorese identified themselves as Catholic in the 1990s, up from only 50 percent on the eve of the Indonesian invasion.[30] It also may explain the Indonesian army's preference for local auxiliaries and militias, who shared the same cultural and religious background as the insurgents and hence could have been expected to win them over more easily. For example, all the militia detainees I interviewed during the INTERFET campaign in 1999 were Catholic, and captured militia documents frequently indicated Catholic beliefs.

The urbanization and intensification of the insurgency in the 1990s indicated the failure of the P4K paradigm under conditions of globalization, in the circumstances of East Timor. In response, the Indonesian army began to apply a later, more sophisticated paradigm, again developed from West Javanese experience (in the "petrus" campaign* of the 1980s, a special forces–led operation against urban organized crime).[31] This approach used a framework of overt counterinsurgency measures to control the population and deny maneuver to the rural FRETILIN guerrillas. Within this framework specialized teams undertook subversion, provocation, agitation, propaganda, and assassination against the urban clandestine movement.

The campaign against Darul Islam in West Java was conducted with little international scrutiny and hence limited scope for influence by global or regional governments, economy, or media. Darul Islam had no overt international support—at the time, most Islamic nations were still colonies or were absorbed in their own independence struggles (Egypt and Algeria are obvious examples), and no globally influential Islamist movement existed. Indeed, the functional equivalent was probably the pan-Arab nationalism embodied by Nasser's Arab Socialism in the 1950s. But Sukarno's Cold War political maneuvers within the Non-Aligned Movement generated support for Indonesia from both Eastern and Western blocs. The United States saw Indonesia as a potential bastion against

---

* "Petrus" is the Indonesian abbreviation for "penembakan misterius" or "mysterious shootings." The petrus campaign was a series of extra-judicial killings, mostly in Java in the late 1980s, in which special forces teams disrupted organized crime networks in a lethal counter-network operation which, while effective in shutting down some criminal networks, created a political and human rights outcry that ultimately forced the campaign's suspension.

communism in Asia and hence perceived its stability as vital. Conversely, the Soviet Union and China saw Indonesia as a leading nonaligned nation and sought to draw it into the communist sphere through political and military support. Darul Islam (partly because of the close proximity of its base areas to Jakarta) was the strongest threat to the Republic's stability over this period, so there was little criticism or pressure on the Indonesian government from either bloc, since both wanted the country stabilized.

By contrast, FRETILIN's "united front" strategy beginning in 1986 and the eventual formation of the Timorese National Resistance Council led to the development of a vocal, broadly based international support movement, which was able skillfully to exploit the developing globalized media to influence public opinion in Western countries. The circumstances of Indonesia's invasion of East Timor—a preemptive response to a perceived communist threat—provided less international credibility than the situation (in the case of Darul Islam) of self-defense against an internal insurrection. Inside East Timor itself, the Clandestine Front emphasized civil disobedience, propaganda, and the provocation of disproportionate response from the occupying security forces, which was then exploited through the international media to discredit and pressure Indonesia. Moreover, the collapse of the Eastern Bloc by 1992 meant that Indonesia's role as a bulwark against communism—which had encouraged U.S. support and muted Western criticism—no longer applied. In this situation of greater globalization, leading to increased international scrutiny, closer economic ties with Western nations, and the loss of Cold War immunity from criticism, the Indonesian army's counterinsurgency methods became increasingly injurious to Indonesian political interests, though they remained highly effective in strictly tactical terms.

THE IMPACT OF GLOBALIZATION ON COUNTERINSURGENCY

These Indonesian examples reflect a broader trend in the impact of globalization on insurgency and counterinsurgency.

Insurgents have always sought global recognition and support. For example, the American War of Independence, like the Spanish and Portuguese *guerrilla* against Napoleon's occupying forces, was founded on international support.[32] The Greek war of national liberation against the Ottoman Empire in the 1820s drew influential private supporters from Britain, including the poet Lord Byron.[33] Islamic rebels in the Caucasus sought British government support against the Russians in the 1850s. Similarly, throughout the 1950s, guerrilla movements worldwide—many portraying themselves as liberation movements—sought recognition and support from the international community through media coverage, diplomatic support, political activism, and lobbying.

But the process of globalization, accelerated through advances in transport and telecommunications in the last two decades of the twentieth century, has so increased connectivity that ideas, capital, goods, services, information, and people can be transferred in nearly real time across national borders. This has created a more interdependent global economy than ever before, along with an emerging global culture and an embryonic international public opinion. Insurgents have not been slow to realize the opportunities that globalized communications—including the new maneuver space of the Internet and satellite television—provide as a means to impose political and economic costs on governments undertaking counterinsurgency.

The effect of this change has been to reinforce the fundamental importance of both theatre-level and international information operations as part of counterinsurgency. All counterinsurgent actions in a given theatre must now be tightly integrated into a unifying "perception management" plan that unites disparate activities into a coherent "hearts and minds message." The increasing presence of media and independent information sources (such as picture-message-enabled mobile phones and digital video cameras) means that local tactical actions can now have immediate strategic effects. More important, in-theatre information operations must now be coordinated with measures to influence international public opinion though similar perception management activities at the national and international levels. Insurgent movements have long recognized this, and they continue to seek and exploit international support. Governments engaged in counterinsurgency must do likewise in order to succeed.

Mao Zedong's dictum of the Three Unities (unity of political action within the insurgent forces; spiritual unity between the insurgents and the people; and unity of political action targeting the enemy's cohesion) applies here.[34] But a "fourth unity" might be added: unity of perception management measures targeting the increasingly influential spectators' gallery of the international community.

The Indonesian army's counterinsurgency methods, even in East Timor, contrary to popular belief, have not been especially harsh by world or historical standards. Indeed, the performance of the Indonesian army's *rajawali* companies in Aceh in the campaigns of 2001–2 was marked by a high degree of professionalism and restraint, as well as skilled perception management (both in theatre and in relation to the international community).[35] Moreover, the methods evolved in response to Darul Islam were perfectly acceptable to international opinion in the cultural and moral climate of the 1950s, characterized by Cold War confrontation and the decline of European and American colonial empires. Indonesian methods were, for example, somewhat less harsh on the local population than the wholesale resettlement programs, collective punishments and punitive twenty-hour curfews employed in Malaya, Palestine, Cyprus, and Vietnam or the unconventional warfare "pseudo" operations of Kenya and Rhodesia, in which special forces troops masqueraded as guerrillas. They were also far cleaner in terms of minimizing collateral damage to innocent populations than were the counterclandestine operations undertaken by the French in Algeria or by other counterinsurgency forces in their campaigns of the same period. Rather, the Indonesian army's failure in applying these methods against FRETILIN—an enemy highly skilled in perception management at the international level—may primarily reflect a failure to adapt to variations in circumstances brought about by globalization.

At the same time, the very success of P4K may have created reluctance within the Indonesian army's organizational culture to question the doctrine's foundations. Indeed, it may be that operational success raises barriers to future adaptation: most successful reorganizations of military forces and their tactics have been responses to failure and defeat, not success. For example, Prussian reforms after defeat by Napoleon, U.S. reorganization and professionalization after Vietnam, German tactical innovation on the Western Front in 1918, and Soviet resurgence after 1941 all seem to indicate that militaries evolve primarily through response to the shock of defeat. Conversely, French complacency after 1918, Israeli complacency after 1967 and British complacency in respect to an assumed innate ability to conduct counterinsurgency, all seem to indicate that tactical success can become a barrier to effective military adaptation. The Indonesian army's unwillingness to abandon its remarkably successful repertoire of counterinsurgency techniques, developed at much cost in the fight against Darul Islam, is neither surprising nor particularly reprehensible—rather, it typifies the behavior of virtually every professional military. It is therefore applicable well beyond the circumstances of the Indonesian army.

CONLUSION

Indonesia's approach to counterinsurgency, then, has derived partly from its experience in suppressing Darul Islam. The tactics developed in West Java that proved effective in the geographical and political circumstances of the 1950s have proved ineffective—indeed, positively injurious to Indonesian interests—in other circumstances. Globalization and particularly the influence of world media and international public opinion undermined the approach's effectiveness in East Timor, and this highlights the continuing impact of globalization in contemporary counterinsurgency.

Given the constraints of space, this article has merely touched on certain aspects of the Indonesian army's approach to insurgency and counterinsurgency. However, one key conclusion is that Indonesia's approach to counterinsurgency is both unique and relatively poorly understood in Western military circles. Nevertheless, understanding that approach is important for understanding the policies and reactions of Indonesian leaders today. A second conclusion is that although the P4K approach of the 1950s showed an innovative brilliance rarely achieved in any counterinsurgency campaign, it was later misapplied in situations that appeared similar but were in fact radically different. The lesson is that counterinsurgency planners must seek to understand the essential nature of any problem, diagnosing the problem before attempting to treat it, and avoiding "template" solutions. That said, the actions of the Indonesian army in Papua and Aceh today show that the P4K paradigm remains influential and may still be a useful indicator of that army's likely responses to insurgency.

Introduction to "Reflections on the Engagement at Motaain Bridge"

People's perceptions of war are shaped by their own combat experiences. Besides academic fieldwork as a researcher in several insurgencies, my own perceptions are derived from my service as an Australian infantry officer, as an adviser with conventional and special forces in Southeast Asia and the Middle East, and later as a civilian adviser in Iraq and Afghanistan. The chapter that follows describes one early combat experience, from the UN-approved stabilization intervention following the Timorese vote for independence from Indonesia. I wrote this report in early 2000 in a classified version and finalized it in 2003 as an unclassified "combat action monograph" for the Australian Army History Unit.

The writing of combat monographs by returning field officers as a means to capture the microdetail of combat has a long tradition. It goes back at least as far as the classic *Infantry in Battle*, compiled by the U.S. Army Infantry School after World War I and edited by the future Chief of Staff of the Army and later Secretary of State George C. Marshall.[1] In adapting to counterinsurgency, combat monographs like this one can play a valuable role in augmenting formal lessons learned systems.

The chapter describes and analyzes a minor but highly sensitive skirmish on the frontier of East and West Timor in which Australian forces encountered Indonesian army and police forces and their "militia" proxies—guerrilla fighters who opposed the international intervention but whose campaign never developed into a full-blown insurgency. I have discussed the overall intervention campaign in general terms elsewhere.

This chapter dissects one incident in great detail, makes observations, and draws lessons from experience. I should emphasize that these are personal observations only, recorded at the time.[2] The details of this particular combat engagement are less important than the illustration of method. The point is to illustrate the usefulness of collecting data from field personnel, as immediately as possible after a combat action, before micro-details and nuances become tidily rearranged in the minds of participants, and to allow researchers and analysts an opportunity to develop the detailed understanding of combat—as it actually is, rather than how it ought to be—as a basis for adaptation.

Although this UN-approved campaign was not a full-blown counterinsurgency, largely because skillful maneuvering by the Australian force commander, General Peter Cosgrove, prevented it from becoming one, its lessons are directly relevant to today's campaigns. It shared many characteristics (ethnic conflict, religious and sectarian violence, regional separatism, the interplay of stabilization with reconstruction and combat operations) with conflicts in Afghanistan and Iraq. At the level of junior commanders, many lessons and observations that are relevant to peace enforcement or stabilization operations like these in Timor also directly translate to counterinsurgency.

While the incident described was neither my first nor my last experience of infantry combat, it illustrates some of the kinds of experience that my generation of officers—the generation who learned their trade in peace operations, rapid-deployment interventions, and small wars in the 1990s—have brought to bear in understanding the new counterinsurgency era in Iraq and Afghanistan. It also provides some field-level context for chapter 3's discussion of Indonesian counterinsurgency tactics in Timor.

Reflections on the Engagement at Motaain Bridge, 10 October 1999

4

The largest combat engagement of the INTERFET campaign in East Timor, and the only direct clash between the Australian army and the Indonesian army, occurred on 10 October 1999 outside the village of Motaain—a cluster of about twenty palm-roofed houses—on the East-West Timor border. The firefight occurred around a small stone bridge over the Mota Biku River and a portion of coastal palm jungle just within East Timor, to the east of the village.

In this combat action monograph I have sought to describe the engagement accurately in detail. Sources include my company war diary (Support Company, Second Battalion, Royal Australian Regiment), after-action debriefs of participants recorded at the time, interrogation notes compiled by investigators after the firefight, extensive combat video footage taken by military combat cameramen and civilian news crews, and the report of the UN committee on border demarcation. Using these sources, I have sought to check my personal impressions, wherever possible, against externally verifiable fact.

BACKGROUND

To understand what occurred at Motaain, some background is necessary. INTERFET was an Australian-led, UN-approved regional intervention mission to stabilize the situation in East Timor during the mass bloodshed, destruction, and population displacement that followed the

UN-sponsored referendum of 30 August 1999 in which East Timorese voted for independence from Indonesia. This vote prompted massive retaliation from the Indonesian armed forces and their "militia" allies: local irregular armed groups operating as partisan auxiliaries to the regular Indonesia military. These militia groups, led and directed by members of the Indonesian military, had intimidated and killed thousands of members of the local population before the referendum, in an attempt to prevent a vote for independence, and then carried out the bulk of their destruction after the referendum failed to deliver the result they had tried to control.

Peter Cosgrove, an Australian major general (and later general and chief of defense force), was the force commander. The mission began on 20 September 1999, with the predawn seizure of key points across East Timor by the international force, and ran as a stabilization operation until mid-2000, when the UN Transitional Authority, under Sergio Viera de Mello (later tragically killed in Iraq in 2003) took charge of the mission, which continues to this day.*

Once INTERFET had invaded East Timor and secured the major cities—within the first few weeks of the campaign—the militia operated as guerrillas, some from within East Timor and some from camps on the West Timor side of the border, from where they infiltrated the border area and attacked international troops and installations and Timorese civilians. They continued these activities for several years after the Australian-led stabilization force was replaced by a new UN peacekeeping force, but they never amounted to a serious challenge to the stability of the new nation of Timor Loro'sae.

In terms of military doctrine, this was not a counterinsurgency mission, even though the enemy operated as guerrillas and applied classic insurgent tactics. Rather, the mission involved elements of insurgency prevention—nipping the proto-insurgency in the bud before it had time to grow—and stability operations.[1] Nonetheless, since in logical terms counterinsurgency is a subset of stability operations and since the enemy applied guerrilla tactics throughout the operation, the INTERFET

---

* AUTHOR'S NOTE (2009): The INTERFET operation, a multinational stabilization mission, was replaced by the United Nations Transitional Authority [sic] East Timor, a transitional governance and stabilization operation that continued until the formal establishment of East Timor's independence on 20 May 2002, when it was replaced with the United Nations Mission in Support of East Timor, a reconstruction mission that ran until May 2005.

campaign holds lessons for counterinsurgency tactics, and these lessons are the focus of this chapter.

10 October 1999 was day 21 of the INTERFET campaign, or "D plus twenty" in operational terminology. In the preceding three weeks, my company's parent battalion, Second Battalion, Royal Australian Regiment (2 RAR), had secured Komorro airfield and Dili Harbor as the lead combat element of the INTERFET intervention force, having several minor brushes with local guerrillas and Indonesian regulars in the first few days, then spreading out to secure the East Timor capital, Dili, as the remainder of the force arrived.* One of our rifle companies (about 110 infantry soldiers) secured Baucau airfield, in the east of the country, in an independent operation less than twenty-four hours after the initial lodgment. After a multibattalion cordon and search in central Dili and an airmobile clearance of Liquissa, a town near the north coast, our battalion was relieved in place by our sister battalion (3 RAR), handed over responsibility for security of western Dili, and then concentrated in an assembly area back at Komorro airfield just outside the city.

On 1 October, the battalion and its supporting artillery, armor, combat engineers, and logistic units, plus a Special Air Service Regiment element, had mounted the largest Australian airmobile operation since the Vietnam War and the largest ever undertaken using solely Australian army helicopters.† This operation had secured the towns of Balibo and Batugade in the western border area, establishing an Australian presence astride the militia groups' main escape route from East Timor. This was important, because at this time the Indonesian military was evacuating its militia auxiliaries to hastily established guerrilla bases in the jungle along border, from where it hoped subsequently to wage an infiltration campaign to destabilize East Timor. Preventing or disrupting such a campaign was

---

* AUTHOR'S NOTE (2009): Australian infantry battalions number about seven hundred people and consist of four rifle companies; a support company made up of specialist troops such as reconnaissance, heavy weapons, snipers, communications and assault engineers (known as "pioneers"); and an administration company, including medical, logistics, and transportation platoons and a battalion headquarters. Second Battalion, Royal Australian Regiment, in which I commanded Support Company (operating as a rifle company for the initial lodgment in Dili and then reverting to normal tasking), was a high-readiness light infantry battalion that was part of the Townsville-based Rapid Deployment Force, which was maintained at seven days' notice for intervention operations across Southeast Asia and the Pacific. The Rapid Deployment Force was organized around an airborne brigade and operated similarly to a U.S. parachute infantry, light infantry, or ranger unit, except that it also included armored cavalry, helicopter, and engineer units.

† AUTHOR'S NOTE (2009): The Special Air Service Regiment is the Australian equivalent of the British Special Air Service and of Tier 1 national mission units (such as Delta Force or the Naval Special Warfare Development Group) in the U.S. joint special operations command. It was founded in 1956 and has seen extensive combat service in every Australian war since that time.

thus important if we were to prevent the emergence of a full-blown insurgency later.

This crucial operation had also carried risk: it had dangerously isolated our battalion from the rest of the force. At this point, more than ten thousand Indonesian regulars and an unknown number of militia guerrillas were still operating in East Timor, many of them between our position and the rest of INTERFET. The situation was extremely precarious—in a strategic sense, this was probably the most dangerous period of the whole campaign. The boldness of this move by General Cosgrove to seize the border area cannot be overstated.

Because we were so heavily outnumbered in the border region, seizing the initiative was critical, so we quickly pushed patrols out on foot into the jungle and the surrounding villages (mostly destroyed), to dominate the area and prevent further militia destruction and killing of the local population. By aggressive and active patrolling, we sought to convince the numerically stronger enemy that we were a larger and less vulnerable force than was actually the case.

By 10 October, therefore, the battalion had been operating at an extremely high tempo for twenty-one days and nights without any rest. Most people were getting three to four hours' sleep each night, and fatigue was becoming a major problem. This was due partly to lack of transportation: virtually all movement was on foot, and helicopters and vehicles were in short supply. Personal loads being carried were also very heavy: on the day of deployment, the average load carried by a soldier in my company (Support Company, operating as a reinforced rifle company for this operation) was 71 kilograms (156 pounds). This sounds like an outrageous amount, but was recorded in writing by loadmasters who carefully weighed each soldier's equipment before embarkation from Australia. The lightest load in my company was recorded at 126 pounds; my personal load was 137 pounds; and the heaviest load—that of a member of a sustained fire machine gun detachment carrying a heavy machine-gun tripod and ammunition—was a punishing 212 pounds. These loads were somewhat higher than those carried by the rifle companies, due to our heavier weapons and equipment, but only marginally so.

These crushing loads were exacerbated on day 5 by the issue of new combat body armor. In our home garrison base of Townsville, in north Queensland, we had rarely been able to train with helmets and body armor. These were in short supply, and as the battalion only had a week's notice for the operation, our sister battalion 1 RAR—which had been "on-line battalion" (Australia's highest-readiness rapid deployment unit, maintained on seven days' notice to deploy worldwide) until a week out—had the lion's share of this equipment. The new armor was much more effective than our older Kevlar flak jackets—it was American issue and included ceramic armor plates over the chest and back. But it was very heavy and, being rigid, made carrying a pack extremely uncomfortable, often leading to numbness and loss of circulation in soldiers' backs and arms. A related factor was that we were carrying a full combat load of ammunition for extended periods—something that, again, we had rarely done in training and had been unable to do during the week of predeployment workup. Live (correctly, "ball") ammunition is considerably heavier than blank ammunition, of course, and besides the extra weight to be carried, this was having an effect on our load-bearing equipment (webbing and ammunition pouches), a new design that turned out to be insufficiently robust to carry such loads for extended periods.

The terrain (steep, razor-backed ridges, secondary jungle), and climate (high humidity, daytime temperatures around one hundred degrees Fahrenheit with little cooling off at night) contributed to high water consumption and increased fatigue still further. Average water consumption in the first ten days of the operation, according to the battalion's second-in-command, was eighteen liters per man per day. During the Dili phase, this meant that rifle companies needed water resupply at least once, sometimes twice per day. Once the battalion arrived in the border area, water resupply was much more difficult. The withdrawing enemy had destroyed or poisoned all water sources, military water purification equipment was not available, and the main supply route back to Dili was not yet properly established—it ran more than a hundred miles on single-lane, badly damaged roads with few intact bridges and enemy forces still at large along the whole route. So we were very much on our own for the moment, and everyone, to a greater or lesser extent, was dehydrated.

Food was also a problem. Frontline troops had seen no fresh rations at this stage. (My company, which spent much of the operation in small teams in a remote jungle area near the border, was not to have their first fresh meal until day 62 of the operation.) Although troops in rear areas such as Dili had started to receive fresh rations, the supply situation was still tenuous, and in the forward areas all rations at this stage were combat rations (canned or dehydrated food carried in individual packs). Combined with the water shortage, the lack of food left energy levels across the battalion quite low—many of us were living on our personal energy and adrenaline reserves at this point. Due to the tempo of operations, meals were often eaten cold—I managed my first hot combat-ration meal of the operation on day 11.

The Intelligence Picture

Several intelligence sources had warned us of guerrilla camps on the border, opposite our battalion's area of operations. There had been night infiltration attempts by Indonesian regulars and militia, at least one of which reached the battalion main headquarters and resulted in shots being fired inside Balibo town itself. There had also been persistent rumors of an imminent large-scale militia counteroffensive designed to deal with our battalion before the rest of INTERFET was in a position to support us. These rumors panicked the local population but had repeatedly proven untrue. A lack of human intelligence experience or familiarity among some commanders had led to a distrust of all local information sources and an inability to distinguish between unfounded rumor and more accurate information. Many commanders also had great difficulty in distinguishing information accuracy from source reliability.

However, on 7 October we began to receive specific, detailed information on heightened militia activities at Motaain. Indonesian regulars and key guerrilla leaders had been sighted there, encouraging and training militia groups and apparently preparing a coordinated attack. Our sources told us that the local population and East Timorese refugees in the area had been mistreated and terrorized. This information originated from three independent sources using two distinct intelligence collection methods, one an INTERFET asset and the other a local source who had previously proven reliable. The intelligence officer and myself therefore regarded this as relatively firm—albeit time-sensitive—information. Importantly, our attitude to this information was colored by our perception that Motaain was in East Timor (and therefore inside the battalion's area of operations), as shown by the village's marked position on our issued maps (see "The Mapping Situation" below), which indicated that it was well within our side of the border.

As officer commanding support company, one of my tasks was to act as the battalion's "patrol master," responsible for the coordination of intelligence, surveillance, and reconnaissance assets and patrol operations within the battalion area. The intelligence officer was responsible for assessment and tasking of certain intelligence assets, while I controlled and tasked other intelligence assets and directed the battalion's snipers, reconnaissance and surveillance patrols, and company fighting patrols. In the early morning of 10 October, with the intelligence officer, I briefed the commanding officer on the new information about Motaain coming from multiple sources and our assessment that the village was a center of militia activity. He considered the information and decided to send a patrol to Motaain to investigate. His intent was to gather independent verification of the intelligence reports, assist the battalion in dominating its area of operations, and disrupt militia plans for the rumored offensive, while protecting and reassuring the local population.

He tasked the rifle company closest to Motaain (Charlie Company) to conduct the patrol but directed the intelligence officer and myself to accompany the patrol. As an Indonesian linguist, my task was to conduct any negotiations or mediation as necessary and question any detainees or local sources. I was also to speak with the local population and reinforce key information and psychological operations themes. Later that morning, the army public relations team located in Balibo sought permission to accompany the patrol. The commanding officer agreed, and the army camera team, several civilian news teams, and their media support unit escort were approved to accompany the patrol, in Land Rover patrol vehicles provided by 2 RAR battalion headquarters.

The force that approached Motaain early that afternoon, therefore, was a mixed group from several units who had never worked together before, had very limited time for orders, and no opportunity to rehearse. Critically, the command relationships within the group were not clear-cut and were based on personal goodwill rather than a clear command chain. The patrol group consisted of the following.

- One platoon and company tactical headquarters from Charlie Company, 2 RAR. The officer commanding Charlie Company (OC Charlie) was in overall command of the patrol (by agreement with me during the orders process—this had not been specified by the commanding officer but was worked out by us on the ground).
- The company tactical headquarters, Support Company, 2 RAR. This group included me, my radio operator, the intelligence officer, and a civil-military operations team under the command of an artillery forward observation officer. Again by agreement during the orders process, I took command of the non–Charlie Company personnel in the patrol, including the linguists, intelligence operators, civil affairs team, and escorts.

- One platoon from Support Company 2 RAR, mounted in armored personnel carriers from B Squadron 3rd/4th Cavalry Regiment, as a quick reaction force held on standby at Balibo. As the battalion quick reaction force, this platoon was under battalion control. But as this was one of my own platoons (the assault pioneer platoon), I maintained constant communications with the platoon commander, and he was tracking my movements during the patrol.
- The civilian news media, escorted by 2 RAR regimental police in armed Land Rovers, and with personnel from the media support unit. These media groups followed behind the patrol but moved entirely on the main coast road and remained about one hundred yards behind the patrol until the aftermath of the battle.

The Mapping Situation

A final key piece of background concerns the mapping situation. At this point in the operation, we were working with very poor quality maps by Australian standards. The maps we were using were blurry color photocopies produced by our brigade intelligence staff from 1:50,000-scale Indonesian maps dating from the early 1990s. Nevertheless, compared to the maps I had become used to during earlier deployments to Indonesia in the 1990s, when I had commanded Australian Army mobile training teams with the Indonesian army, these maps were very professionally produced. (The map for this operation was Indonesia Map 2407–122/121 *Batugade* 1:50,000.)

We had repeatedly found these maps to be out of date and inaccurate. Errors of fifty to one hundred meters in the lateral and vertical positioning of key features were common, and villages and settled areas were particularly inaccurately marked. This was partly because Timorese villages comprise mainly palm and thatch huts with wickerwork wooden fences—they decay quickly, are easy to relocate, and at this point in the operation had been burnt to the ground by the enemy in many cases, and were already being overgrown by the jungle.

We had repeatedly requested better mapping products, including air photographs, but none had reached us by this stage in the operation. (Ironically, after the firefight a flood of hyperaccurate surveys and air/satellite photography was produced that would have been very useful on the day.)

Importantly, the map showed Motaain as a small village some five hundred meters east of the border with West Timor. In fact, on the ground, there was no village at that location, and the river at that point, shown as a major feature running through the center of the village, was (at that time of year, anyway) a dry and hardly noticeable gully amid the long coastal "elephant grass" that my company's soldiers—we had just returned from a deployment to northern Papua New Guinea a few months before the Timor operation—called by its Papuan name, *kunai*. The actual location of Motaain was across a large stone bridge, beyond a major flowing river, just inside West Timor—a major difference from what was shown on the map, though no more major than that of many features on the map.

A final issue was that the maps we were using were right on the edge of a grid convergence zone. In other words, due to distortion in the projection used to convert the curved three-dimensional surface of the earth to a flat two-dimensional picture, the grid squares were slightly "stretched" on the edge of the grid zone, and hence were not actually square but slightly rhomboid on the ground. Moreover, the maps were not based on the Universal Transverse Mercator (UTM) map projection, the standard grid system used by military and civilian satellite navigation systems, but on an older projection (the Lambert Conical Projection), and the grid lines did not match UTM grid lines. This was unfortunate, because our satellite navigation sets gave readings only in latitude and longitude (not marked on the photocopied maps) or by UTM grid. Thus GPS readings could be (and often were) up to three hundred meters off and were very difficult to relate to the map other than by educated guesswork.

THE PATROL

We departed from the half-ruined Portuguese coastal fortress at Batugade in the early afternoon, the hottest part of the day. This was Charlie Company's fortified patrol base, so we moved through their forward defenses and an outpost manned by the mortar platoon, part of my company. We moved west along the coast road for about one hundred meters and then cut into the coastal jungle on the north, or coast, side of the road. The temperature, in our body armor with full ammunition load, was extremely hot in this jungle, which was secondary growth with little shade and extremely still, humid air.

The air had a faintly rotten odor. Bodies of refugees and other local people killed by the enemy were frequently washing up on the beach at this time, and for several weeks afterward, and a large amount of dead livestock plus the occasional human corpse lay in the jungle and the burnt-out villages. The alternating bright sunlight and shade combined with the limited field of vision (a few feet at most) was quite disorienting. We were also pushing into an area of known militia presence and were expecting contact with the enemy at any moment. I was counting paces for what is known as dead reckoning, a technique for jungle navigation that is used when no landmarks are visible, but I was soon unsure of my precise location, because the ground was flat and evenly vegetated, with no elevation change, creeks, or other features for reference, and we were moving in a meandering single file in the thick jungle.

After three hundred meters we emerged from the *kunai* grass, rejoined the coast road, and pushed along it in staggered file: a patrol formation in which half the patrol walks on one edge of the track and half on the opposite edge. I was with my detachment of specialist troops, about two hundred meters behind the front of the patrol, and well back, due to the long spaced patrol formation. A monsoon drain, a narrow canal about three feet deep and full of mud and rotting detritus, ran along the left side of the road, with dense palm jungle immediately beyond it. On the right side of the road was a thin screen of trees, some palms, and then a narrow black beach and the coppery grayness of the ocean, calm and oily at this time of day. The air was heavy and hot but considerably cooler than it had been in the *kunai*.

As we moved along the road, the two patrol vehicles carrying the civilian media crews pushed up close to the back of the patrol, and I turned back briefly to consult with the drivers, with sweat running down my face and into my eyes. Each vehicle mounted a 7.62 millimeter MAG 58 general-purpose machine gun, and I wanted to be able to call on this supporting fire in case of problems. I consulted my map—you always have a very clear recollection of the last moments immediately before a firefight—and, talking with the vehicle commander, I realized we were considerably further along the road than I had expected. I had been expecting to see a major village (i.e., Motaain) within a few hundred meters, but we had moved a long way and seen nothing but a couple of burnt-out huts since we had left the jungle. The vehicles had moved directly along the road and thus had a better feel for their location.

I asked my radio operator to raise OC Charlie, close to the front of the patrol, using the battalion command net radio, and ask him to stop while we confirmed our location. While the radio operator was doing this, I looked up and realized that the forward elements of the patrol were still moving forward along the road, talking to some locals on the edge of the road and about to disappear out of sight around a sharp bend to the left.

I could not halt my portion of the patrol without splitting the formation, which is a bad idea when you're expecting contact with the enemy. In any case, I was not in overall command. We could not raise OC Charlie on the radio, so I began to move quickly through the formation toward the front, taking my radio operator. I quickly overtook the rear of the leading platoon and moved to within about fifty meters of OC Charlie, wanting to stop the patrol and confirm our precise location before continuing. As I moved forward, in my memory it seems as if the entire landscape had fallen silent, as in the moments before a tropical rainstorm. There had been loud cicadas and birdsong in the jungle, but now even those sounds were hushed, and my feet on the rough tarmac road seemed to make no noise at all.

At that moment, as I was running down the road toward the head of the column, dripping with sweat in the airless heat, the gunfire began like a thunderstorm bursting.

THE FIREFIGHT

I remember what seemed to be a single shot, possibly two, followed by a longer burst of shooting, and then, suddenly, a huge volume of fire—thousands of rounds in rapid succession—all coming our way. The fire was skimming along the roadway at about waist height and higher, chopping leaves and small branches off the roadside trees and kicking up dust. Bizarrely, my memory is of small fragments of dry palm leaves spinning in the air, and my sense of the enemy fire is that it was bright and hot, though in reality I could not have seen it—the sunlight was so bright that even tracer fire was hard to see.

The instant the firing broke out, I ran forward and jumped off the left side of the road into the stone-lined monsoon drain. This was excellent cover, with deep, cement-edged walls, and half-full of rotting vegetation and black mud. However, because it ran directly toward the enemy, it would have been a death trap if they had managed to get a machine gun firing along it or land a grenade inside it. I perceived all this in the moment of jumping into the drain but it felt incredibly safe to be off the road. Psychologically, it was rather difficult to keep moving forward, although we all did. My immediate concern was for my radio operator and the rest of my party, ensuring that they had all got off the road safely and out of the fire, which was still pouring along the roadway just above our heads at a fast clip, sounding exactly like the sound you hear when you sit in the butts at a rifle range. Strangely enough, this was a very comforting and familiar sound, evoking lazy sun-filled afternoons with my platoon on the army rifle range at Greenbank as a young officer, when you came back from the range pleasantly tired, slightly sunburned, and relaxed.

As soon as I had confirmed that my people were all safe, I got my radio operator to try again to raise OC Charlie on the radio. The radio operator had already reported "contact, wait out" to battalion headquarters in their underground command post back at Balibo castle and received an acknowledgment, so I knew our radio worked, but I could not get OC Charlie to answer his radio. The enemy rifle fire was still very intense, smashing into the trees above the drain and cracking loudly, just over our heads. I had seen OC Charlie go off the right side of the road, which was a raised causeway and bending around to the left at that point, so he had moved directly toward the enemy and out of cover. I thought it quite likely that he and his party had been killed in the first burst of enemy fire, and that I would need to assume command of the whole patrol. I therefore needed to be up front where I could see instead of 150 meters back.

Ordering my own party to follow me up in their own time along the monsoon drain, I therefore took my radio operator and we began to move quickly forward, through the firefight, which was now intensifying further, along the drain. Crawling fast along a monsoon drain in full kit is quite tiring and can be very disorienting, particularly as shots were now striking the edge of the drain and occasionally skipping along inside it, ricochetting off the sides. We moved along the drain for what felt like about two hundred meters, and found ourselves close to the edge of a large river, near a stone bridge. I realized with a shock that we were right on the border, within about twenty meters of West Timor. The two of us had obviously attracted the enemy's attention, and we were taking quite a lot of fire. So we moved back a little, and then with something of a terrifying lurch, dashed across the roadway together, over the top and down beyond into the area where I had seen OC Charlie disappear. We were about five feet apart. As we crossed, I felt about twenty enemy rounds pass between us—the impression was of loud, hot whip-cracks a foot or so away. The fire seemed to be coming from houses on the other side of the river. I looked briefly at my radio operator, who had enormous round eyes and looked as haggard and sweat-drenched as I am sure I did.

Sliding down off the roadway, we found ourselves huddling against an embankment in a small triangular garden area, about 150 by 75 meters, with a brick or stone wall ahead of us, lined by a series of large trees. Interestingly, in my mind's eye as I look back on the event, I cannot remember any more than one or two very large trees—the trees I eventually sheltered behind. In fact, there were many trees, and in the video footage of the battle, you can see rounds striking them and knocking quite large branches off onto the ground. I cannot remember this at all, even though I must have jumped over the same falling branches as I ran forward through the firefight. But in my mind, the area was completely open and nakedly free of cover, and I saw only the open ground and the cover beyond it, as if my mind had simply tuned out everything not immediately relevant to its survival.

Almost as soon as my radio operator and I arrived on the enemy side of the roadway, we realized that we were exposed to fire from the enemy positions across the river. A large burst of fire struck the embankment, around the area where we had thrown ourselves, and my radio operator pushed my head down as another burst hit the area around our heads. It may have been at this point that I was hit in the left knee by a stone splinter from one of the bullet splashes. (I felt nothing at the time and did not notice it until after the battle, when the artillery observer with my group pointed out the blood on my trouser leg, and I rolled it back to find a huge black bruise and a sharp little chip of stone sitting under my skin against the side of a bloodied kneecap.)

We clearly needed to move, as it seemed as if every militia position in the village was firing at us. One in particular—I was convinced it was the same guy who had fired at us as we crossed the road—seemed determined to hit us and was repeatedly firing bursts of machine-gun fire at us, and getting closer with every burst. So we dashed forward to the large trees on the far side of the garden, this time accompanied by the battalion intelligence officer and a combat cameraman who had appeared from out of the jungle behind us. At the trees, we found OC Charlie with his tactical headquarters, alive and well but under significant pressure.

At this point, I believe we killed the enemy who had been firing at us ever since we had left the monsoon drain. I say "I believe" we killed him, because to this day I don't have a clear memory of it. Indeed, it was only later when I cleaned my rifle and found that it had been fired and four rounds were missing from my magazine that I began to think back and started to remember the details. My impression is that we closed up to the stone wall, and I remember a feeling of fury, exactly like road rage, toward the militia who had been firing at us. I felt particularly protective of my radio operator, weighed down as he was with the heavy radio, and I have a blurry memory of waiting with murderous triumph for the same guerrilla fighter to pop up again in his firing position, and of several of us firing at once. I cannot say whether I hit anything, but he dropped out of sight behind the wall and did not appear again. My ears began to ring with a deafening loudness and did not stop for several days—even now, several months later, they still ring occasionally.

At this point OC Charlie and I pulled out our maps, got under cover, and had a brief discussion in the shelter of the wall. It was clear to both of us that we were within a hundred meters of the border and that at least some of those firing at us were Indonesian army forces as well as militia. I realized this with a dreadful sinking feeling, because killing militia was one thing, but a firefight with Indonesian regular troops could easily lead to a general war between Australia and Indonesia. We were sitting right on an international flashpoint. Tensions with Jakarta were on a razor's edge, the worst in thirty years: our ships, submarines, and aircraft were playing hide-and-seek with theirs all over the Timor Sea; our troops were intermixed with the remnants of the Indonesian occupation force throughout East Timor; and they outnumbered us eight to one. This was clearly a strategic crisis point and needed immediate action to quell it before it could spin out of control.

My radio operator had been giving a running commentary to battalion headquarters throughout the engagement so far, and the commanding officer now wanted a direct situation report from me. I briefed him on the position, explained what had occurred, and said that I thought we were now close to the border and potentially facing the Indonesian army. He told me that Brigade and Force Headquarters had been informed and that we were to push forward and clear the village, killing any militia. It was clear to me that he was still working on the notion that we were at the outskirts of Motaain in its fictional location well inside East Timor. I had mistakenly given my position about three hundred meters to the east earlier in the firefight, before seeing the bridge and realizing the mapping error—so this was my fault. Making him understand this in the heat of battle proved difficult, especially as Brigade had apparently directed him to close with and destroy the militia.

It was at about this point that he released the quick reaction force— the assault pioneer platoon mounted in armored personnel carriers—to move forward and reinforce us. It would take them almost an hour to reach us, though, so I knew we had to act quickly to stop the present firefight before it escalated. We could hear trucks coming and going in the rear of the enemy position throughout the battle. At the time, I assumed the Indonesian armed forces were reinforcing their forward troops. As it turned out, this was actually the militia pulling out under covering fire of the Indonesian regulars, who covered them long enough to make good their escape and then began to slacken off their rate of fire. But at the time, I knew we were outnumbered and expected a flanking or rear attack from them at any moment—having trained the Indonesians as commander of an advisory team a few years earlier, I knew their tactical style, and it was always to outflank aggressively.

Shortly thereafter, what I expected seemed to be happening, as a large burst of firing broke out behind us. After a hurried consultation with OC Charlie, I agreed to go back once again through the firefight, take charge of the rear part of the patrol, and fight off the outflanking move in our rear. As we dashed back across the open ground and over the roadway again, I had an extremely uncomfortable plucking sensation at the base of my neck as I smothered the fear of being shot in the back. I remember deciding at that point not to turn my back on the enemy again.

However, even in that moment I felt the enemy fire begin to slacken off, as Charlie Company tactical headquarters opened fire again into the flanks of the enemy in the village, who seemed fixated on our forward platoon, which was pinned down on the home side of the stone bridge. The enemy seemed taken unawares by the headquarters engaging them from a flanking position in depth, and I believe it was at this point that the enemy suffered the bulk of their killed and wounded.

With the firing behind our backs, back down the monsoon drain we went again, to the rear of the little perimeter the patrol had formed when the firefight began. Here we found the two armed patrol vehicles closing up to our rear, having had a fleeting firefight with a group of militia fighters who had infiltrated to the rear of our location and popped out of the jungle ahead of the vehicles, whose gunners saw them crossing the road and engaged. This group of enemy, their outflanking move having been stopped by the patrol vehicles covering our rear, had then fled away from the firefight, eastward along the beach.

As there was no longer an immediate threat to our rear, I gathered up everyone I could find, formed them into an ad hoc perimeter covering the rear of the triangular walled garden, and then ran forward through the firefight for the third time. As I did so the fire began to die down into a lull. After again reaching the stone wall, and having a brief whispered discussion with OC Charlie, I agreed with him that we needed to try and organize a cease-fire. The Charlie Company medic, who spoke some Indonesian, had been calling on the enemy to put their weapons down for some time, but I am not sure they understood, and things were still on a hair trigger, with every weapon facing in and a tense "Mexican standoff" developing.

I agreed with OC Charlie that I would take a small party forward across the bridge to negotiate. Gathering together my radio operator, the artillery forward observation officer who also commanded the civil affairs team, and his radio operator, I pulled everyone together into the shelter of the bridge abutment and briefed them on the plan. The combat cameraman joined us at this point, and I gave him permission to follow at a distance. I told the group to stay well behind me and that if there was any firing they were to go to ground, abandon me on the bridge, throw smoke grenades to create a smokescreen, then work their way back to the home side of the river. My theory was that as I was walking first, I would be most likely to be hit, and while that would be unfortunate for me, it would be disastrous if the whole party were killed in trying to recover me.

We then set off, in a loose square formation, myself leading and calling out in Indonesian "*Jangan tembak, kami mau cakap saja*" ("Don't shoot, we just want to talk"). I remember feeling faintly ridiculous and wishing we had something white to fly to indicate our intention to parley, but we had nothing available and so simply moved forward with our weapons in outstretched arms, hoping the Indonesians would not misunderstand our intent.

For me, this was the most frightening part of the whole engagement. My heart was thumping so hard I could barely walk, and I felt shaky in the legs, with a dry mouth that tasted of dust and ashes. After all the fire that had gone down, the deafening noise of the firefight, and the killing and wounding of people, I felt the afternoon silence flooding back, pressing in on me, and I wanted simply to take cover rather than walking blindly forward like an idiot into the unknown. Particularly, I felt worried that my little party would be engaged and that my radio operator or one of the others would be killed, and it would be my fault. Alternatively, the Indonesians might misinterpret our action as an attempt to surrender and take us prisoner. Having seen the dismembered bodies of local people who had been captured by the militia, and which had washed up on the beach over the past few weeks, this prospect did not fill me with confidence.

As we came around the slight curve in the bridge, we saw an Indonesian army light-machine-gun team lying on the side of the road near the first houses, struggling with their weapon, which had jammed. I do not know if they would have fired if they had been able, but by the time they cleared the jam the cameraman had appeared, and they clearly thought better of it. By this stage, my heart felt as if it was knocking a hole in my ribs, and I was keyed up to an enormous extent.

Then, a few yards ahead, around the corner appeared an Indonesian army lieutenant, a police captain, and several Indonesian regular soldiers, clearly, from their uniforms, members of the Indonesian Strategic Reserve Command. As we closed up with them, Australian troops began appearing out of the tree line also, including the lead platoon commander and several other soldiers. The Indonesians were smiling, and with enormous relief, I closed up with them and we began to talk. As I came close, I put my rifle down on the ground and walked forward unarmed with arms at my sides—my radio operator picking up the rifle behind me. The firefight was over, but the hardest part of the day was still to come.

It felt as if it had only been a few minutes since the start of the firefight, but glancing at my watch I realized it was after 4:00 P.M.—The gun battle had lasted almost ninety minutes.

THE NEGOTIATION

As we met, I briefly grasped hands with the senior Indonesian police and army officers, touching my heart in the Javanese style. We were all smiling with relief, although the senior police officer looked sullen. After exchanging greetings, I said that there seemed to have been some kind of misunderstanding, and asked the army officer (a first lieutenant) why his troops had fired on us. He said, with disarming frankness, that we had caught his people by surprise and they had reacted by firing at us because they did not know who we were. By this stage no militia were visible any more, and I wanted to confirm the cease-fire before we discussed the guerrilla presence. We were speaking in Indonesian, but I was very conscious of the Australian Army cameraman recording the negotiation— very useful from one point of view but still disconcerting knowing that any mistake I made would be permanently recorded and widely known.

I was still very stressed—extremely hot, incredibly thirsty, as one always is after a firefight, still sweating, and shaking slightly from the aftereffects of the gunfight and the fear I had experienced leading the party across the bridge. I paused for a drink of water, which one of my sergeants, a mortar fire controller who had been with me through the firefight, kindly offered me from his water bottle. I took a couple of deep breaths, and then continued negotiating.

The Indonesians were indeed Strategic Reserve Command troops, from Java, clearly unused to Timor and unfamiliar with their location. The senior officer (Lieutenant Eddy) said they had only been there for less than two days. He was quite unclear as to his location but was sure he had been told that his position was in West Timor. His impression was that the border ran through the center of the stone bridge and that the contact had literally been a crossborder shoot, with our people on the East Timor side and his people on the West. Still, he had no map, there was no visible border marking, and I was still at this point fairly sure that we were at least a hundred meters inside East Timor.

On a positive note, he admitted that his men had fired first and that they had started the firefight. This was important, since (ambiguously enough) because of the way the international community, led by the United States, had pressured Indonesia to permit the international intervention, we were ostensibly supposed to be cooperating with the Indonesians in putting down the militia. There were even Indonesian liaison officers at INTERFET headquarters in Dili, listening to the contact unfold over the radio and tracking it in the command post.

At this point, I and the Indonesian commander had reached agreement on a cease-fire, each promising that we would not advance beyond our present positions, would not engage each other further, and would withdraw from immediate contact as soon as we had confirmed the situation and completed battlefield clearance: the process of cleaning up dead, wounded, weapons, and expended ordnance that always has to happen after a firefight. I felt considerable relief at this—even though the consequences of the firefight still had to be worked through, at least we had agreed on a cease-fire and the immediate strategic danger of war with Indonesia was averted.

In terms of casualties, we had seen two stretchers being carried out of the houses, at least one of which contained a dead man. I was unable to determine whether he was militia, police, or army, but the Indonesians later admitted to the loss of a policeman killed. We quickly offered the Indonesians the use of the medical team who had accompanied our patrol to treat their casualties, but they declined the assistance.

This puzzled and saddened me at the time, because it almost certainly cost the unnecessary death of at least one of the Indonesian wounded who could have been treated, stabilized, and evacuated by our people on the spot but was instead trucked to the primitive hospital in Atambua. This was an hour's drive away, and at least one of the wounded did not survive the journey. There were at least two other casualties on the Indonesian side, according to reporting we received later. So this means a total of one to five people killed or wounded on the Indonesian side. On our side, we had no serious casualties, despite having been outnumbered—probably because we had remained largely static and in cover and the Indonesians' aim had been quite high in the initial burst of fire.

Strictly speaking, the position of the border was a secondary issue. At this time, East Timor was still legally part of Indonesia—the Indonesian parliament had yet to vote on the issue, and Australia had recognized East Timor as the twenty-seventh province of Indonesia more than a decade earlier. So there was, in fact, no international border involved. Rather, it was an administrative boundary between two village districts within Indonesia, lying on the interprovincial boundary between Nusa Tenggara Timur Province and East Timor Province. However, INTERFET had agreed with the Indonesian army representatives in Dili that we would not cross the boundary, and it seems that even the level of cooperation between INTERFET and the Indonesian military in East Timor (largely mythical as it was) was not replicated in Nusa Tenggara Timur Province.

It was clear to me, though, that public opinion in Indonesia and Australia would consider this an international border issue rather than simply a case of two ostensible allies being drawn into a gunfight by the presence of local guerrillas. So we needed to clearly establish the position of the interprovincial boundary and (if possible) record the Indonesians admitting that we were still on the East Timor side.

By this time, the tactical situation had changed. The assault pioneers had arrived, mounted in the big M113 armored personnel carriers, and were deploying around the walled garden and along the road. This substantially increased our troop presence in the battle area and seemed quite intimidating for the Indonesians. The noise and gravitas of the armored vehicles as they maneuvered and positioned themselves, with their deep-throated engines and heavy machine guns, seemed to stamp our side's ownership and dominance on the area and had an obvious intimidatory effect on the Indonesian negotiators.

The press had also now arrived, in the form of several TV news media crews, as well as the army combat camera team who had been with us throughout the battle. A small crowd of media people had begun to gather on the home side of the stone bridge, getting in people's way and filming the negotiations as they continued. I asked the forward observer and his civil-military operations team to move them somewhat to the rear and maintain control over them. This was partly for their own safety, as the situation was still a relatively tense standoff, but mainly to ensure that we controlled the information flow about the battle for as long as possible. I had no illusions that we would be able to maintain control for any length of time—the civilian mobile phone system was still functioning, and almost certainly, at least some of the reporters had already filed an initial report.

I was conscious that at this moment, even as the battlefield clearance was still under way, General Cosgrove in Dili and the Australian government in Canberra probably already knew in some detail about the firefight. They almost certainly knew more than our own brigade commander, who was still embarked on a navy amphibious ship in transit to his new headquarters location at Suai. There was still a possibility that the incident, if reported in an inflammatory way, could lead to a direct shooting war with Indonesia. So it was imperative that we gain positive control over the media information flow as soon as possible and put our own "spin" on the reporting of it.

Another change was the arrival of a senior Indonesian officer, the Atambua military district commander, Colonel Sigit Yuwono. He arrived looking very dapper in an office uniform rather than combat fatigues, with a silver-tipped swagger cane and a rolled wall map of the area. However, he was also clearly agitated, and the corners of his map showed traces of masking tape where it had been torn from the wall of a command post or office. He and I laid our respective maps on the roadway near the bridge and, poring over them, went again over the same issues I had discussed with Lieutenant Eddy before Colonel Sigit's arrival. We then moved on to a more detailed discussion of the border issue. All of this was happening in full sight of the media, and I was conscious of being in public view. So I made an effort to use both Indonesian and English for all key points, to ensure that both the domestic Indonesian media and the global English-language media received the same basic information. I had learned on a previous operational tour as an intelligence officer with the British Army contingent in the UN peacekeeping force in Cyprus that even when apparently a very long distance from the action, TV cameras and microphones can pick up an extremely high degree of detail during an incident.

The discussion over the map turned out to be useful because on the Indonesian map it was clear that there was a major discrepancy between Colonel Sigit's map, which was a Dutch map from the mid-1930s, and the Indonesian-published maps that we were carrying. The Dutch map had form lines only, with no topographical contours or grid references, but it showed Motaain very clearly as a major village on the West Timor side of the border, with a river running immediately to its east and a bridge marked as the border crossing. This matched the verbal account of the border that the Indonesian junior officers had given us but was entirely different from the depiction on our maps, which showed Motaain as a minor village well inside *East* Timor with the river to its west. Clearly, either the border had moved at some point, the village had moved (which happens, in the tropics, more often than one might suppose), the river had changed its course, one or both maps were simply incorrect, or all of the above! All this discussion was played out in front of the media.

After some time, I agreed with Colonel Sigit that we would make a joint statement to the media. I agreed to this because, for some reason, the Indonesians seemed very willing to admit that their troops had started the firefight and that our troops (regardless of how the maps were interpreted) had at all times been inside East Timor. What they were completely unwilling to admit was the presence of the militia or any relationship between the guerrillas and the Indonesian regular troops and police. This was understandable, as this would have been a public admission that they had been training and supporting the militia and would have undermined their whole strategic position.

In fact, of course, all through the operation we had seen the closest possible cooperation between the militia and the Indonesian regulars. For example, the very day after this firefight, my company ambushed an eleven-man infiltration party near the Nunura River, a major infiltration route (then and now).[2] This party was made up of militia but was equipped with the latest Indonesian army weapons and equipment and led by two Indonesian special forces soldiers.

Other information made it clear that the battle had involved a significant militia presence. For example, I had just debriefed the leading Australian section commander (i.e., squad leader) and forward scout on the initial moments of the battle. It seems that as the leading section rounded the corner, they saw a man on the road, level with the first houses of the village, armed with an SKS or M16 rifle and wearing camouflage pants and the T-shirt of the Besi Merah Putih militia group. The moment he saw the patrol, this guerrilla fighter opened fire on them. They went to ground and returned fire, and then a storm of small-arms fire burst out of the houses in the village. Similarly, OC Charlie had moved forward as I was beginning the negotiation, on the other side of the village. In doing so, he encountered two men dressed entirely in khaki (a common militia uniform color not worn by either the Indonesian army or police) and armed with SKS rifles (a common militia weapon not possessed by the Indonesian army). All of this, in the absence of a militia prisoner or corpse, was purely circumstantial evidence, but (along with the hurried evacuation of the militia by truck, which our forward section had witnessed) the evidence was nevertheless very strong that the Indonesian regulars had been protecting and supporting a sizeable guerrilla group.

Given the information spin issues associated with the engagement, I thought that we should try to get a public admission on the border issue from the Indonesian commander before the situation developed too far. It was probably too much to expect any discussion of the militia issue. After some discussion, I managed to convince him to agree on a four-point joint statement, to the effect that

- The two sides' maps were different and showed the border differently
- The firefight was initiated by the Indonesian troops when the Australians were still in East Timor, and neither side crossed the border at any stage
- The Australian troops returned fire from the East Timor side of the border
- The situation was now stable, and both sides had agreed to a cease-fire and to maintain their current positions

Having agreed on this joint statement, Colonel Sigit and I then called an impromptu press conference on the bridge, surrounded by the media crews. This would normally have required higher headquarters approval, but there was a real-time imperative to get our side of the story out before the civilian media began to spin it, so I made the judgment to go ahead on my own initiative. I later got some sharp criticism from my commanding officer about this, but I still think it was the right thing to do—Sigit had made it clear that he was about to give a press conference, whether I agreed or not, so if I had not taken part, the Indonesian version of the story would have gone out before ours, with their interpretation only. So I agreed to take part, we made our joint statement, he speaking in Indonesian and I making the same points in English and confirming his statement. We then answered a few questions.

By this stage, my injured knee was stiffening badly. It was almost sunset, and I was absolutely exhausted after the ninety-minute gun battle and the subsequent drawn-out negotiations. The quick reaction force commander had deployed his platoon and the armored personnel carriers around the battle site, and battlefield clearance (on our side at any rate) was complete. Charlie Company were shaking out into a dispersed formation in the general area and preparing to pull back a little to prevent any further outbreak of fighting. After a brief consultation with the commanding officer by radio, he directed me to return to Balibo and brief him in person.

Driving up the winding hill road to Balibo in one of the open Land Rover patrol vehicles, I began to experience a reaction after combat: a trembling, shivering fit of chills much like an attack of fever, as well as physical weakness (particularly in the legs), thirst, and gritty eyes. Luckily, I had experienced this before and knew what to expect, and I also had a forty-five-minute drive to get over it. I was nevertheless extremely tired by the time the Land Rover drove through the archway into the stone courtyard of the old Portuguese colonial fortress of Balibo castle.

THE AFTERMATH

In the deepening twilight, the whole castle was buzzing with excitement, with a small group gathered around the underground command post doorway listening to the radio traffic relating to the battle. Other onlookers, mainly headquarters people, were standing around the courtyard, and a gaggle of staff officers, along with the commanding officer, were standing by the battle map, which was taped to the damp dungeon-like wall of the command post.

With the intelligence officer, I briefed the commanding officer in detail on the engagement, using the big wall map in the tactical operations center, and we then sat down to write a contact report for brigade and INTERFET headquarters.

In retrospect, this was premature, as the report contained a number of inaccuracies—not least the actual point where the firefight had started and the location of the village of Motaain. The number of enemy casualties was also still unclear at this stage. Unfortunately, as a formal contact report, this document entered the official record of the campaign. Subsequently, as we were able to walk over the scene in daylight and reconstruct the events, it became clear that some aspects of the report were wrong. To Brigade headquarters, and perhaps to General Cosgrove, it thus appeared that we had held something back or falsified details of the initial report. This was not the case, but it made higher headquarters suspicious and contributed to a more thorough grilling when the investigation began.

By the time I had finished the contact report and it had been sent, the moon was already up, the night was very dark, and the castle was quiet. The commanding officer told me to go to bed—normally I would have had a three- to four-hour command post shift to do, involving sitting in the command post and supervising the clerks, radio operators, and staff officers through the night. In fact, this was the only night of the operation (apart from nights spent out on patrol with my company) when I missed doing a shift. But I was grateful for the break.

My sleeping space was tucked into a corner of the castle wall, under a waterproof shelter sheet known as a "hutchie" and up on a small stone ledge. Making my way there, I finally removed all my combat equipment. I was still shaking, primarily from the chill of the night air after taking off my body armor, but also with the tail end of my reaction to combat. It was dark, so I was unable—for reasons of night battle discipline, which in the Australian Army forbids cooking or the use of light after dark in a forward area—to cook a meal or make myself a cup of coffee. So I had a biscuit and some cold tinned tuna for dinner, drank some water, sat for a while staring at the wall with a blank mind, and then rolled myself in my silk sleeping bag liner and tried to go to sleep. This proved difficult, as I kept replaying the events of the day in my mind, seeing again the flash of fire and the movement of the troops, shuddering as I remembered walking across the bridge.

A thunderstorm was playing about the distant mountaintops along the border, and the thunder and lightning unsettled me, sounding like a distant battle. My knee was also hurting considerably and was stiffened by the wound from the stone chip (which I had managed to extract without difficulty, using my clasp knife).

The enemy was still occasionally infiltrating right into Balibo town at this stage of the operation, and there may have been at least one alarm during the night due to actual or suspected probing. In any case, in the early hours I woke with a start and saw in the bright moonlight what I thought were two guerrillas standing about four feet away, looking at me. I snatched up my rifle, which when sleeping I kept, loaded, between my body and the wall, attached by a lanyard to my wrist. I was about to put a burst of fire into the "enemy" when I realized that I was looking at the two young banana plants, each about six feet high, that grew next to my sleeping spot. It was lucky I did not fire, as I would almost certainly have hit those sleeping on the opposite side of the castle courtyard. After giving myself this unnecessary and rather embarrassingly unprofessional fright, I spent the rest of the night sitting wedged into my corner of the castle wall, knees drawn up, unable to sleep.

THE INVESTIGATION

The next few days turned out to be unequivocally the worst of my army career, indeed of my life up until that time.

By midmorning, it was clear that the previous day's firefight was considered a major international incident and that there would be an investigation by INTERFET headquarters and possibly also by the UN. Reports of the battle were on the radio, and apparently on TV, on the Internet, and in world newspapers as well. One paper (I believe it was the front page of the Queensland daily newspaper, the *Courier Mail*) carried a large full-color photograph of me negotiating with Colonel Sigit and the banner headline "Brink of War," with an article describing the state of extreme international tension between Australia and Indonesia. This was not good, to say the least.

The process of the investigation is perhaps better described as an inquisition. It occurred in three stages. First, I drove down to Batugade with the commanding officer, and he and I discussed the battle with OC Charlie. The commanding officer told us that investigators were coming down from Dili—the first time anyone had yet visited our battalion from the headquarters—and advised OC Charlie and I to be completely honest and open with them, as there was nothing to be afraid of. This, of course, immediately caused alarm bells to start ringing in our minds.

Later, we met with the three investigators from INTERFET headquarters: two Colonels—one an operations officer, the other the senior military policeman in Timor—and a military police warrant officer. The atmosphere was frostily adversarial, and it was immediately clear to all of us that we were in serious trouble.

Each of us was interviewed separately and then made to write a detailed statement on his part in the engagement. The investigators had watched the combat camera crew's video footage of the incident—we had not—and the television news footage and therefore had us at a disadvantage. They continually corrected our recollection in matters of detail, using phrases like "contrary to what you just said, the video evidence shows..." and so on. This was extremely uncomfortable, as none of us had any intention of misleading the investigators—indeed, before the interrogations began, we rather naïvely felt quite satisfied with our performance during the battle.

The key issue appeared to be the border, which we all felt was a bit odd, since there was in fact no international border there and in any case there was pretty clear topographical evidence that the maps were inaccurate. Certainly, from my point of view, the key issue was that the militia had been at Motaain in strength and had fired on us first and that we had returned fire, killing several without loss to ourselves. But from the investigators' point of view, this had been primarily an international boundary issue, and it was clear that there was a major political storm going on back in Australia, with questions in Parliament, criticism of the government in the media, and a sharp exchange of diplomatic notes with the Indonesians.

After this initial grilling, we drove forward along the coast road to a point just short of the incident site, where I dismounted and walked forward alone, as I was the only linguist, and we needed to talk to the Indonesian garrison on the bridge site to ensure there was no chance of another clash with them. I found it extremely unnerving to walk forward alone through the previous day's battle site toward the bridge. The Indonesians were on the bridge and waved to indicate that they were comfortable with our presence.

The investigators then came forward to join me, and we walked over the ground with them. Again, now that we were able to walk around in the open rather than crawling in the monsoon drain or taking cover behind the wall, our recollection of events proved somewhat inaccurate. For example, my whole calculation of the location where the firefight began (based on dead reckoning and counting paces while crawling up the monsoon drain) turned out to be incorrect—in fact, we were about two hundred yards further forward than I had thought. Similarly, already mentioned, there was the matter of the trees that I had completely failed to notice while under fire.

The initial investigations were followed, a few days later, with a joint UN border commission with representatives from Australia, Indonesia, and other countries with UN observers in Timor. We were called in to discuss the incident with the commission members, a process that involved a fairly tortuous discussion about the negotiation phase down at the battle site. Ultimately, the commission reported in detail on the position of the border, broadly confirming the Indonesian view of the border location but stating that the contact had occurred entirely in East Timor. There was no mention of militia.

I have always considered this commission verdict, more or less, a political whitewash. It was typical UN behavior, similar to the behavior I had witnessed time and again on the Green Line in Cyprus and to a lesser extent in Bougainville. If the commission's interpretation of the border was correct, then at least the forward scout and possibly the whole of our lead section were inside West Timor once the firefight ended. This was clearly not the case at the start of the battle, when we were all inside East Timor, even by the Indonesian interpretation, but it was certainly so by the end, when we had advanced some way through the firefight. My small team had definitely penetrated the border when crossing the bridge to negotiate. Conversely, the masses of evidence pointing to a significant militia presence during and before the firefight seem to have been completely ignored.

It seems likely to me, based on previous UN experience, that the commission decided to seek a resolution through compromise—we won't mention the militia, you won't complain about the border being crossed in hot pursuit. The second firefight—the militia who appeared to our rear attempting to outflank us, were cut off by the vehicles covering our rear, and then escaped by fleeing along the beach—was simply ignored as if it had never happened.

THE RESULTS OF THE BATTLE

Particularly in operational and intelligence matters, it is very difficult to know the effects of your own actions. The enemy never tells you the effect you are having, and you have to piece together the results of any operation or intelligence action from a patchwork of incidental detail that does not emerge until much later.

With the advantage of hindsight, the results of the battle seem to have been relatively positive for INTERFET. Later in the operation, we picked up a defector who had been part of the guerrilla group at Motaain that day. He said that the village had been used as a militia training area for some weeks before we arrived, and he named an Indonesian special forces sergeant (already known to me through another source) who had been responsible for training and supporting the militia. Motaain was a rallying point for guerrillas exfiltrating out of East Timor once we arrived, and the Besi Merah Putih and Aitarak militia groups both had elements there. These groups had been training at Motaain in preparation for an infiltration into East Timor. This defector confirmed for us that the militia had withdrawn from Motaain during the battle, cancelled the planned infiltration, and relocated to a new training camp outside Atambua, about another ten miles further back from the border inside West Timor. Another captured infiltrator told us that there had been several militia camps right on the border in early October, and that they had all moved back after the Motaain bridge battle, so that they were now located at a distance of ten to twenty kilometers inside Nusa Tenggara Timur Province.

The threatened "militia offensive" never occurred. Some local people with contacts across the border told us that the offensive had been planned but cancelled after Motaain, which had disrupted the preparation for it. I always found this hard to believe. Mounting a major offensive of this type would have been extremely foolish for the militia, and our aggressive patrolling after we arrived may well have convinced them not to take us on but rather to wait us out—by holding on until we inevitably left East Timor—before going on the offensive. Conversely, keeping the fear of a militia counteroffensive uppermost in our minds was in the local people's interest—it kept us there, protecting them. So our actions at Motaain *may* have prevented the offensive, but I doubt that any such offensive was ever really intended.

In a more general sense, we had given a good account of ourselves in our first major clash with Indonesian regulars, police, and militia. Although there were other firefights, this was the largest and the only one where large numbers of both Indonesian regular troops and militia fighters were involved. We had identified the "center of gravity" for the militia as their relationship with the Indonesian military and the support they derived from their sponsors. At Motaain the militia saw their protectors taking a kicking, and we know from sources that remain classified today that this led to a loss of confidence between the two groups and contributed to the subsequent political disintegration of the militia movement, hence its failure to evolve into a full-blown insurgency.

On a formal intergovernment level, the firefight made people realize the risk of having an ill-defined land border. First, INTERFET declared a self-imposed moratorium on ground operations within a thousand meters of the border. This was a real restriction on our operations in some areas—particularly for my company, which spent almost the whole of the campaign in a remote area of jungle right on the frontier—but we were always able to get a dispensation from force headquarters when we needed one. A joint commission studied the border, our topographical survey squadron mapped it in great detail and confirmed the errors in the maps we had all been using, areas of dispute and discrepancy were identified and the two sides (and later the UN and the East Timor government) began to resolve them. Agreed crossing points, known as "Junction Points," were established to control movement and information across the border. These still exist and seem to have become a permanent feature of the Western border area.

So the short answer to the question "What were the results of the battle?" is that we don't really know. The evidence we do have, however, suggests that the firefight may have pushed the militia back from the border, hampered preparations for infiltration, undermined the guerrillas' confidence in the regular Indonesian military, and (possibly) led to the cancellation of a planned militia counterstroke. We do know that the battle led to the formalization and detailed mapping of a previously ill-defined border, removing potential sources of friction between Indonesia and newly independent East Timor.

LESSONS LEARNED

Although the overall results of the firefight were broadly positive, the engagement was most definitely not one of my better performances, and I took from it several lessons worth noting. I have listed them here (in no particular order).

Combat performance. It is a truism that people never perform as well in actual combat as they do in training. Certainly, training comes through and influences people's behavior, helping them adjust to an infinitely more complex and hostile environment. But fear, exhaustion, uncertainty—in Clausewitz's word, friction—undermines performance. Luckily, the same factors affect the enemy, so, if you cope better with friction and the inevitable degradation of performance than the enemy can, you come out on top. If I consider my own performance on the day of Motaain, it was certainly not one of my better days. But it seems the Indonesian forces and militia were having an even worse day, so things turned out all right for us.

Fear. Motaain was not my first firefight; I had previously experienced hostile action on other operational deployments. But Motaain was by far the heaviest engagement of my experience to that date. [Of course, it pales into insignificance compared to what I and thousands of my peers experienced subsequently in Iraq and Afghanistan.] I noticed on that day, and subsequently on other occasions, that troops in their first firefight—particularly young, well-trained regular troops—tend to experience less fear than more seasoned troops who have already seen combat. I suspect this is because inexperienced troops do not have as clear an understanding of what could possibly happen to them, so they feel more invulnerable. As their experience of combat develops, troops tend to take fewer risks and to consider their options more carefully. They have seen people getting killed and injured and have a much clearer perception of the risks they run. Hence their tactical behavior tends to be less reckless and more considered. Youth is a factor here—that sense of immortality and invulnerability that defines young men can actually be a precious commodity in combat. I have watched even very young soldiers grow old in weeks after a few firefights, while their older peers who have not experienced the same intensity remain callow. The quiet, self-contained confidence of experienced troops is ideal for a complex operation, say an ambush or a cordon and search, but in a major one-off combat engagement, there is no substitute for youth, and inexperience (provided the standard of training is high) can actually be an advantage. This was not a major factor in Timor, where combat action was relatively infrequent, but it would be a significant issue in a more intensive operation.

Patrol planning. It is clear to me and will surely be obvious to the reader that our patrol planning for this operation was deeply flawed. At the time, given the apparent accuracy of the information and the fact that it appeared time sensitive, we saw a degree of urgency in the situation and a need to mount the patrol quickly. Could we, in fact, have waited another twenty-four hours? With the benefit of hindsight, I suspect we could have, and this would have allowed more detailed reconnaissance and deliberate planning rather than the more hurried process we actually adopted. This might have revealed the error in our maps, as well as the presence of significant Indonesian regular military forces alongside the militia, and might have given us pause. At the very least, we might have gone in with armored vehicles in the patrol from the outset instead of using them as backup.

Navigation. Poor maps are no excuse for poor navigation. Our mapping products are outstanding in Australia, in terms of accuracy and production quality, so that we become spoiled and expect to rely on our maps. In most of the world, this is a mistake. Most maps have neither the accuracy nor the clarity of the maps we use in training, and when we work with poorer maps—maps that require a degree of skepticism and interpretation in use—we can be caught out, as I and the other Australian commanders undoubtedly were on this occasion. My dead reckoning in the jungle was inaccurate, due to the fact that we entered and left the woods at no fixed, recognizable landmarks. I was not carrying a GPS, but in hindsight I should have insisted on a satellite fix from one of the other officers as soon as we hit the road again. I continued counting paces along the road and trying to identify my location using "map to ground," but I was at least thirty seconds to a minute too late in realizing our true position—and as it turned out, this was long enough that the firefight became inevitable. True enough, I was not in overall command and neither OC Charlie nor the lead platoon commander spotted the error either, but that is not the point. Navigation in combat conditions is not like navigation in training—there is nothing like someone shooting at you to make you lose count of paces and bearings—and we need to train our young commanders accordingly. We must give them experience of working with poorer maps and of making navigational decisions under stress. We must also develop skills in geographic intelligence and ensure that commanders are aware of the need to interpret, assess, and evaluate topographic data.

Contact drills. One benefit of "contact drills," the set of tactical plays that infantry small-unit tactics prescribe for firefights of this nature, is that they relieve the soldier of the obligation to think about his actions at the moment of the first shot. This is invaluable, because if you think rationally about your options under the stress of a "fight-or-flight" moment like that, you may well decide that flight is the better option. As it was, an efficient contact drill brought us all into cover within moments, all moving forward toward the enemy and laying down fire. It allowed us to regain the mental "high ground" following the enemy's initiation of the firefight. The fact that the Indonesians fired high probably helped, but I have no doubt that an effective contact drill saved lives at Motaain. Contact drills are considered somewhat basic and boring in infantry units. On the contrary, we should be doing them every day, in a variety of terrain and tactical situations, until they become absolute second nature.

Weapons employment. The enemy's marksmanship in this engagement was exceptionally poor. They fired literally thousands of rounds over the ninety minutes of the firefight without hitting a single Australian. Their fire was high throughout the contact, often a sign of inexperience, and they laid down so much fire that they actually damaged their own situational awareness. They were making so much noise and creating such obscuration of the battlefield (through dust and knocked-down vegetation) that they could not hear or see us, hence could not detect our movement and return fire until we started to kill them. This fact allowed us to get away with a fairly poor standard of marksmanship ourselves. Our shooting was better than theirs, but it was not good. Much of it was high, particularly in the initial stages, and we made little use of our heavier weapons such as rockets and forty-millimeter grenades. We did so mainly in order to avoid damage to civilian property, and out of deliberate restraint due to our uncertainty about whether civilians were in the village, but we could still have employed smoke, flanking fire, and point destruction (discussed below) to greater effect. In hindsight, a heavier weight of fire from us in the early stages of the conflict may have foreshortened it, avoiding much of the protracted firefight and potentially saving some Indonesian lives.

Point suppression. The majority of Indonesian casualties seem to have been inflicted by Tactical Headquarters or my detachment of specialist troops rather than the leading platoon itself. I found this highly instructive, because our doctrine tells us that the lead element in a firefight should go to ground, take cover, lay down a heavy suppressing fire, and thus allow the other elements to maneuver and defeat the enemy. The opposite was true in this firefight—the lead element was pinned down during the battle and unable to effectively suppress the enemy. Instead, it was elements such as headquarters, firing from a position in depth and undetected by the enemy, who did the damage. There was virtually no "maneuver" in the sense of movement, but a precisely applied weight of accurate fire from concealed positions in depth. This led me to begin developing the idea of "unobtrusive killing areas" in urban fighting—areas that appear safe but are actually vulnerable to fire from well-placed undetected enemy positions in depth. Results from simulation support the idea that such unobtrusive killing areas are where most casualties are lost in this type of fighting, and that undetected weapons firing from depth positions do the killing, not maneuver by forward elements.

Personal equipment. Many of us carried far too much personal equipment throughout the campaign. This battle was no exception. I had learned on previous operations to minimize personal equipment, but even those of us with previous experience were still carrying far too much kit. The ridiculous weights carried on initial deployment—two-thirds of body weight or more in many cases—were actually quite unnecessary. As described, the loads were so excessive that the soldiers needed water resupply at least daily. The justification for carrying such enormous weights was that the resupply system could not be trusted to supply us for several days—yet we relied on that very resupply system for our daily water resupply. If the system could reliably supply water (a bulky and heavy item shipped all the way from Australia), then surely we could have relied on it for other things also. None of us managed to eat a meal of any kind for the first forty-eight hours, yet we all landed in Dili with three days' combat rations that remained uneaten. We need to recapture our traditional austerity in our approach to equipment—we are in danger of getting soft and (literally) killing ourselves and our soldiers with kindness.

Protective equipment. Similarly, throughout the campaign, our heavy helmets and body armor made it impossible to catch or keep up with the lightly equipped enemy fighters who carried a rifle and one water bottle at most. They consistently outran, outmaneuvered, and outpaced us. The official reason given for the requirement to wear protective equipment was "duty of care." In other words, the generals and politicians didn't want to have to explain to someone's parents that he had been shot while not wearing body armor. But the very weight and bulk of the armor tired us, destroyed our agility, and made us a bigger target for longer. At Motaain, no one was hit by enemy fire. But our lack of agility in the firefight may have resulted, at least in part, from the fact that we were burdened and dehydrated from wearing the heavy, stifling armor. I don't expect that the Defence Department will accept the risk of doing away with body armor any time soon. Hence the clear lesson here is that we must train constantly in the armor, develop upper-body core strength, adapt to the extra burden, and ruthlessly minimize other kit.

Webbing equipment. Before Motaain, I carried typical Infantry commander's webbing—lots of navigational equipment, maps, and orders and plans kit, as well as minimal ammunition, water, and first aid equipment. I wore issue belt webbing but supplemented this with British-issue Northern Ireland chest webbing when on patrol, with extra water and ammunition. Many people who wore chest or vest webbing in firefights, including Motaain, came away wanting to ditch it and revert to the issue belt webbing. This was because the chest webbing, by placing the pouches directly below your chest, lifts you an extra ten centimeters or so off the ground. This sounds like a minuscule amount, but with someone shooting at you, it feels enormous. With belt webbing, it is the pouches that are lifted off the ground, while you can hug the earth to your heart's content. After Motaain, I wore the lightest possible belt kit, with ammunition, water, and large amounts of medical kit only. My commander's kit and minimal survival equipment I stuffed into my pockets. I slept out many nights in the jungle with only this equipment, suffering no significant inconvenience. The lesson here, again, is that we are killing ourselves with comfort and convenience—a little more austerity and a willingness to suffer discomfort in order to better kill the enemy would be well worthwhile.

Media. Handling of the media during and after this contact was a key element in limiting the damage caused to our relationship with Indonesia, preventing the outbreak of war, and generating information dominance over the militia and the Indonesian army. It was not until afterward that I attended a media awareness course, but in hindsight I am not sure how much good the standard media course would have been in any case. The standard course, as conducted at Staff College, focuses on routine interviews, press conferences, and handling sensitive political issues. By contrast, the training I found most valuable was an exercise I did with the British army while preparing for Cyprus. This was a simulated combat situation with numerous issues competing for one's attention, including a real-life BBC television crew led by the well-known war correspondent Kate Adie. In addition to handling the media, I had to make tactical decisions under pressure, handle the information operations side of the incident, and maneuver my troops. This was the most pressure I had experienced in training during my time in the army until that time, and the experience stood me in excellent stead at Motaain. I believe such training should be mandatory for all combat arms officers.

The other lesson from the media aspect of this incident was that the armed forces no longer control information flow on the battlefield. Our hierarchical command-and-control system functioned well, but the networked media reporting system outpaced it dramatically. This does not necessarily mean that we need to mimic the media system—theirs is purely a reporting network, whereas ours requires decision-making, assessment, and response at various levels. But it does mean that we need to recognize that sources and flows of information around the battlefield are not ours to control. We must still seek to apply information and influence to the greatest extent possible, but we must also recognize that the chaos and confusion inherent in this situation is ultimately outside our control.

Language. Language skills were critical here. Without sound language skills (including interpreting and negotiating skills) we could not have organized a cease-fire, confirmed the border location, neutralized unfavorable media coverage, or (ultimately) avoided the threat of wider conflict. But language capability in and of itself was not enough. We also needed cultural understanding of the Indonesians (the sort of understanding that went into our efforts to avoiding exacerbating their loss of face, sidestepping the militia issue, defusing the stand off situation), as well as area studies knowledge of how Timorese and Indonesian society works. Importantly, we needed to combine these skills with professional competence—we needed not specialist linguists but bilingual infantry and intelligence operators. Given the current Australian military language training and management system, we do have some of these people, but nowhere near enough. Moreover, the people we *do* have emerge largely by accident, without centralized or coherent planning by the military. If we want to be successful in future, we cannot afford to continue leaving this to chance.

Intelligence work. Our application of field intelligence improved over the course of the campaign. By the end, we had a well-developed system of field and human intelligence and I had a personal network of local sources and agents—a major asset in prosecuting countermilitia operations. In the early stages and at the time of this incident, however, field intelligence was still rudimentary and based almost entirely on interrogations of militia detainees, defector debriefings, and casual contacts with local sources. Because we had been in the area of operations only a short time, we had limited collateral information and limited ability to judge the reliability of sources, and many of our best sources were yet to be developed. In particular, senior commanders were unwilling to place any reliance on local sources and tended to place too much reliance on assets controlled by us. This is typical of inexperienced commanders, who confuse our degree of control over a particular collection asset or agency with the accuracy of its information. Overreliance on technical means to the exclusion of human sources—requiring more finesse in interpretation—also led to distorted intelligence. In the case of Motaain, the basic intelligence picture existing before the battle, which was derived primarily from local human sources, proved to be almost completely correct.

It was impossible to verify the rumors of an impending militia counteroffensive, but every aspect of the information that could be verified was proved accurate. The sole inaccuracy—and it was one we introduced ourselves through reliance on mapping and failure to ask the locals for directions or use local guides—was the location of the village in relation to the border. Yet because of senior commanders' inexperience in intelligence work, this error (actually our own) was blamed on local sources and we had great difficulty convincing the commanding officer to even consider local information thereafter or to engage with local community leaders—a great opportunity lost. I also had difficulty gaining permission to raise and train a group of local guides, although I eventually managed to create a small local irregular group under the control of my intelligence, surveillance, and reconnaissance team. More familiarization with intelligence methods and procedures, as well as a larger number of professionally trained intelligence officers within Infantry and other combat arms units, would have avoided this problem. We must remedy this issue as a matter of priority.

Psychology of combat. A key lesson for me from this firefight was that personal recollection alone is an unreliable guide to what happens in combat. Unless you happen to be right on the spot where a particular incident occurs, you have no way of knowing about it or even being sure that it actually happened. Conversely, if you *are* on the spot, the psychology of combat is such that you probably can't remember it in detail. You are like the victim of a car accident—able to remember specific moments with blinding clarity but often unable to sequence these recollections. Moreover, such recollections are often simply wrong. Consider my failure to notice the trees, my inability to remember shooting the militia fighter until several days later, my incorrect assessment of the point at which the contact began. Only by using video evidence, the transcripts of radio logs, and the company's war diary, along with other people's recollections, can I be sure that any of this account even approaches reality—and even then, it is undoubtedly biased.

It may be that I am particularly weak-minded in this regard, but other people's evidence supports this impression. For example, as the battalion patrol master, I often debriefed patrols after combat action. Almost invariably, in the first few minutes after a firefight, most members of the patrol would have different views of what had happened—down to the number of enemy, the location of the contact, who shot whom, the sequence of events, and so on. After leaving them to discuss things among themselves, in almost all cases I found that they agreed on the fundamentals of the incident. But, again almost always, it was the dominant personalities of the group, or those who were most experienced in combat, whose version of events seemed to emerge. I was never entirely confident—without some form of collateral evidence—that the patrol's version of events was accurate. Incidentally, if this is the difficulty of an immediate debrief, pity the military historian trying to piece together an incident years later! We always tend to remember things happening in a neater, more coherent fashion than was actually the case. I claim no particular accuracy for this account, except to say that it does not differ, except in minor detail, from other accounts and collateral information. We may well all be wrong.

Investigations. The final lesson from Motaain is that any incident in a modern conflict, particularly a low-intensity campaign like Timor, will be investigated in detail if it involves loss of life. This admittedly came as a surprise to me at the time, but in retrospect it was inevitable and, from a government point of view, entirely justified. Later incidents were also investigated in detail, and some, such as the Special Air Service ambush at Suai on 9 October, are still under investigation. The manner in which this investigation of Motaain was carried out was somewhat unnecessarily harsh, however. An intelligence approach rather than a military police approach to the problem—applying more finesse to interrogation and less harshness—might have brought better results. As it was, the morale of all the participants was severely dented for most of the rest of the tour, and many of us are still reluctant to discuss the incident.

Deiokes and the Taliban

5

Local Governance, Bottom-up State Formation, and the Rule of Law in Counterinsurgency

I want to begin by talking about something that happened around twenty-eight hundred years ago on the western edge of the Iranian plateau, near Saghez in the Zagros Mountains. Then we're going to take a virtual detour via the theory of counterinsurgency and state-building, and then travel by way of the Horn of Africa in the 1990s to the far eastern side of that same great Iranian plateau, around Kandahar in Afghanistan, in 2009.

HERODOTUS'S ACCOUNT OF DEIOKES

Herodotus of Halicarnassus, writing in the fifth century B.C., gave an account of Deiokes, whom he identifies as the first king of the Medes. Here's Herodotus:

> There was a certain Mede named Deiokes, son of Phraortes, a man of much wisdom, who had conceived the desire of obtaining to himself the sovereign power. In furtherance of his ambition, therefore, he formed and carried into execution the following scheme. As the Medes at that time dwelt in scattered villages without any central authority, and lawlessness

This chapter is an edited version of the 2009 Wallace Wurth Memorial Lecture, University of New South Wales, Sydney, 2 September 2009. This annual public lecture in honor of the university's former chancellor Wallace Wurth, first delivered in 1964, is a major event of the university's calendar. In 2009, the lecture was also the keynote address for the symposium "Catalysing the Rule of Law in Afghanistan: Challenges and Opportunities," cosponsored by the university's Centre for Interdisciplinary Studies of Law and the Asia Pacific Civil-Military Centre for Excellence.

in consequence prevailed throughout the land, Deiokes, who was already a man of mark in his own village, applied himself with greater zeal and earnestness than ever before to the practice of justice among his fellows. It was his conviction that justice and injustice are engaged in perpetual war with one another. He therefore began his course of conduct, and presently the men of his village, observing his integrity, chose him to be the arbiter of all their disputes. Bent on obtaining the sovereign power, he showed himself an honest and an upright judge, and by these means gained such credit with his fellow-citizens as to attract the attention of those who lived in the surrounding villages. They had long been suffering from unjust and oppressive judgments; so that, when they heard of the singular uprightness of Deiokes, and of the equity of his decisions, they joyfully had recourse to him in the various quarrels and suits that arose, until at last they came to put confidence in no one else. (*Histories* 1.96)

Now, what Herodotus is describing here is a member of a local elite (a "man of mark in his own village") using the delivery of justice—dispute resolution, mediation, settling of disputes among the community—as a means to acquire local legitimacy and political power from the bottom up in a traditional society, one where people live "in scattered villages without any central authority." Herodotus goes on:

The number of complaints brought before him continually increasing, as people learnt more and more the fairness of his judgments, Deiokes, feeling himself now all-important, announced that he did not intend any longer to hear cases. . . . Hereupon robbery and lawlessness broke out afresh, and prevailed through the country even more than heretofore; wherefore the Medes assembled from all quarters, and held a consultation on the state of affairs. The speakers, as I think, were chiefly friends of Deiokes. [A snide little aside here from Herodotus.] "We cannot possibly," they said, "go on living in this country if things continue as they now are; let us therefore set a king over us, that so the land may be well governed, and we ourselves may be able to attend to our own affairs, and not be forced to quit our country on account of anarchy." The assembly was persuaded by these arguments, and resolved to appoint a king. (1.97)

So Deiokes is now starting to successfully transition from local justice to bottom-up state formation: translating the social good and community service of dispute resolution, mediation, and order into popular support, and thence into the formal authority, the rule of law, and the political structure of a state—in this case, a monarchy founded on law. Herodotus again:

> It followed to determine who should be chosen to the office. When this debate began the claims of Deiokes and his praises were at once in every mouth; so that presently all agreed that he should be king.... Thus Deiokes collected the Medes into a nation, and ruled over them alone. (1.98, 1.101)

Now, we should say that classicists, archaeologists, and historians don't all agree about this fellow Deiokes. He may be the same person as Dai-ukku, a leader mentioned in the ancient Assyrian cuneiform records, during the reign of Sargon II in the middle of the eighth century B.C., as governing a province in Mannea, along today's Iran-Iraq border. (Interestingly, Diyako, meaning Deiokes, is still a relatively common boy's name among Kurds in the same part of Iran.)

But what we *can* say—and we'll come back to this—is that Herodotus seems to be tapping into a long-standing trend here, one that links the origins of insurgency warfare with the origins of government: local nonstate actors gaining influence through the local exercise of law and order, especially dispute resolution and mediation, and then translating that influence into formal political authority through processes of state formation from the bottom up.

COUNTERINSURGENCY THEORY: A DETOUR

Now, I warned you we'd be taking a detour into counterinsurgency theory, but I also promise to make it as brief and painless as possible.

Bernard Fall, a French counterinsurgency theorist of the 1950s and 1960s, wrote in 1965 that "a government that is losing to an insurgency isn't being out-fought, it's being out-governed."[1] This is one of the neater expressions of an insight that is fundamental to classical counterinsurgency theory, namely that insurgents challenge the state by making it impossible for the government to perform its functions, or by usurping those functions—most commonly, local-level political legitimacy; the rule of law; monopoly on the use of force; taxation; control of movement; and regulation of the economy. Robert S. Thompson and David Galula, two leading classical theorists, described counterinsurgency as a competition for government, with both the state and the insurgent trying to mobilize and control the population. Here's Fall:

The communists, or shall we say, any sound revolutionary warfare operator (the French underground, the Norwegian underground, or any other European anti-Nazi underground) most of the time used small-war tactics—not to destroy the German Army, of which they were thoroughly incapable, but to establish a competitive system of control over the population.[2]

Fall fought in the French Resistance in World War II, and later in French Indochina, and was killed in February 1967 in South Vietnam while working as a counterinsurgency researcher.

About twenty years after Fall was killed, Joel Migdal in his book *Strong Societies and Weak States: State-Society Relations and State Capabilities in the Third World* (1988) took a deeper look at the functioning of states in society. Now, if you accept the basic Fall-Galula-Thompson insight that counterinsurgency is a competition for governance between a state and an armed nonstate challenger, then it becomes really important, in actually running a counterinsurgency campaign, to compare the strength and effectiveness of the insurgents with those of the government they're fighting. But that's really hard if you think in structural terms, because governments are *structurally* very different from insurgent movements. Governments have fixed locations, a capital, provincial and district offices, a bureaucracy and public service, armed forces and police, and so on, whereas the insurgents may have only a shifting, shadowy network of cadres, fighters, sympathizers, and supporters. They're usually smaller than governments, and it's often difficult to pin down exactly how many fighters they can put in the field at any one time. So all of that makes it extremely hard to compare relative strength and effectiveness.

Migdal solved this problem for us by taking a *functional* rather than *structural* approach. He identified four functions of government. It has to penetrate society, regulate social relationships, extract resources, and apply those resources to identified group ends. These functions are relevant to any form of governance, including nonstate governance systems like tribes or clans, and of course these functions are independent of structure. The beauty of this approach is that the same four functions are exactly what insurgents also have to do if they want to establish the competitive system of control that Fall talks about—and although their structure differs greatly from the government's, Migdal's approach makes it much easier to compare the two—as "apples with apples."

Jump forward about another twenty years, and Stathis Kalyvas in his book *The Logic of Violence in Civil War* (2006) examines the same phenomenon from the standpoint of the third actor in the insurgency triad: the local noncombatant population. Using an exhaustive series of field-work studies from numerous conflicts, he shows that one of our common assumptions—namely, that insurgent movements are strongest in areas where people support the insurgents' ideology, while governments are strongest in areas where people have a positive view of the state—actually reverses the causality of what really happens. The insurgents aren't strongest where people support them: rather, people support them where they are strongest. Likewise, people support the government in areas where government presence is strongest. In other words, support *follows* strength, not vice versa.

Obviously, this finding has huge implications for traditional "hearts-and-minds" and "battle-of-ideas" approaches in which you try to make people like you in order to gain their support. Kalyvas shows that that's not how it works at all. He taps into the same thing Herodotus is talking about—the fear of disorder and anarchy—and shows that local populations in an insurgency are in a lethally uncertain environment, buffeted on all sides by armed groups who want their support and will kill or punish them if they don't get it. Community leaders are forced to cooperate with the strongest local group and to switch sides as needed, as a means to survival.

As an aside here—and we'll talk about Afghanistan in more detail in a minute—when I read Kalyvas, it reminds me of conversations I've had with Afghan tribal elders and community leaders over the years. Once, last year, I was with a local leader and eleven of his district elders. This guy had fought with the Taliban and had just defected to the government side a few weeks before, and we were all sitting down and talking about the situation, and I asked him what made him decide to leave the Taliban and join the government. And he said—"Oh, you don't get it. I wasn't with the Taliban before, and I'm not with the government now. I was always just trying to protect my people, to look after them. Before, I thought we were better off with the Taliban. Now, we think we're better off with the government—but that could change." So this is a classic "swing voter" approach. Other people take a "hedging" approach: in both Pakistan and Afghanistan, I've talked to Pashtun leaders from tribes where most families have one son fighting with the Taliban and one with the government, just to cover all bases.

Now, Kalyvas unpacks the motivation that drives people to behave like this, and his work shows that people will do almost anything, and support almost anyone, to reduce that feeling of fear and uncertainty by establishing a permanent presence, through a predictable system of rules and sanctions that allow people to find safety by compliance with a set of guidelines. Even if those guidelines are harsh and oppressive, if people know they can be safe by following a certain set of rules, they will flock to the side that provides the most consistent and predictable set of rules. Obviously, people don't want to be oppressed, and they want to be treated kindly and have a prosperous life. But as Kalyvas shows, these are actually secondary considerations—what people most want is security, through order and predictability, and they will kill to get it.

We could describe what we're talking about here as a theory of normative systems—or following Fall's usage, we might talk about "systems of competitive control." If you add into the mix Migdal's functionalist state-in-society approach and Kalyvas's insight that support follows strength, and throw in for good measure Mao Zedong's observation that "political power grows out of the barrel of a gun," then we come to a pretty good understanding of what it takes to prevail in an insurgency—something that I call the theory of competitive control.

THE THEORY OF COMPETITIVE CONTROL

Simply put, this is as follows: *In irregular conflicts* (i.e., conflicts in which at least one warring party is a nonstate armed actor), *the local armed actor that a given population perceives as most able to establish a normative system for resilient, full-spectrum control over violence, economic activity, and human security is most likely to prevail within that population's residential area.*

In other words, whoever does better at establishing a resilient system of control, that gives people order and a sense of security where they sleep, is likely to gain their support and ultimately win the competition for government.

The expression "resilient, full-spectrum control" is important here. Let me explain it by talking a bit about Al Qa'eda in Iraq. Just like any other insurgent or terrorist group, Al Qa'eda in Iraq tried to gain control by manipulating and controlling Iraq's Sunni population, whom they saw as their power base. They did that through a system of rules and sanctions based on a particularly severe and decontextualized form of sharia that was alien to the population. It included rules like—if you smoke we'll cut your fingers off; if you're a woman and you push your headscarf back behind your hairline we'll throw acid in your face; if you fail to give us your daughter in marriage we'll cut your head off; if we think you're a spy we'll skin you alive in public; if you're a tribal leader who refuses to cooperate with us we'll bake your seven-year-old son alive in an oven. All these things actually happened in Iraq in 2006–7, and in fact I've left out some of the worst things Al Qa'eda in Iraq did, but the point—as I think you'll agree—is that Al Qa'eda in Iraq had a system of control based almost entirely on intimidation. They terrorized people, and they had control in areas where they could maintain that pall of fear over the population, and—as Kalyvas would have predicted—where there was a threat to the Sunni community from Shia death squads, people even supported Al Qa'eda in Iraq out of fear that, horrific though they were, the alternative of chaos and oblivion was worse.

But the control they established was in a very narrow band—pure intimidation. They were a toggle switch: they could (1) cut your head off, or (2) not cut your head off. Beyond that, they were basically incapable—and that made their control very brittle. When we finally succeeded in breaking their reign of terror and lifting the pall of fear off the community, people turned on them in a flash, and they were destroyed.

Now, contrast this with an organization like Hezbollah, which has a much more resilient, full-spectrum system of control. Sure, they have a terrorist wing, and they will kill you if you step out of line. But they also have a community militia that will protect you and keep crime down, and they have charities that will help you if you are poor, and they can get you a job, and teach your children in their schools, and treat you in their hospital if you are sick, and represent you in parliament through their political party, and you can watch their television channel, al-Manar, and listen to their radio station and read their newspaper. Al Qa'eda were thugs. Hezbollah—and groups like them including Jaysh al-Mahdi, Muqtada al-Sadr's Shia movement in Iraq—are much, much more than that. In fact, they are acting very much like a government, which is after all another normative system based on wide-spectrum systems of control.

So Al Qa'eda in Iraq and Hezbollah are at opposite ends of a spectrum here and, as we'll see in a minute, the Taliban are somewhere in between but far closer to Hezbollah in their approach than to Al Qa'eda in Iraq.

But speaking of normative systems, clearly the rule of law is the ultimate normative system of control. It lays down rules, associates each rule with a sanction if you break the rule, sets up a system of published laws that aid predictability and consistency, and establishes a judiciary (in democracies, an independent judiciary), a police force, prisons, lawyers, judges, et cetera—all in the interests of making people feel safe and secure through a standardized, and ordered normative system. And this is a huge factor in social stability that ultimately becomes the basis for government. Rule of law, in this sense, as Herodotus clearly knew, is literally the foundation of both the state and of social order.

Now, if Noam Chomsky or some of my other predecessors in giving this lecture were here, this would be a great opportunity for them to interject and say "Aha, you've admitted it: government is just another oppressive protection racket, no better or worse than rebels, insurgents, or so-called terrorists. In conducting counterinsurgency you're no better than the enemy, and you're engaging in a fundamentally illiberal and oppressive activity, because you're trying to establish a system of control just like them. States with their police and courts and armies and parliaments are just like insurgents, except that they own the means of legitimacy."

Well, I think that drawing any moral equivalence between what some insurgents do—as we've seen, beheading people or baking children alive—and what legitimate governments do, like enforcing speeding and taxation regulations and upholding the laws against homicide and robbery, is gravely misplaced. But functionally, as Migdal would have it, there is certainly an equivalence, and this where rule of law, state-building, and the character of the state really come into play. To answer the objection that counterinsurgency is fundamentally immoral and oppressive, though, we need one final bit of theory here, which is the observation that counterinsurgency techniques mirror the state that uses them.

COUNTERINSURGENCY MIRRORS THE STATE

An *insurgency*, according to current U.S. military doctrine, is "an organized movement aimed at the overthrow of a constituted government through the use of subversion and armed conflict....Stated another way, an insurgency is an organized, protracted politico-military struggle designed to weaken the control and legitimacy of an established government, occupying power, or other political authority while increasing insurgent control." *Counterinsurgency*, meanwhile, is just an umbrella term that describes the full range of measures that governments take to defeat insurgencies. These can be political, administrative, military, economic, psychological, or informational, and these are almost always used in combination. There's no standard set of techniques in counterinsurgency. In fact, the precise approach any particular government takes to defeat an insurgency depends very much on the character of that government.

Indeed, any given state's approach to counterinsurgency depends on the nature of that state, and the concept of "counterinsurgency" can mean entirely different things depending on the character of the government involved. And I would submit that this means that good governments can do counterinsurgency badly, but bad governments can't do it well. Oppressive governments tend to enact brutal measures against rebellions, and military dictatorships tend to favor paternalistic or reactionary martial-law policies, whereas liberal-democratic states tend to be quick—perhaps too quick—to hand control to locally elected civilians in a bid to return to "normalcy." You only need compare the approach taken by Syrian president Hafez al-Assad in crushing the *ikhwan*, the Muslim Brotherhood, at Hama in 1982, or by Saddam Hussein in massacring Kurdish civilians at Halabja in 1989, with British policy in Northern Ireland or our own policies in Iraq and Afghanistan to see this. So I think counterinsurgency *can* be oppressive and inhumane, but it's not inhumane by definition—that depends on the character of the state involved.

Okay, we're nearly done with theory, but let's visit the Horn of Africa as promised, and what I want to look at here is the contrast between theory and reality, and more specifically between top-down versus bottom-up nation-building.

TOP-DOWN VERSUS BOTTOM-UP: SOMALIA VERSUS SOMALILAND

It may surprise you to realize this (or not), but in the past it has actually been rare for counterinsurgents to compare notes with peace-building specialists, members of the international development community, and rule-of-law experts. That's changing, but one of the side effects of that academic stovepiping has been that, even though Herodotus was writing about this stuff more than twenty-five hundred years ago, we currently lack a generally recognized theory of opposed nation-building or of bottom-up state formation. Because of this, when the international community becomes involved in reconstruction and stabilization, institutions like the UN, the World Bank, the IMF, and governments tend to focus on top-down, state-centric processes that have a structural focus on putting in place the central, national-level institutions of the state rather than a functional focus on local-level governance functions. Now, empirically, these top-down, state-centric approaches seem to be much less useful than bottom-up, community-centric approaches.

Current experience—in Iraq, Afghanistan, and the Horn of Africa (specifically, the different experiences of Somaliland and Somalia) actually suggests that bottom-up, civil-society-based programs that focus on peace-building, reconciliation, and the connection of legitimate local nonstate governance structures to wider state institutions may have a greater chance of success in conflict and postconflict environments than traditional top-down programs that focus on building the national-level institutions of the central state.

For example, as the anthropologist Ioan Lewis has shown, in Somalia since 1992 the international community has engaged in a series of failed attempts at top-down nation-building that have been captured and perverted by local elites, many of whom have been the same warlords who made the problem in the first place. Meanwhile, just to the north in Somaliland, a series of local clan peace deals in 1992 led to district-level agreements in 1993, regional charters, and the formation of provincial and then "national" government in 1994. This has resulted in a relatively high degree of peace, order, economic recovery, and the rule of law in Somaliland and to some extent in Puntland, despite lack of international recognition and involvement. In fact, Somalia is virtually a laboratory test case, with the south acting as a control group against the experiment in the north. We have the same ethnic groups, in some cases the same clans or even the same people, coming out of the same civil war and the same famine and humanitarian disaster, resulting from the collapse of the same state, yet you see completely different results arising from a bottom-up peace-building process based on local-level rule of law versus a top-down approach based on putting in place a "grand bargain" at the elite level.

Likewise, in Iraq in 2007, the Coalition forces during the Surge went in with the intent to create security for Iraqis, that would then lead to a national-level peace deal, a "grand bargain" that would resolve the conflict. Instead, the opposite occurred: a series of local agreements and reconciliation processes created peace and security at the local level (with our security presence acting as a critical enabler, as Kalyvas predicted), which resulted in an improvement in security overall—again, bottom-up and civil-society-led, not top-down and national-government-based. And of course, local agreements that are enforceable are just another form of normative system, sanctioned by society, and upheld in a very similar manner to the rule of law—in fact, police, courts, and a judiciary system, along with local representative councils, were some of the first institutions that these communities found it necessary to create.

THE TALIBAN AND THE RULE OF LAW

So, finally, we come to Afghanistan, and here we have seen exactly the same thing. International assistance efforts focused on building police and courts and ministries and institutions at the level of the central state, as well as international aid programs became bogged down in bureaucracy, duplication, and inefficiency. This breakdown created a vacuum at the local level, which the Taliban filled. They came in at the grassroots level and took over the functions of security, mediation, dispute resolution, and community policing, and they brought the world's most convenient and attractive cash crop—the poppy—to the Afghan farmer. The Taliban thus successfully sidestepped our top-down approach and were able to outgovern the Karzai government at the local level.

To paraphrase Bernard Fall, in Afghanistan the government is losing to the Taliban, and it's losing because it's being outgoverned, not outfought. Let me give you some examples.

Across the south of Afghanistan today, about fifteen Taliban sharia law courts are operating at the local level. Now, when you hear the term "sharia court" you may think of people having their hands cut off for stealing, women being stoned for adultery, beheadings, and so on. And that *does* happen. But in fact, the majority of the work of these courts is commercial or civil rather than criminal law. They issue title deeds and resolve land disputes, settle water and grazing disputes, handle inheritances and family law, issue ID cards and even passports (in the name of the Islamic Emirate of Afghanistan), and basically deliver a local dispute resolution and mediation service, with a reputation for harsh but fair and swift justice. In other words, the courts form part of a resilient, full-spectrum system of control. They are, in fact, doing precisely what Deiokes did and, like him, they are translating local dispute resolution and mediation into local rule of law and thus into political power.

For example, a friend in Kandahar tells me that there's a Taliban court just outside the city that formally subpoenas people to testify in court, and people go—even from within the supposedly Coalition-controlled urban area of Kandahar City—because they know they'll be punished if they don't—by local Taliban enforcement squads who act, and work, a lot like local police. There is in fact a silent campaign of intimidation, coercion, and control happening right under our noses. So who's in charge in Kandahar? In some places local warlords or drug dealers and in some places the Taliban, but clearly not the government.

In Migdal's terms, the Taliban have penetrated society and are playing a major role in regulating social relationships. They are also extracting resources and applying these resources to identified group ends—Taliban tax assessors, associated with the local Taliban governors whom the Taliban have appointed for each village and district, go out on a regular basis and assess people's property and crops and then levy taxes—usually around 10 percent—in a firm but generally equitable manner. So the Taliban, at the local level, are acting a lot like a government.

How is the actual government doing? Well, the Afghan government levies no taxes, relies largely on corruption and shakedowns of the population, has no functioning local court system, doesn't have a presence at the local level in about two-thirds of the country, and when it does have a presence, its local representatives tend to act so corruptly or oppressively that they alienate the population. And that's even leaving aside the significant loss of legitimacy resulting from an election that a lot of people saw as fraudulent and flawed. In other words, in terms of Migdal's functional approach, the Taliban are the real government of much of Afghanistan. Remember Bernard Fall? We can beat the Taliban in any military engagement, but we're losing in Afghanistan not because we're being outfought but because the Afghan government is being outgoverned. Unless we take drastic action to counter corruption, prevent abusive and oppressive practices by local officials (especially the police), reform local-level systems, and create legitimate local government structures that can function in the interests of the population, there's little doubt that we are eventually going to lose.

Two other things the Taliban have done really demonstrate that they understand the government's weakness in this area and see the importance of the competition for local legitimacy. First, the Taliban have established an ombudsman system, such that if a local Taliban commander does something abusive or wrong, people can go and have their complaint heard by an independent authority, and that Taliban commander will be punished and the people will be compensated. Now, that push for fairness and accountability is a direct challenge to the state—it's saying, the government will exploit you and abuse you, the Coalition forces will bomb you, and there's really nothing you can do about it. But we are fair, predictable, and just.

Secondly, the Taliban has a code of conduct, known as the *layeha*, that reads a lot like a military justice or field service regulation. We first saw this back in 2006, and in May 2009 we captured an updated, expanded version of it. This is a set of rules, guidelines for behavior, and admonitions to treat the population fairly and a set of legal authorities that lays out how Taliban groups are to operate. This is a code of conduct that the local people know about, and combined with the ombudsman system and the Taliban court system, it means that there is a high degree of accountability here. Now, don't get me wrong: the Taliban are oppressive and intimidatory as well. They will put a gun to your head and force you to comply. But then, a lot of local-level officials and drug dealers and warlords and other people associated with the government are oppressive and intimidatory as well. And this is a competition: you don't have to be perfect, but you do have to do better than the other side.

SOME CONCLUSIONS

Let me start drawing together some of the threads we've been talking about. Herodotus's account of Deiokes is something of an archetype—a semimythical description of how rule of law, the delivery of justice, and the establishment of locally legitimate presence becomes the foundation not only of social order but of the state itself. As Fall, Galula, and Thompson have shown, counterinsurgency is a competition for government, and as Migdal and Kalyvas have shown, you win that competition by penetrating society, regulating people's actions through a normative system of rules and sanctions that create predictability and order, and establishing a presence that causes people to feel safe and makes them flock to your side. You can get things right at the level of counterinsurgency technique, but if the state is fundamentally oppressive, corrupt, or illegitimate, that won't help you.

As I have said, this is a competition for control, and the side that best establishes a resilient, full-spectrum system of control that can affect security, rule of law, and economic activity at the local level is most likely to prevail.

And, as our current experience in Afghanistan, Iraq, and Somalia shows, in places where local people have taken a bottom-up, peace-building approach based on local peace deals, enforceable agreements among local groups, and normative systems that protect the community from threats and disorders, the results have been far better than in places where the international community has taken a top-down approach focusing on the institutions of the central state. Yet that top-down approach does seem to be the international community's default setting in these types of situations.

To conclude, let me give you three implications that I think arise from all of this. First, counterinsurgency and counterterrorism people need to start talking more with the peace-building and development community, and they both need to talk much more with the rule-of-law community. These academic and policy communities have been intellectually segregated for far too long, and the more we share insights, the better we'll do in the field. We need to look at our theories of top-down state-building and recognize what empirical evidence from the field is telling us: that bottom-up, community-based, civil-society approaches are having much greater success than top-down, state-based approaches. This doesn't mean we can do without top-down structures, but it does mean we need to put a lot more effort into bottom-up issues, especially rule of law.

Second, in terms of Afghanistan, all of this suggests that we need to give top priority to anticorruption action, governance reform, creating a functioning government at the local level, and establishing sufficient presence to make people feel safe. Until now, we have had policies that basically focused on fighting the main force Taliban and extending the reach of the Afghan government. But as we've seen, it's not the main guerrilla units that are the problem, it's that the Taliban is outgoverning the Afghan government. And if our strategy is to extend the reach of a government that is corrupt, is oppressing its people, and is failing them, then the better we do at that strategy, the worse things are going to get.

Finally, we need to recognize that we're facing a crisis of legitimacy here, founded on a failure to connect at the local level with ordinary Afghans. Our efforts have been captured by an elite—the same warlords the Taliban overthrew in 1996—and the elite is doing what elites do, acting in an extractive and exploitative way toward its population. The election result has just underlined that fact and made visible to the international community something that lots of Afghans have known all along.

I don't think the war is lost, and I don't think the situation is hopeless. The additional troops, resources, civilian specialists, and money, as well as the better leadership, that the international community is putting into Afghanistan will create a window of opportunity. But I do think we have to urgently seize that opportunity and use it to focus on fixing what's wrong at the local level of the Afghan government, or that window will close again, and it will all be for naught, and the cost to the Afghan people will be immense. We can still turn this around, but we have to act now, and we have to focus on governance, rule of law, anticorruption action, and protecting the people at the local level. It's not rocket science, and these are hardly original ideas. But translating them into action is really, really hard, and we need to get on it.

PART II

A GLOBAL PERSPECTIVE

The struggle against the guerrilla is not, as one might suppose, a war of lieutenants and captains. The number of troops that must be put in action, the vast areas over which they will be led to do battle, the necessity of coordinating diverse actions over these vast areas, the politico-military measures to be taken regarding the populace, the necessarily close cooperation with various branches of the civil administration—all this requires that operations against the guerrilla be conducted according to a plan, established at a very high command level, capable at any moment of making quick, direct intercession effectively felt in the wide areas affected by modern warfare.

—ROGER TRINQUIER (1964)

Countering Global Insurgency

6

Since the United States declared a global "War on Terrorism" following the 9/11 terrorist attacks, some analysts have argued that terrorism is merely a tactic, thus a war on terrorism makes little sense. Francis Fukuyama's comment that "the war on terror is a misnomer...terrorism is only a means to an end; in this regard, a war on terrorism makes no more sense than a war on submarines" is typical.[1] This view is irrelevant in a policy sense (the term "War on Terrorism" is a political, not an analytical, expression) but nonetheless accurate. Indeed, to paraphrase Clausewitz, to wage this war effectively, we must understand its true nature: neither mistaking it for nor trying to turn it into something it is not.[2] We must distinguish Al Qa'eda and the broader militant movements it symbolizes—entities that *use* terrorism—from the tactic of terrorism itself. In practice, as I will demonstrate, the "War on Terrorism" is a defensive war against a worldwide Islamist jihad, a diverse confederation of movements that uses terrorism as its principal—but not its sole—tactic.

This chapter argues that the present conflict is actually a campaign to counter a globalized Islamist insurgency.[3] Therefore, counterinsurgency theory is more relevant to this war than is traditional counterterrorism. As this analysis shows, a counterinsurgency approach would generate a subtly, but substantially different range of actions in prosecuting the "War on Terrorism." On this basis, the analysis argues for a strategy of "disaggregation" that seeks to dismantle, or delink, the global jihad.* Just as the so-called containment strategy was central to the Cold War, likewise a disaggregation strategy would provide a unifying strategic conception for the current war—something that has been lacking to date.

THESIS

My principal thesis is this:

- The "War on Terrorism" is actually a campaign to counter a global Islamist insurgency. So counterinsurgency, not counterterrorism, may provide the best approach to the conflict.
- However, classical counterinsurgency is designed to defeat insurgency in one country. Hence, traditional counterinsurgency theory has limitations in this context. Therefore, we need a new paradigm, capable of addressing globalized insurgency.
- Classical counterinsurgency uses systems analysis, but traditional reductionist systems analysis cannot handle the complexity of insurgency. However, the emerging science of complexity provides new tools for systems assessment—hence, complex systems analysis may provide new mental models for globalized counterinsurgency.

---

* AUTHOR'S NOTE (2009): Since I first wrote this monograph in 2003, my thinking on terminology has shifted significantly. In particular, I have ceased using the terms "jihad" or "jihadist" to describe the enemy. I explained why in my note on terminology in my preface to *The Accidental Guerrilla* (New York: Oxford University Press, 2009), where I also explained that throughout that book I used the term *takfiri* to describe the enemy's ideology and the phrase "*takfiri* terrorist" to refer to those who use terrorism to further that ideology. As I explained in that note, the doctrine of *takfir* disobeys the Qur'anic injunction against compulsion in religion (Sûrah al-Baqarah: 256) and instead holds that Muslims whose beliefs differ from the takfiri's are infidels who must be killed. Takfirism is a heresy within Islam: it was outlawed in the 2005 *Amman Message*, an initiative of King Abdullah II of Jordan, which brought together more than five hundred ulemas (Islamic scholars) and Muslim political leaders from the Organization of the Islamic Conference and the Arab League in an unprecedented consensus agreement, a "unanimous agreement by all Muslims everywhere as represented by their acknowledged most senior religious authorities and political leaders." Al Qa'eda is *takfiri*, and its members are universally so described by other Muslims whom they routinely terrorize. In my view, and (compellingly for me) in the daily vocabulary of most ordinary local people, religious leaders, and tribal leaders with whom I have worked in the field, "takfirism" is the best descriptor for the ideology currently threatening the Islamic world. I prefer it to the terms "jihad," "jihadist," *jihadi, or mujahideen* (literally "holy war" or "holy warrior"), which cede to the enemy the sacred status they crave, and to *irhabi* (terrorist) or *hiraba* (terrorism), which address Al Qa'eda's violence but not its ideology. It is also preferable to the terms *salafi* or "salafist," which refer to a belief that true Muslims should live like the first four generations of Muslims, the "pious ancestors" (*as salaf as-salih*). Most extremists are *salafi*, but few *salafi* believers are *takfiri*, and even fewer are terrorists: most, while fundamentalist conservatives, have no direct association with terrorism.

- Complex adaptive systems modeling shows that the global nature of the present Islamist jihad, and hence its dangerous character, derives from the links in the system—energy pathways that allow disparate groups to function in an aggregated fashion across intercontinental distances—rather than the elements themselves.
- Therefore, countering global insurgency does not demand the destruction of every Islamist insurgent from the Philippines to Chechnya. Rather, it demands a strategy of disaggregation (delinking or dismantling) to prevent the dispersed and disparate elements of the jihad movement from functioning as a global system. Applying this approach to the current war generates a new and different range of policy options and strategic choices.

The argument is in four parts. In Part 1, I demonstrate that a worldwide Islamist jihad movement exists, and in Part 2, I show that it is best understood as an insurgency. In Part 3, I use complex adaptive systems theory to develop a systems model of insurgency. On the basis of this systems model, in Part 4, I then propose "disaggregation" as an appropriate strategy for countering the global Islamist insurgency. The chapter ends with conclusions and recommendations.

PART 1: ANATOMY OF THE GLOBAL JIHAD

We are not fighting so that you will offer us something. We are fighting to eliminate you.
—Hussein Massawi, Hezbollah (2003)

A Global Movement

Usama bin Laden, leader of the World Islamic Front (commonly known as Al Qa'eda, "the Base," or Qa'idat al-Jihad, "the Base of Jihad") declared war on the West on 23 February 1998. The declaration was made in a statement entitled "World Islamic Front Declaration of War against Jews and Crusaders."[4] Bin Laden's deputy Ayman al Zawahiri, former leader of the organization Egyptian Islamic Jihad, subsequently published a strategy chapter describing a two-phase strategy for global jihad against the West. Neither statement was treated particularly seriously at the time, but in retrospect each provides an insight into a developing global pattern of Islamist militancy.

Bin Laden's declaration of war announced a global campaign against the United States and the West. It issued a fatwa to all Muslims, calling for jihad, thereby indicating that bin Laden claimed religious authority (needed to issue a *fatwa*) and political authority as a Muslim ruler (needed to declare a jihad).[5] Subsequent Al Qa'eda statements refer to bin Laden as the sheikh or emir (prince or commander) of the World Islamic Front, indicating a claim to political and military authority over Islamist militant fighters throughout the world. Thus Al Qa'eda's statement declares a worldwide state of war against the West and simultaneously claims political and military authority over the forces engaged in that war. Unlike a traditional declaration of war, the declaration also claims authority over a worldwide Islamist movement for jihad.

Zawahiri's statement, issued shortly after 9/11, announced a specific strategic program for this war. Zawahiri, identified as the principal Al Qa'eda operational planner, articulated a two-phase strategy.[6] In the first phase, the global jihad would focus on the greater Middle East Area: "this spirit of *jihad* would...turn things upside down in the region and force the US out of it. This would be followed by the earth-shattering event, which the West trembles at: the establishment of an Islamic caliphate in Egypt."[7] Thus the first stage of the campaign would reestablish the caliphate, the historical source of spiritual and temporal authority for all Muslims, which existed from the death of Muhammed (in A.D. 632) until A.D. 1924, when it was dissolved by the Turkish Republic after the fall of the Ottoman Empire.[8]

The second stage of the strategic plan would use the "restored" caliphate as a launchpad for jihad against the West, in order to remake the world order with the Muslim world in a dominant position. "If God wills it, such a state...could lead the Islamic world in a jihad against the West. It could also rally the world Muslims around it. Then history would make a new turn, God willing, in the opposite direction against the empire of the United States and the world's Jewish government."[9]

A related document, "General Guide to the Struggle of Jema'ah Islamiyah" (Pedoman Umum Perjuangan al-Jama'ah al-Islamiyah), issued by Al Qa'eda's Southeast Asian ally Jema'ah Islamiyah (JI) in 2001, articulates a similar interpretation of the caliphate concept. This document states JI's objectives as the establishment of an Islamic state in Indonesia, followed by the creation of a pan-Islamic state in Southeast Asia (*daula Islamiya nusantara*) covering Malaysia, Indonesia, the Philippines, Thailand, and Singapore. Once this Islamist superstate is created, JI's aim is to further the establishment of a global pan-Islamic caliphate.[10]

Many aspects of Al Qa'eda's program could be disputed. The legitimacy of its claimed authority over Muslims and Islamist fighters, the veracity of its claim to have initiated the jihad, the viability of its two-phase strategy, the true extent of its intended pan-Islamic caliphate, or the sincerity of its stated aims could be questioned, for example. Nevertheless, according to open-source information, Al Qa'eda has a presence (in the form of sympathizers, sleeper cells, terrorist cadres, or active fighters) in at least forty countries. Earlier U.S. statements claimed an Al Qa'eda presence in sixty countries, and recent assessments have concluded that Al Qa'eda is still functioning globally, though disrupted by the destruction of its base in Afghanistan.[11] Indeed, a recent article in the Al Qa'eda military journal *Al-Battar* argued that the destruction of the Afghan sanctuary has enabled a global expansion for Al Qa'eda:

> In the beginning of their war against Islam, [the Crusaders] had announced that one of their main goals was to destroy the Al-Qaeda organization in Afghanistan; and now, look what happened? Thanks to God, instead of being limited to Afghanistan, Al-Qaeda broke out into the entire Islamic world and was able to establish an international expansion, in several countries, sending its brigades into every Islamic country, destroying the Blasphemers' fortresses, and purifying the Muslims' countries.[12]

ISLAMIST THEATRES OF OPERATION

This worldwide pattern of militant Islamist movements appears to function through regional "theatres of operation" rather than as a monolithic bloc. Theatres are regions where operatives from one country cooperate with operatives from neighboring countries or conduct activities in neighboring countries. Evidence suggests that Islamist groups within theatres follow general ideological or strategic approaches that conform to the pronouncements of Al Qa'eda and share a common tactical style and operational lexicon. But there is no clear evidence that Al Qa'eda directly controls operations in each theatre. Indeed, as will be seen, the global jihad appears to be not a single monolithic organization but a much more complex phenomenon.

The principal Islamist theatres so far identified are as follows.

- **The Americas.** North America is most prominent as the scene of the 9/11 terrorist attacks, but significant other Al Qa'eda activity has occurred elsewhere in the Americas, including attempts to infiltrate the United States from Mexico and Canada. Latin America has also been identified as a major center for Islamist training, infiltration, supply, and political subversion.[13] In particular, Al Qa'eda has a strong presence in the triborder area of Argentina, Paraguay, and Brazil—where there is a large Arabic Muslim population. There are regional Al Qa'eda affiliates (like the Mohammed Atta Brigades in El Salvador), there is evidence of cooperation between Al Qa'eda and Hezbollah, and there is evidence that the Panama Canal and Western hotel chains have been reconnoitred by Al Qa'eda affiliates in preparation for a possible attack.[14]

- **Western Europe.** This theatre (except the Iberian Peninsula, which seems to be linked more closely to the North African theatre) appears to function primarily as a theatre for political organization, subversion, and fundraising. The 9/11 hijackers passed through western Europe before the attack and are thought to have trained and prepared there. The United Kingdom has long been a significant area of Al Qa'eda activity, including political subversion, recruitment, organization, and web-based propaganda activity. Few terrorist or insurgent attacks directly linked to Al Qa'eda have occurred in western Europe, although terrorist cells and militant underground groups exist.* There is also a growing pattern of sectarian violence by radical Islamists against liberals within Western European society, most notably in the Netherlands and Belgium.

---

* AUTHOR'S NOTE (2009): Tragically, of course, since this monograph was written, we have seen numerous actual or attempted terrorist attacks in western Europe, including the London subway attacks of 7 July 2005, the failed London attack of 22 July 2005, and the August 2006 airline plot, along with plots in France, Belgium, and the Netherlands. Western Europe appears to be very much alive and well as a terrorist operational theatre as of 2009.

- **Australasia.** Although Australians and New Zealanders suffered heavily in the October 2002 Bali bombing, Australasia has seen no direct terrorist attacks. However, at least one Al Qa'eda–linked JI cell has been uncovered in Australia; several arrests of alleged radical and terrorist cells within Australia's immigrant populations have occurred; Australians fought with the Taliban and (in the 1980s) with Afghan mujahideen against the Soviets; and JI has used Australia for training, fundraising, and political subversion. There is also evidence that JI has used remote locations in Australia to test chemical and possibly biological warfare agents. In 2000, New Zealand police arrested several refugees of Middle Eastern origin, after discovering evidence that they were conducting reconnaissance of the Lucas Heights nuclear reactor in Sydney with the intent to create a nuclear incident during the 2000 Olympic Games.
- **Iberian Peninsula and Maghreb.** The Iberian Peninsula and the Maghreb (Muslim Northwest Africa) appear to function as a single theatre, with North Africans implicated in the May 2004 Madrid bombing, a subsequent Islamist attempted bombing and gun battle with police, and an assassination attempt on judges of the Spanish supreme court. Besides the Madrid attacks, this theatre has been fairly active, with major terrorist bombings in Casablanca, Morocco; ongoing Islamist insurgencies in Algeria, Mauritania, Mali, Niger, and Morocco; and terrorist attacks in Tunisia. Al Qa'eda has a subordinate "regional franchise" in this theatre, and the theatre is used for training and political subversion as well as active terrorism and insurgency. There is also ongoing sectarian violence between Muslims and Christians in Nigeria.
- **Greater Middle East.** This theatre—including Turkey, the Levant, Israel, and Palestine, Egypt, the Arabian Peninsula, and Iran—is by far the most active. Ongoing Islamist insurgencies exist in Iraq, Jordan, Egypt, Saudi Arabia, Yemen, Turkey, Lebanon, and Israel and Palestine. Terrorist activity—including bombings, suicide attacks, kidnappings, beheadings, and raids on expatriate housing—is frequent throughout this theatre. Al Qa'eda has designated regional affiliates in Iraq, Saudi Arabia, Egypt, and Kurdistan and probably also has a presence in Iran, Yemen, Jordan, and Israel and Palestine. The 9/11 hijackers passed through Iran and may have received assistance from elements within that country. However, importantly,

much of the insurgent and terrorist action in this theatre is not sponsored, directed, or controlled by Al Qa'eda. Moreover, there is an entire separate (though interlinked) pattern of Shia terrorism and insurgency across this region, and some Shia groups—especially Lebanese Hezbollah and Hamas—have global ambition and reach.[15] Indeed, there is "increasing evidence that, in spite of their religious differences, Hizballah and Al Qa'eda could be sharing operational information and cooperating in fundraising and recruitment efforts."[16]

- **East Africa.** Kenya and Tanzania suffered simultaneous terrorist bombings on U.S. embassies in August 1998. These attacks were coordinated by Al Qa'eda from a base in Sudan, which in addition to an Al Qa'eda presence has an ongoing Islamist insurgency against Christian and animist Sudanese. Kenya suffered a subsequent attack on the Kikambala Palace Hotel in Mombasa in 2002 and probably has an ongoing Al Qa'eda presence. Al Qa'eda has also claimed a presence in Somalia, Eritrea, and Ethiopia. Muslim (although not Islamist) militias in Somalia and its separatist province of Puntland provide a "failed state" environment favorable to the development of Islamist terrorist and extremist cells.* The East African and Middle Eastern theatres overlap substantially, with strong connections between Yemen, Sudan, and the Horn of Africa. Nevertheless, there is a distinct regional dynamic in East Africa that is separate to the Middle Eastern dynamic, and this area is a jihad theatre in its own right.

- **The Caucasus and European Russia.** The separatist insurgency affecting Chechnya, Georgia, Azerbaijan, and other parts of the North Caucasus was initially nationalist rather than Islamist in character but has been infiltrated and co-opted by elements allied to Al Qa'eda. After the 1994–96 Chechen War, Chechnya briefly enjoyed autonomous self-government, but it became a haven for Islamist movements and a launching pad for terrorist attacks within

---

* AUTHOR'S NOTE (2009): Since 2004, the situation in the Horn of Africa has developed significantly, with the emergence in Somalia of the Union of Islamic Courts (UIC), which gained control of Mogadishu in 2005 and expelled the internationally recognized Transitional Federal Government to Baidoa. In July 2006, the U.S.-backed Ethiopian invasion of Somalia overthrew the UIC, but since that time al-Shabab, "The Youth" (Harakat al-Shabab al-Mujahideen), has emerged from a group of members of the UIC who went underground and formed an insurgency after the UIC was toppled. Somali piracy has also become a focus of international attention, with the deployment of an international naval task force in the wake of numerous attacks by pirates on international shipping in the Gulf of Aden. In Kenya, Tanzania, and some other parts of the East African coast, Al Qa'eda operational cells or other extremist presence has also been noted.

European Russia. This led to the second Chechen War, commencing in 1999 and still ongoing, which has seen further Islamist infiltration of Chechnya, Georgia, and Azerbaijan. Incidentally, the use of Chechnya as a terrorist haven during its period of self-rule compromised—perhaps fatally—the Chechen separatist cause, which is now seen largely as a cover for Islamist terrorist activity.* Numerous terrorist attacks have occurred across European Russia, carried out by groups linked to the Chechen insurgency. These have included a spate of suicide bombings, aircraft bombings, and hijackings; the 2002 Dubrovka theatre siege; and the atrocious 2004 massacre of hundreds of school children in Beslan, North Ossetia.

- **South and Central Asia.** Bin Laden's declaration of war of 23 February 1998 was cosigned by leaders from Afghanistan, Pakistan, and Bangladesh, and South Asia has long been a key jihad theatre. Afghanistan was the principal Al Qa'eda sanctuary until October 2001. A symbiosis developed between the Taliban government and numerous Islamist groups that shared facilities, and allied themselves, with Al Qa'eda. Prominent among these was Lashkar e Tayyiba, which since the fall of the Taliban has become Al Qa'eda's principal South Asian ally. The Provincially Administered Tribal Areas (PATA) and Federally Administered Tribal Areas (FATA) on the Afghan-Pakistan border have become a haven for Al Qa'eda, who are cooperating with Taliban remnants fighting as guerrillas in the area. Bin Laden and Zawahiri are believed to be in Pakistan's Northwest Frontier Province, hiding in an area administered by a federation of six Islamist parties that rejects Pakistani sovereignty, supports the Taliban remnants, and indirectly protects Al Qa'eda. Pakistan itself has experienced Islamist subversion, agitation, and terrorist activity, as has neighboring India. The ongoing separatist insurgency in Jammu and Kashmir has been infiltrated by Islamist elements, and Kashmir has become a major training and administrative area for Al Qa'eda affiliates. The neighboring republics of former Soviet Central Asia (Kazakhstan, Kyrgyzstan,

---

* AUTHOR'S NOTE (2009): As of 2009, the Chechen War is in remission in Chechnya itself, though Chechens and Daghestanis continue to fight, both in the Caucasus and in Afghanistan and Pakistan. Russian operations have severely disabled the insurgency, and Russia officially ended its counterinsurgency operation on 16 April 16 2009. Violence is still sporadic but at a much lower level than at the original time of writing. The appointment as president of the Chechen Republic of Russian-backed local strongman Ramzan Kadyrov, son of the assassinated former president Akhmat Kadyrov and a former insurgent and militia leader, has contributed to the suppression of violence but has also prompted claims of severe human rights abuses and political repression.

Uzbekistan, Turkmenistan, and Tajikistan) and the Xinjiang Uighur region of China have also seen Islamist subversion, terrorist activity, and low-level insurgency.*

- **Southeast Asia.** There are Islamist insurgencies in Indonesia, the Philippines, and southern Thailand, with substantial terrorist activity in these countries and in Singapore, Malaysia, and Cambodia. There is also a broader pattern of Islamic militancy, Muslim separatist insurgent movements, and sectarian conflict. This includes major separatist movements such as the Free Aceh Movement. Indonesia has a substantial underground Islamist movement, Darul Islam, which dates back to the World War II and is still active in several regions of Indonesia. The principal terrorist grouping in this regional theatre is JI, which operates across the entire region, maintains links to Al Qa'eda and other global groups, cooperates with and co-opts local movements and grievances, and has links into other theatres including South Asia and the Middle East. As discussed above, JI has articulated a pan-Islamic agenda that aligns closely with that of Al Qa'eda. However, the two groups are better understood as allies, rather than seeing JI as an Al Qa'eda subordinate or franchise. The Abu Sayyaf Group is a Philippines-based ally of JI, and there are two other major Islamic separatist groups operating in the Mindanao region of the Philippines. Several other armed Islamic sectarian groups have engaged in armed conflict, insurgency and subversion in this region.††

The first three theatres (the Americas, western Europe, and Australasia) do not have ongoing active insurgencies. Indeed, Australasia and western Europe appear to be predominantly theatres of subversion, fundraising and organizational development (representing Al Qa'eda's strategic hinterland) whereas North America appears to be a primary target for terrorist activity.

---

* AUTHOR'S NOTE (2009): This description of the situation in South Asia is of course markedly out of date. I have described the situation as of 2008 in detail in *The Accidental Guerrilla*, chap. 2; however, the situation is rapidly developing and continues to change unpredictably in the wake of the August 2009 Afghanistan presidential election and the troop surge announced by President Obama and key NATO allies in December 2009.

†† AUTHOR'S NOTE (2009): The insurgency situation in Southeast Asia has also developed significantly, with JI in Indonesia collapsing in terms of popular support and operational capability, although it retains the ability to strike at Western targets within Indonesia. The Abu Sayyaf Group in the Philippines has also been degraded through successful cooperation between local law enforcement, local military forces, national governments, and U.S. military, law enforcement, and intelligence agencies. The insurgency in southern Thailand has worsened, in part because of political instability at the national level, and was described in detail in *The Accidental Guerrilla*, chap. 4.

The remaining six theatres, however, all have active Islamist insurgencies as well as Al Qa'eda presence and terrorist activity. Indeed, globally, there is a greater than 85 percent correlation between the presence of Islamist insurgency in a given theatre and terrorist activity or Al Qa'eda presence in the same area. Thus, with the exception of the 9/11 attacks themselves, all Al Qa'eda–linked terrorist attacks have occurred in theatres with ongoing Islamist insurgencies. Not all Islamist insurgency is linked to Al Qa'eda—but most Al Qa'eda activity occurs in areas of Islamist insurgency.

Besides this correlation with insurgency, there is a clear correlation between the geographical area of the historical caliphate, the broader pan-Islamic caliphate posited by Al Qa'eda, and Islamist insurgency (see fig. 6.1).

As the map indicates, every single Islamist insurgency in the world sits within the claimed pan-Islamic caliphate, while the most active theatres correspond to the historical caliphate. Taken at face value, this map seems to show that Al Qa'eda is indeed executing the strategy outlined by Zawahiri: re-establishing an Islamic caliphate and then using this as a springboard to extend Islamic control over the remainder of the globe. In fact, the reality turns out to be much more complex. Nonetheless, the map accurately portrays the existence of a global spread of Islamist movements, at least some of which are linked to a broader, globally focused movement that seeks to overturn the world order through subversion, terrorism, and insurgency.

Links between Theatres

The mere existence of a global spread of similar movements does not in itself constitute evidence for a global insurgency. To demonstrate the existence of a global jihad, it is necessary to show that these dispersed Islamist terrorist and insurgent groups are linked in some way. Indeed, the links are critical because (as discussed in the next section) the global nature of the jihad actually resides in the links, not the individual groups themselves. There are eight basic types of links that join these theatres, and groups within them, into an aggregated pattern of global jihad:

- **Ideological Links.** Insurgent and terrorist groups aligned with Al Qa'eda have common ideological roots. They are broadly Salafi in orientation, and many follow variants of Saudi Wahhabism. Even groups such as the Taliban, which is Deobandi in origin, adopt

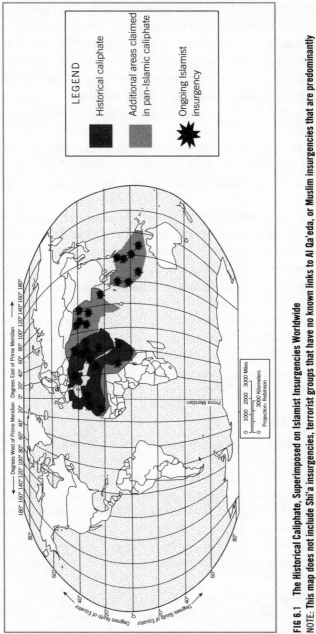

FIG 6.1   The Historical Caliphate, Superimposed on Islamist Insurgencies Worldwide

NOTE: This map does not include Shi'a insurgencies, terrorist groups that have no known links to Al Qa'eda, or Muslim insurgencies that are predominantly separatist or nationalist in character.

a purist, authoritarian outlook. Ideologues such as Sayyid Qutb, Maulana Mawdudi, Abdullah Azzam, and the mediaeval theologian Ibn Taymiyya are influential in their thinking. These "Jihadists" are so called because they tend to elevate the "lesser jihad" (armed struggle against unbelievers) into a virtual sixth pillar of Islam.[17] Besides Islamic influences, these groups are influenced by communist revolutionary technique (adopting Soviet organizational methods and consciously acting as a "vanguard party" in the Leninist mode) and military theory. Many Islamist insurgents, particularly in Afghanistan, apply Che Guevara's concept of "focoist insurgency," while Carlos Marighela's *Mini-manual of the Urban Guerrilla* has also been very influential. Al Qa'eda applies "leaderless resistance," first advanced by the American right-wing theorist Louis Beam, to an unprecedented degree. Finally, concepts such as "propaganda of the deed," which originated with the nineteenth-century European anarchists, are influential. The most important element of ideological commonality is that the Islamist groups described (and shown on the map in fig. 6.1) identify themselves with Al Qa'eda, subscribe to its strategic program, and seek a global pan-Islamic caliphate as a prelude to remaking the Western-dominated world order.[18]

- **Linguistic and cultural links.** Because of their shared Islamic faith, jihad groups share Arabic as a common language.[19] This allows groups from remote parts of the world to communicate effectively, train together, and share intelligence or planning resources. It also contributes to a shared consciousness—religious, political, and cultural. These groups also share an Islamic civilizational overlay, providing a common language, social outlook, and political theory for groups from diverse national cultures. Moreover, as these groups originate from what Michael Vlahos has called distinct "military subcultures" within Islam, they share a common sense of alienation from mainstream Islam's traditions of quietism or political moderation.[20]

- **Personal history.** The personal histories of individuals across the jihad movements are closely linked. Many older mujahideen fought together against the Soviets in Afghanistan during the 1980s or trained together later in Afghanistan. Many key ideologues and leaders in the global jihad studied under Wahhabi clerics in Saudi Arabia and still maintain relationships with these mentors—for example, JI leader Abu Bakar Bashir maintains a close relationship with his former teacher and seeks guidance before most major decisions. The senior leadership of Al Qa'eda all share this experience, and many have links dating back to the 1970s and opposition to the Egyptian and Saudi governments. Later generations of mujahideen fought together in Kosovo, Bosnia-Herzegovina, or Chechnya. Even within one country, many jihadists share a common military or personal history. For example, many JI members come from established families in the Indonesian Darul Islam movement (described above), went to school together, fought together in sectarian conflicts in Maluku or Sulawesi, and trained together in boarding schools or camps like Camp Abubakar in the Philippines. Thus friendships, webs of acquaintance, and networks of mutual obligation stretch worldwide between and among groups. Similarly, within jihad theatres, groups cooperate and develop bonds of shared experience and mutual obligation.

- **Family relationships.** Unsurprisingly, because of this shared history, many members of the global jihad movement are related to each other by birth or marriage. Often alliances between groups are cemented by marriage, as in the marriage of Usama bin Laden to the daughter of Taliban leader Mullah Omar. Similarly, some Indonesian jihadist leaders have wives from the Arabian Peninsula, particularly the Hadhramaut area on the Saudi-Yemen-Oman border. Again, intermarriage is common among Southeast Asian, South Asian, and Chechen jihad groups, cementing bonds of friendship and obligation between theatres. Sons of prominent leaders in the jihad movement often follow their fathers, and widows often avenge their husbands by becoming suicide bombers. This pattern has become so common in Chechnya and European Russia that such *mujahidat* (female jihad fighters), known as "Black Widows," have been implicated in numerous attacks and have gained independent status as a distinct subcategory of jihadist.[21]
- **Financial links.** Groups in different theatres frequently fund each other's activities. For example, Al Qa'eda is suspected to have provided funding to JI for the 2002 Bali bombing and is known to have funded terrorist groups in the Philippines. Similarly, some Islamic nongovernment organizations, including traditional Islamic *hawala* banking networks, charitable organizations, and religious networks, are used (wittingly and unwittingly) as conduits for funding between and within jihad theatres globally.[22] Many of these

nongovernment organizations are based in the Arabian Peninsula, including significant (and legitimate) charities such as al-Haramein and the Islamic Relief Organization. Indeed, oil wealth in the Middle East has provided the bulk of terrorist and insurgent funding over time, making the Arabian Peninsula a central hub in the web of financial links joining dispersed movements. The systems of traditional trade, as well as flows of remittance money from migrant workers worldwide, also represent conduits for insurgent and terrorist funding.[23] In addition, there is an intricate network of private patronage, financial obligation, and mutual commitment that links dispersed groups and individuals in geographically dispersed regions.

- **Operational and planning links.** As this analysis shows, Al Qa'eda is not a central headquarters or high command for the global jihad. Bin Laden does not issue directives to subordinate groups, tasking them to conduct insurgent or terrorist action. Rather, planning and operational tasking appears to happen through a system of sponsorship and financing, with Al Qa'eda providing funding, operational advice, targeting data, and specialist expertise to allied regional and local groups. Similarly, local groups appear to gather intelligence and targeting data and share it across theatres in the jihad. For example, the planned JI attacks foiled in Singapore in December 2001 were averted through the discovery of targeting data in an Al Qa'eda safe house in Afghanistan. A recent terrorist alert in the United States was sparked by the discovery of targeting data on American schools and public buildings on a captured terrorist's computer in Pakistan. The same arrest also prompted the capture of eight terrorists in Britain. So although there is no centralized command-and-control hierarchy, it appears that local groups plan and conduct their own operations but cooperate within and between regions. Simultaneously, global players like Al Qa'eda provide encouragement, tactical support, financing, and intelligence for specific high-value operations.[24]

- **Propaganda.** Al Qa'eda exploits events in jihad theatres across the world for propaganda purposes in its communiqués and media materials. Groups across the jihad contribute to a common flow of propaganda materials, supporting each other's local causes and sharing grievances. For example, the web site Jihad Unspun is managed by a Canadian convert to Islam and provides reportage, analysis, comment, and "spin" on issues across all theatres of the jihad.[25] Al Qa'eda issues a fortnightly propaganda bulletin on its official web site, *Sawt al-Jihad*, and publishes a jihadist women's magazine, *al-Khansa*. Similarly, a flow of cassette tapes, videos, and CDs—many depicting so-called martyrdom operations, as well as terrorist bombings, or the execution of infidel prisoners—moves throughout jihad groups worldwide. For example, the Russian Hell series of videos, many depicting the torture and execution of Russian troops captured in Chechnya, is popular viewing across South Asia, the Middle East, and Indonesia, and is current among certain militant extremist subcultures within the Australian Muslim community.[26] Imagery purporting to portray the oppression of Muslims in Israel and Palestine, Chechnya, Iraq, and the Balkans is also used to stir up resentment and motivate mujahideen in other theatres. The Zarqawi network inside Iraq, subsequently known as Al Qa'eda in Iraq, is also believed to maintain a media section that is responsible for the production of propaganda materials, including videos of the beheading of Western hostages. The Internet has become a potent tool that groups use for sharing propaganda and ideological material across international boundaries, contributing to a shared consciousness among dispersed groups within the jihad.*

- **Doctrine, techniques, and procedures.** Terrorist and insurgent groups worldwide can access a body of doctrine, techniques, and procedures that exists in hard copy and on the Internet, primarily in Arabic but also in other languages. It includes political guidance (like the "General Guide to the Struggle of Jema'ah Islamiyah," described earlier), military manuals (like the encyclopedic *Military Studies in the Jihad against the Tyrants*, discovered by police in Manchester, England, in 2002), and CD-ROM and videotaped materials.[27] In addition, Al Qa'eda publishes a fortnightly online military training manual, *Al-Battar*.[28] There is thus a common

---

* AUTHOR'S NOTE (2009): Al Qa'eda and its associated movements have maintained a focus on propaganda since their formation, with the Al Qa'eda senior leadership group often acting more like a propaganda hub than like a command center, identifying themes in Western debate and playing these back at the West. Usama bin Laden has not issued a video communiqué for several years, and the West's ongoing pressure against Al Qa'eda leaders in the Pakistan-Afghanistan border area has undoubtedly suppressed, to some extent, their activities. But the propaganda model has also shifted over time. A single narrative of oppression, redemption, and resistance against an infidel West bent on the destruction of Islam has taken hold in some parts of the world's Muslim community, fueled in part by the wars in Iraq and Afghanistan and by the ongoing violence in Israel and the Palestinian territories. This has empowered local activists who generate their own propaganda in general alignment with broad Al Qa'eda themes but do not take propaganda guidance from a central Al Qa'eda leadership. In this sense, what was once a jihadist "start-up" enterprise has now become self-sustaining and semi-independent.

tactical approach across Islamist groups worldwide, and tactics that first appear in one theatre permeate across the global movement, via the Internet and doctrinal publications.*

Local, Regional, and Global Players

Within each country in a jihad theatre there are local actors, issues, and grievances. Many of these have little to do with the objectives of the global jihad, and they often predate the jihad by decades or centuries. For example, Russians have been fighting Muslim guerrillas in the Caucasus since the 1850s, while there has been a Moro separatist issue in the Philippines for centuries. Local insurgent and terrorist groups—in some cases, little distinguishable from bandits—continue to operate in these areas, often with no connection to the global jihad. These local elements will probably remain intact, at some level, even if the global jihad movement is completely destroyed.

But what is new about today's environment is that, because of the links described above, a new class of regional, theatre-level actors has emerged. These groups *do* have links to the global jihad, often act as regional allies or affiliates of Al Qa'eda, and prey on local groups and issues to further the jihad. They also rely on supporting inputs from global players and might wither if their global sponsors were significantly disrupted. For example, in Indonesia the regional Al Qa'eda affiliate, JI, has fueled, exacerbated, and fostered sectarian conflicts in the Poso region of central Sulawesi in order to generate recruits, anti-Western propaganda, funding, and grievances that can be exploited within the Southeast Asia theatre. In turn, JI has received funding, guidance, expertise, and propaganda support from Al Qa'eda. In general, Al Qa'eda seems not to have direct dealings with local insurgent groups but to deal primarily with its regional affiliates in each theatre. This makes the operational (regional or theatre) level of the jihad a critical link.

Sitting above the theatre-level actors are global players like Al Qa'eda. But Al Qa'eda is simply the best known of several worldwide actors.

---

* AUTHOR'S NOTE (2009): This dispersion of tactics has only increased since this chapter was written, with the proliferation of tactics developed in Iraq (such as suicide bombings and the use of roadside improvised explosive devices) into Afghanistan, Pakistan, Somalia and elsewhere. We have also seen the physical movement of fighters between theatres—former members of AlQa'eda in Iraq into Yemen, Chechens and Uzbeks into Pakistan and Afghanistan, Indonesians and Malaysians into the Philippines, Somalis into Kenya, and so on. These fighters bring with them knowledge of tactics, techniques and procedures and contribute to a general tactical style or "way of war" as practiced by these groups.

Al Qa'eda has competitors, allies, and clones at the global level who would be able to step into the breach should Al Qa'eda be destroyed tomorrow. For example, the Shia group Hezbollah has global reach, has worked closely with Sunni movements worldwide, sponsors approximately 80 percent of Palestinian terrorism (including that performed by Sunni groups such as Hamas), and has strong links to Iran. Hezbollah is one of several groups that could replace Al Qa'eda in its niche of "top predator" as the jihad evolves.[29] Similarly, financial, religious, educational, and cultural networks (based largely in Arabia) function at the global level in unifying the effect of disparate actors across the jihad, and often have greater penetration and influence than Al Qa'eda itself.

Thus, this analysis indicates that there *is* a global movement, and almost all Islamist insurgency and terrorism worldwide is linked to it. However, it comprises a group of aligned independent movements, not a single, unified organization. Global players link and exploit local players through regional affiliates—they rarely interact directly with local players but sponsor and support them through intermediaries. Each theatre has operational players who are able to tap into the global jihad, and these tend to be regional Al Qa'eda affiliates. Saudi Arabia is a central node, with greater "reach" than Al Qa'eda itself, although Saudi influence is a systemic effect, not necessarily based on conscious activity.* As Al Qa'eda is disrupted, its clones and competitors will probably tend to move into its niche and assume some of its role.

Understanding the Jihad Phenomenon

So far, this chapter has shown that a globalized network of Islamist groups exists, that this network tends to operate through distinct regional theatres, and that there are multidimensional links that connect the operations of dispersed groups across theatres. In other words, the multifarious groups and activities of Islamists—including terrorists, subversives, political activists, and insurgents—in fact form a single global system. But we have also seen that this jihad is not a single unified movement or a hierarchical organization. Al Qa'eda is not the headquarters for a unified worldwide organization. Indeed, many of the links that unite the

---

* AUTHOR'S NOTE (2009): Despite the undoubtedly central role of Saudi Arabia in the early thinking of many *takfiri* terrorist groups, in practical terms, the epicenter of violent extremism worldwide increasingly resides in Pakistan. Many major terrorist attacks since 9/11, especially in Europe, India, and Central Asia, have included links to groups sponsored by or operating in Pakistan. There is debate over whether the center of gravity of the global jihadist endeavor has truly shifted to Pakistan, but there is little doubt that South Asia is one of the most important, and dangerous, theatres of terrorist activity.

dispersed movements are personal, private, historical, or ideological—
not hierarchical or organizational.

In seeking to understand the jihad, Western analysts have often struggled to characterize it. Is it a formal organization? Is it a mass movement?
Is it a loose confederation of allies? Is it—as Peter Bergen argues—a franchised business model with centralized corporate support and autonomous regional divisions?[30] Is it—as others have argued—merely a myth,
a creation of Western counterintelligence agencies and authoritarian governments?[31] The picture of the jihad this chapter has drawn suggests that
far from being a mythical bogeyman, the network is all too real, global
in reach, and unprecedented in scale. But Western models—mass movement, hierarchical organization, business structure—are unable to fully
describe it. Rather, the analysis would suggest, traditional Islamic or Middle Eastern social models may be more applicable.

Karl Jackson (during fieldwork in 1968) and I (during fieldwork in
1995–97) both independently demonstrated that a model of traditional
patron-client authority relationships is applicable to Islamic insurgent
movements.[32] Under this model, the global jihad could be seen as a
variant on a traditional Middle Eastern patronage network. In this con-
struct, the jihad comprises an intricate, ramified web of dependency
and—critically—it is the patterns of patronage and dependency that are
its central defining features rather than the organizational groupings—
the insurgent cells or their activities.[33] Many analysts have tended to
see the marriage relationships, money flows, alumni relationships, and
sponsorship links in the jihad as weakly subordinate to a military core
of terrorist activity. Rather, this analysis would argue, the military activity is actually subordinate, being merely one of the shared activities that
the network engages in, while the core is the patronage network.

As noted, analysts tend to apply Western models to the jihad—mass
movement, hierarchical organization, franchised business structure. In
fact, the jihad appears to be more like a tribal group, an organized crime
syndicate, or an extended family than like a military organization.* Like a

---

* AUTHOR'S NOTE (2009): There are strong analogies between police work, counterinsurgency, and counterterrorism.
Insurgents tend to operate like gang structures, and police gang suppression approaches that focus on community security, network displacement and a layered method of overt police presence, criminal informants, and undercover operations
is analogous to counterinsurgency, especially in urban environments. Likewise, some terrorist networks share structural and
operational similarities with organized crime networks, and police methods against organized crime syndicates—financial and
logistical controls, counternetwork operations, detainee exploitation, penetration by informants, and targeted disruption—are
similar to the methods used against terrorists.

mafia clan, the Islamist network resides in a web of traditional authority structures, family allegiances, and tribal honor, not the essentially secondary activity of criminal behavior. Thus, the Islamist network resides in the pattern of relationships itself—jihad is simply one activity that the network *does*; it is not the network itself.

PART 2: GLOBAL ISLAMIST INSURGENCY

If you were afraid to carry out the Jihad in the Arabian Peninsula, what is your excuse for not going to Iraq, Afghanistan, and Chechnya?
—Sheikh Saud al Otaibi, emir of Al Qa'eda in the Arabian Peninsula (2004)

Part 1 has demonstrated the existence of a globalized Islamist jihad network, forming an intricate web of dependencies and patronage, and oriented (as a loose confederation of allies) toward the overthrow of the existing world order and its replacement with a pan-Islamic caliphate. As this part will show, this Islamist jihad is best understood as a global insurgency.[34]

"Insurgency" can be defined as "a popular movement that seeks to overthrow the status quo through subversion, political activity, insurrection, armed conflict, and terrorism."[35] By definition, insurgent movements are grass roots uprisings that seek to overthrow established governments or societal structures. All are popular uprisings that employ the weapons of the weak (subversion, guerrilla tactics, terrorism) against the established power of states and conventional military forces. Many, including the Islamist jihad, draw their foot soldiers from deprived socioeconomic groups and their leadership from alienated, radicalized elites.

Conversely, "terrorism" can be defined as "politically motivated violence against civilians, conducted with the intention to coerce through fear," and is in the tactical repertoire of virtually every insurgency (and, of course, some governments).[36] Western analysts tend to distinguish insurgency from terrorism as research disciplines, but for practitioners, this distinction is (literally) academic. Terrorism is a component in almost all insurgencies, and insurgent objectives (i.e., a desire to change the status quo through subversion and violence) lie behind almost all nonstate terrorism.[37]

By this definition, the global jihad is clearly an insurgency—a popular movement that seeks to change the status quo through violence and subversion, whereas terrorism is one of its key tactics (hence a component part, or subset, of insurgency). But whereas traditional insurgencies sought to overthrow governments or social structures in one state or region, this insurgency seeks to transform the entire Islamic world and remake its relationship with the rest of the globe. It looks back to a golden age, seeking to reestablish a caliphate throughout the Muslim world and, ultimately, expand the realm of Islam (Dar al Islam) to all human society. The stated Islamist strategy is to provoke a clash between the West and Islam, generate a world Islamic front, and so mobilize Muslims—whom the Islamists see as oppressed victims—to overthrow the global status quo.[38] The scale of the Islamist agenda is new, but their grievances and methods would be familiar to any insurgent in history.

In addition, bin Laden's own fatwa of August 1996 explicitly calls for insurgency in the cause of jihad:

> it must be obvious to you that, due to the imbalance of power between our armed forces and the enemy forces, a suitable means of fighting must be adopted, that is using fast moving light forces that work under complete secrecy. In other words, to initiate guerrilla warfare, where the sons of the nation, and not the military forces, take part in it.[39]

The jihad, therefore, can be described as a form of globalized insurgency.

Al Qa'eda and similar groups feed on local grievances, integrate them into broader ideologies, and link disparate conflicts through globalized communications, finances, and technology. In this, Al Qa'eda resembles the Communist Third International (Comintern) of the twentieth century—a holding company and clearinghouse for world revolution. But there is a key difference. The Comintern was a state-sponsored support organization for local revolutions and insurgencies, but the global jihad is itself an insurgent movement. As described, the tools of globalization—the Internet, globalized communications, international finance, freedom of movement—allow tactics, intelligence, personnel, and finances to be shared between groups across the jihad. Likewise, the globalized insurgency exploits events in one theatre for propaganda in others.[40] Moreover, the Comintern was sponsored by the Soviet Union, whereas the Islamist jihad (as discussed later) is itself a virtual state.

Thus the distinguishing feature of the Islamists is not their use of terrorism, a tactic they share with dozens of movements worldwide. Rather, it is that they represent a global insurgency against the world order, that—like all other insurgent movements—uses terrorism, besides other tactics ranging from subversion and propaganda to open warfare.

Competing Paradigms: Terrorism and Insurgency

The study of terrorism as an independent academic discipline emerged in the 1970s in response to the growing phenomenon of international terrorism.[41] Before the 1970s, terrorism was seen primarily as a component within localized insurgencies. The term was used primarily for propaganda purposes—to label an insurgent as illegitimate or portray an insurgent's methods as "beyond the pale."[42] British use of the term "terrorists" to describe insurgents in Northern Ireland, Cyprus, and Malaya served to underline this point. Indeed, in Malaya the principal counter*insurgency* manual was entitled *The Conduct of Anti-terrorist* [not "Counterinsurgency"] *Operations in Malaya*, indicating that the two activities were synonymous.[43] In this period, insurgency and terrorism were seen as practically the same phenomenon, the term "terrorism" was primarily of political and propaganda value.

But the international terrorism that emerged in the 1970s included groups such as the Baader-Meinhof Group (the Red Army Faction), the Italian Red Brigades, the Japanese Red Army, and other groups with little apparent link to any mass movement or insurgency. Rather, they were "disembodied" terrorist groups comprising small cells of alienated individuals within Western society, rather than insurgent movements with definite achievable aims. Although there were still substantial groups of insurgency-based terrorists—such as the PLO, rightly regarded by specialists as one of the most important and dangerous groups[44]—in Western popular culture the conception of terrorism became that of disembodied cells of radicalized, nihilistic individuals. These individuals, almost by virtue of their very alienation from their parent societies, could not and did not tap into a mass base that drew its legitimacy from popular grievances, as traditional insurgents (and today's transnational jihadist terrorists) do. Thus, a new paradigm emerged that has since been highly influential in public discourse.

In this popular conception, shared by many Western legislators and policy-makers, although not by terrorism specialists, terrorists are seen as unrepresentative, aberrant individuals, misfits within society. Partly because they are seen as unrepresentative and partly to discourage emulation, "we do not negotiate with terrorists." Terrorists are criminals, whose methods and objectives are equally unacceptable. They use violence partly to shock and influence populations and governments, and for propaganda and symbolic effect, but also because they are psychologically or morally flawed or evil. In this paradigm, terrorism is primarily a law enforcement problem, and we therefore adopt a case-based approach in which the key objective is to apprehend the perpetrators of terrorist attacks.*

This paradigm has been highly influential in our approach to the "War on Terrorism"—largely because of the word "terrorism" in this name. Thus we have tended to elevate one component of the global insurgency—the use of terrorism as a tactic—until it has become identified as the sole issue, ignoring other aspects of the conflict. Accordingly, we have sought to apprehend Usama bin Laden, and some commentators regard the failure to catch him as evidence of failure in prosecuting the "War on Terror." Likewise, Australia's response to the Bali bombing of 2002 has been primarily focused on "bringing the terrorists to justice"—hence the central role of police agencies in a case-based, legal-evidence-based approach.†

The insurgency paradigm is quite different. Under this approach, insurgents are regarded as representative of deeper issues or grievances within society. Governments seek to defeat insurgents primarily through marginalizing them from their support base, protecting the people from guerrilla intimidation, and "winning the hearts and minds" of the broader population, a process that by necessity often involves compromise and negotiation. We regard insurgents' methods as unacceptable, but their grievances are often seen as legitimate, provided they are pursued peacefully. This is why mainstream society often accepts insurgents

* AUTHOR'S NOTE (2009): This description of terrorism as a popular paradigm was already something of a caricature when it was first written but is even more so now, as a new generation of extremely sophisticated terrorism analysts have emerged over the period since 9/11, with fresh and innovative approaches to understanding terrorist behavior. Still, in its original intent, this passage (like the description of insurgency and counterinsurgency below it) is designed to highlight the differences in popular perception between the methods of counterterrorism (counternetwork operations, manhunting, and the pursuit of individuals and cells as high-value targets through intelligence, law enforcement, and special operations) and counterinsurgency (population protection, political marginalization of the insurgent, addressing of basic grievances, reduction of insurgent recruiting and propaganda opportunities, denial of resources, and so on). In practice, any counterinsurgency campaign today involves highly kinetic, intelligence-led counternetwork operations, while any sensible counterterrorism campaign also seeks to isolate terrorists from support networks and deny them freedom of movement and action. Thus counterterrorism and counterinsurgency techniques merge and blur at the tactical level, even though the two approaches are still seen as competing paradigms by the public, news organizations, and many policy-makers.

† AUTHOR'S NOTE (2009): This is not to suggest that such approaches are invalid or ineffective. Indeed, in Australia's case, police and intelligence assistance to Indonesia proved very important in reducing the JI threat to a far lower level over the period 2002–2007. However, such tactical counterterrorism efforts do not substitute for a broader global strategic approach to reducing the appeal and minimizing the threat of globalized insurgency.

who renounce violence but seek the same objectives through political means—individuals like Nelson Mandela, Xanana Gusmao, and Gerry Adams. Similarly, under this paradigm, we see insurgents as using violence within a carefully integrated politicomilitary strategy, rather than as psychopaths. In this paradigm, insurgency is a whole-of-government problem rather than a military or law enforcement issue. On this basis, we adopt a strategy-based approach to counterinsurgency in which the key objective is to defeat or marginalize the insurgent's strategy rather than to "apprehend the perpetrators" of specific acts.

Table 6.1 summarizes the principal differences between the terrorism and insurgency paradigms. However, as noted, the terrorism paradigm largely represents a popular stereotype rather than an analysis shared by most specialist analysts, some of whom tend to regard terrorism as a subset or subcategory of insurgency.

Clearly, the insurgency paradigm provides a better mental model for the current conflict than does the terrorism stereotype. Indeed, current

TABLE 6.1 Terrorism and insurgency as competing paradigms

Terrorism	Insurgency
Terrorist is seen as an unrepresentative aberration.	*Insurgent* represents deeper issues in society.
No negotiation with terrorists.	Winning hearts and minds is critical.
Methods and objectives are both unacceptable.	Methods are unacceptable; objectives are not necessarily so.
Terrorists are psychologically and morally flawed, with personal (psychopathic) tendencies toward violence.	*Insurgents* use violence within an integrated politicomilitary strategy—violence is instrumental not central to their approach.
Terrorism is a law enforcement problem.	Insurgency is a whole-of-government problem.
Counterterrorism adopts a case-based approach focused on catching the perpetrators of terrorist actions.	*Counterinsurgency* uses a strategy-based approach focused on defeating insurgents' strategy—catching them is secondary.

actions in the "War on Terrorism" appear disparate if viewed through a pure terrorism paradigm. Some (like international law enforcement cooperation, manhunting and drone strikes, and actions to counter terrorist financing) fit the terrorism paradigm neatly, while others (the Iraq War, counterproliferation initiatives, building influence in Central Asia, containment of North Korea and Iran) appear unrelated to an antiterrorism agenda and are thus viewed with suspicion by some. However, if viewed through the lens of counterinsurgency, these actions make perfect sense. They fit neatly into three streams of classical counterinsurgency: pacification, winning hearts and minds, and the denial of sanctuary and external sponsorship.

For example, whatever one thinks of its effectiveness, the intent behind the Iraq campaign may be seen as an effort to restructure the milieu that created the jihad, by removing underlying antidemocratic tendencies that cause Islamist unrest (a form of pacification, in intent if not effect). It may also have been intended to address the principal grievances raised by Al Qa'eda in its "World Islamic Front Declaration of War against Jews and Crusaders" of 23 February 1998, which mostly related to the sanctions regime against Saddam's Iraq (winning hearts and minds). Action against Iraq also allowed the removal of U.S. troops from Saudi Arabia (another key Al Qa'eda grievance) and sent a key message to state sponsors of terrorism (denial of sanctuary and sponsorship). Moreover, at a strategic level, the campaign in Iraq has allowed Western forces to fight the jihad on ground of our choosing, within the territory of the old caliphate now claimed by Al Qa'eda rather than on Western territory or in south or central Asia. This has given the West the strategic initiative— jihadists are focusing on Iraq, not on attacking the West directly.* One might argue with the competence or wisdom of the Iraq enterprise, or the clarity with which its objectives were communicated to the public,

* AUTHOR'S NOTE (2009): The intent of this passage is not to defend the decision to attack Iraq or the poor performance in the early execution of the counterinsurgency campaign following the initial, highly successful Coalition invasion of Iraq. I am on the record elsewhere (*Small Wars Journal* and *Accidental Guerrilla*) arguing that the invasion was a strategic error. Rather, the aim is to show that a counterinsurgency paradigm makes much more strategic sense in explaining the decision to go to war than a traditional counterterrorism approach—thus, a set of strategic ideas associated with traditional counterinsurgency (sanctuary denial, marginalizing the enemy, denial of sponsorship by external actors, and "winning hearts and minds")—may have lain, perhaps at the level of unexamined assumption, behind the war. If these concepts had been explicitly examined within a counterinsurgency lens, some decision-makers might have concluded, as I do in the next section of this chapter, that traditional counterinsurgency actually transfers poorly to the global level. In the event, Western military forces and western political capital have been invested heavily in the outcome of the war. Although we salvaged a draw during the 2007 "Surge" and handed off a relatively stable environment to the Iraqi government in 2008, the Iraq war is far from over for Iraqis, and ultimately its strategic impact may not be clear for a considerable time.

as many analysts and political opponents of the United States have done. Nevertheless, Iraq undeniably fits better into a counterinsurgency paradigm than a traditional counterterrorist one. The same applies to action against North Korea (denial of sanctuary and sponsorship—in this case, transfer of nuclear and chemical technology to Islamists) and other apparently disparate actions in the campaign.[45]

If the "War on Terrorism" is a global insurgency, then the counterinsurgency paradigm (which, as noted, includes action against terrorism as a subset of insurgency) is a better mental model for this war than is counterterrorism. Indeed, the key to defeating global jihad may not lie in traditional counterterrorism (police work, intelligence, special operations, or security measures) at all. Instead, counterinsurgency theory may provide the most useful insights. As I will explain in part 4, a counterinsurgency approach would generate a subtly, but substantially, different range of actions in the "War on Terrorism."

Counterinsurgency Redux

Although counterinsurgency is more appropriate than counterterrorism in this conflict, traditional counterinsurgency techniques from the 1960s cannot simply be applied to today's problems in a simplistic or mechanistic fashion. This is because counterinsurgency, in its "classical" form, is optimized to defeat insurgency in one country, not to fight a global insurgency. The best practice counterinsurgency techniques that emerged from the "wars of national liberation" of 1945–1990, attacked insurgency through unified military, intelligence, political, socioeconomic, "hearts-and-minds" and security measures. For example, pacification programs in classical counterinsurgency demand the ability to coordinate information operations, development, governance, military and police security operations, and overt and covert counterguerrilla operations across a geographical area—often a province or region. At the national level, control of all counterinsurgent actions (political, military, social, and economic) in the hands of a single "Supremo" is recognized as a key element.[46]

This *can* be achieved in one country: Malaya, Northern Ireland, and other campaigns demonstrated this. But to achieve this level of integration requires excellent governmental stability, unity, and restraint. Moreover, it demands extremely close coordination and integration between and within police, intelligence, military, development, aid, information, and administrative agencies. For example, the successful Malayan campaign rested on an overall Supremo with combined military, political, and administrative powers, supported by an intricate system of federal, state, district, and subdistrict executive interagency committees. Likewise, successful classical counterinsurgency in the Americas, Africa, and Asia has been closely tied to improvements in governance, integrated administrative systems, and joint interagency action.

At the global level, no world government exists with the power to integrate the actions of independent nations to the extremely close degree required by traditional counterinsurgency theory; nor can regional counterinsurgency programs be closely enough aligned to block all insurgent maneuver. This is particularly true when the enemy—as in this case—is not a Maoist-style mass rural movement but a largely urban-based insurgency operating in small cells and teams with an extremely low tactical signature in the urban clutter of globalized societies. In today's international system, a unified global approach—even only in those areas directly affected by Al Qa'eda–sponsored jihad—would be intensely problematic. It would demand cooperation far beyond anything yet achieved between diverse states.

Robert Kagan has argued that the current "crisis of legitimacy" affecting U.S. efforts to exercise global leadership in the "War on Terrorism" is a symptom rather than a cause of a deepening geostrategic division between Europe and America.[47] While this division persists, under the international system as currently constituted, any nation powerful enough to act as a global counterinsurgency Supremo would tend to lack legitimacy. Conversely, any collective or multinational grouping (such as the UN Security Council) that could muster unquestioned legitimacy would tend to lack sufficient power to act effectively against Islamist insurgents or their state sponsors. It would be fatally constrained by the very factors (sovereign equality of states, nonintervention in the internal affairs of states, multilateral consensus) that generated its legitimacy. Thus, the entire concept of counterinsurgency—in its classical form, with a single Supremo coordinating actions—is highly problematic when applied at the global level.

Similarly, classical counterinsurgency seeks to deny enemy sanctuaries, prevent infiltration into the area where the conflict is occurring, and isolate insurgents from support. A global insurgency has limited vulnerability to many of these measures, because of the phenomenon of failed and failing states and ungoverned, undergoverned, or poorly governed areas between states (such as the tribal areas on the Pakistan-Afghan border described above). This allows geographical sanctuary for insurgents, while international flows of information and finances provide "cybersanctuaries" (like the Al Qa'eda Internet presence described above) where insurgents can operate.

So a globalized insurgency demands a rethink of traditional counterinsurgency. What is required is counterinsurgency redux, not the templated application of 1960s techniques. Both counterterrorism and counterinsurgency provide some answers, but an integrated approach is needed that draws on both disciplines, modifies them for current conditions, and develops new methods applicable to globalized insurgency.

The next section applies complexity theory to derive a model of how "counterinsurgency redux" might look.

PART 3: A SYSTEMS MODEL OF INSURGENCY

> *This political force... has an elaborate and far-flung apparatus... an apparatus of amazing flexibility and versatility, managed by people whose experience and skill in underground methods are presumably without parallel in history.*
> —George Kennan, "Long Telegram" (1946)

The previous section argued that global insurgency renders the traditional counterterrorism paradigm largely irrelevant, and that it has strained the classical counterinsurgency paradigm, which is ill suited to countering a globalized insurgency. This section reappraises counterinsurgency through the emerging science of complexity.

Systems Thinking

The modern understanding of war is underpinned by systems thinking. This has been increasingly influential since the 1920s, when the Soviet theorist Mikhail Tukhachevskii proposed the theory of "deep operations" (*glubokaia operatsiia*), which viewed friendly and enemy forces as competing systems and sought to dislocate the enemy at the systemic level.[48] Indeed, familiar concepts like Blitzkrieg, strategic bombing, air-land battle, maneuver warfare, and effects-based operations are all systems approaches to warfare.

Classical counterinsurgency is also based on a systems approach. It seeks to identify key processes in an insurgent system and coordinate countermeasures at the systemic level. The most sophisticated example of classical counterinsurgency, under U.S. secretary of defense Robert S. McNamara during the Vietnam War, used highly developed quantitative statistical analysis. Led by an Office of Systems Analysis, this approach broke down the insurgent system into component processes, analyzed each component, and reassembled the components into a net assessment of progress. This (as will be seen) was a highly Cartesian approach to systems analysis and proved incapable of handling the complexity of the insurgency.[49]

But a parallel development—the emerging science of complexity—has created a new understanding of systems and a new language for describing systems behavior. Counterinsurgency is a field in which complexity theory offers fresh possibilities. It is a complex, problematic form of conflict that straddles the boundaries between warfare, government, economics, social stability, and moral acceptability. Hence, it has tended to defy the Cartesian, reductionist analysis traditionally applied to conventional warfare.[50] The new understanding of complex systems might be the tool we need to overcome this problem.

This chapter is not the first to suggest that the "War on Terrorism" is an effort to counter an insurgency, or to propose analyzing insurgency through complexity theory. Several papers making this suggestion have appeared in the academic literature and within the intelligence and strategic policy communities, including complexity-based systems analyses of single-state insurgencies.[51] The new insight in this chapter is that the "War on Terrorism," as a *global* counterinsurgency, demands reappraisal of classical counterinsurgency theory, which was based on Cartesian systems analysis of insurgency in a single state. Because complexity theory provides new tools for systems analysis, it may provide a new approach to countering globalized insurgency.

Insurgencies as Systems

A system is a set of related or interacting variables that function together for a specific purpose. In the most general sense, a system is a group of independent but interrelated elements comprising a unified whole.[52] This is a good description of both human societies and the warlike "system states" within those societies that we know as wars and insurgencies.

Counterinsurgency theory, as described, has long understood that insurgencies are social systems. Complexity theory takes this understanding further by showing that social systems (hence insurgencies) are *organic* systems. That is, social systems share characteristics with living systems like cells, organisms, or ecosystems. They consist of interdependent parts, inputs, processes, and outputs, which exist in a pattern of relationships that define the extent of the system and work together for the whole. So the branch of complexity theory that deals with "living" systems is an appropriate starting point for a complex systems analysis of insurgency.

Organic systems (including social systems like insurgencies) are "complex and adaptive." Their behavior results from the interactions and relationships between the entities that make up the *system in focus* and the *environment*, [that is,] the larger system of which the "system in focus" is a part. For example, the body is composed of subsystems such as the nervous system and cardio-vascular system, while at the same time it is part of an environment with an ecosystem and a social system."[53]

Importantly, the argument is not that insurgencies are *like* organic systems or that organic systems are useful analogies or metaphors for insurgency. Rather, the argument is that insurgencies *are* organic systems, in which individual humans and organizational structures function like organisms and cell structures in other organic systems. Insurgent systems share many features with other organic systems:

- **Insurgencies are social systems.** They form in a society when preexisting elements (grievances, individuals, weapons, and infrastructure) organize themselves in new patterns of interaction involving rebellion, terrorism, and other violent political activity. The *elements* in an insurgency are preexisting, but the *pattern* is new—like waves in water, the insurgency resides in the pattern of interaction rather than the elements themselves. Thus, though we tend to objectify insurgencies as if they were separate from parent societies, this is not the case. Rather, insurgency is a "system state"—a particular interaction of preexisting elements. It has no existence independent of its parent society, any more than a wave has an existence independent of the water in which it moves.
- **Insurgencies are energetically open but organizationally closed.** Insurgencies are open to energy flows from the environment. That is, matter and energy flow into the system as inputs like recruits, sympathizers, weapons, grievances, and doctrine. These inputs are transformed within the insurgent movement (through processes like indoctrination, intelligence collection, operations, and logistics) and emerge as outputs: casualties, social dislocation, destruction, further grievances, and media coverage. Like other organic systems, insurgencies maintain a distinct organizational boundary with their environment. Insurgent movements are networks composed of nodes (individuals, units, locations) and links (communications channels,

causal linkages, demographic and spatial connections). There are detectable boundaries between the movement and its environment. Successful insurgent systems exhibit *homeostasis*: the ability to maintain relatively stable internal conditions despite fluctuations in the external environment. Again, this is characteristic of organic systems—a healthy human or animal maintains a stable core body temperature, whatever the weather outside.

- **Insurgencies are self-organizing systems.** In insurgent systems, outputs from one system element become inputs for another. For example, some groups feed off the anguish and dislocation created by other groups; the outputs of the overall insurgency become inputs for counterinsurgent action. The existence of one system element allows the existence of another, and vice versa. This interdependence creates *autopoiesis*, where "the function of each component is to participate in the production or transformation of other components in the network."[54] The circular causal relationships—"feedback loops" or "vicious circles"—generated by this interdependence provide the driving force that maintains the insurgency.

- **Insurgencies are nonequilibrium, dissipative structures.** Insurgencies are nonequilibrium systems that exist on the "edge of chaos." That is, they depend on inputs of energy and matter from the external environment. Deny these inputs, and the feedback loops driving the insurgency lose energy, until the overall insurgency breaks down. Insurgencies are *dissipative structures* that depend for stability on a throughput of energy. The more energy (violence, grievances, insurgent action, counterinsurgent reaction) circulating in the system, the more stable it becomes and the less effective countermeasures become. Once energy is drained from the system, it becomes chaotic, its structure begins to collapse, inroads can be made into disrupting it, and the underlying drivers can be addressed.

- **Insurgencies are greater than the sum of their parts.** Like other organic systems, insurgencies exhibit *emergence*—characteristics and behaviors that emerge at a given level of analysis, and which could not be predicted by analyzing the component parts. Emergence is a common qualitative property of systems. For example, the taste of sugar emerges at the molecular level: analyzing the component atoms (carbon, hydrogen, and oxygen) gives no clue to the taste of the sugar those atoms form. This means that stakeholder analysis, nodal analysis or link analysis, beloved of intelligence operators and military planners, provides some but not all the answers. It also explains why Cartesian approaches to insurgency (like McNamara's approach in Vietnam) often fail—analyzing the parts gives an incomplete understanding of the whole.

- **Insurgent theatres are ecosystems.** A theatre of irregular warfare is an ecosystem in which many groups and entities interact (like organisms in a biological ecosystem); outputs from one become inputs for another and contribute to emergent systems behavior. For example, as discussed, some groups in a theatre feed off outputs from others, using these as inputs for their own purposes. This creates feedback loops that drive insurgent theatres in particular directions, regardless of the subjective intentions of local groups. So localized groups who subjectively compete can actually be "cooperating" at the systemic level. For example, until recently, Al Qa'eda and the Zarqawi network of Tawhid wa'l Jihad [subsequently, Al Qa'eda in Iraq] competed for the allegiance of Sunni insurgents in Iraq. Although Zarqawi and Al Qa'eda initially competed and disliked each other, their actions were mutually reinforcing at the "ecosystem" level, in terms of overall effects.[55]
- **Insurgent theatres have an adaptational, evolutionary dynamic.** In insurgent theatres, a "survival of the fittest" dynamic emerges. Because multiple groups compete for control over population and terrain, adaptability in changing circumstances is at a premium. As discussed later, the most dangerous insurgents in a theatre may be not the strongest but the most adaptable, the best able to leverage an asymmetric advantage—hence the most survivable. And we know from systems analysis of biological adaptation that the more diverse a system's elements are, the greater its ability to adapt.

Elements of the Insurgent System

Based on this model, insurgencies as organic systems comprise seven elements:

- **Nodes.** Nodes are physical components and structures of the system. In the case of an insurgency, they include individual fighters, units, cells, sympathizers, and intelligence assets; social groups like tribes or clans, or infrastructure. These may or may not be open to counterinsurgency measures.
- **Links.** Links define patterns of interaction in the insurgency. They include communication channels (Internet, satellite, radio, couriers),

causal links (where actions by one element cause actions by others), and demographic or geographic links (spatial or ethnic patterns within an insurgency). Some links are internal to the insurgent network; others connect the insurgency to external support. Because insurgencies are networks, links are critical. Interdict the links, and the insurgency's energy, structure, and resilience dissipate. Again, some links are vulnerable; others are not.

- **Boundary.** The insurgency's boundary defines the limit between the insurgent movement and its environment. This boundary may be permeable, but it is distinct—there is a definite "inside" and "outside" to an insurgent movement. Because the insurgency depends on energy and matter from the environment, attacking the boundary may deny energy to the insurgency and ultimately cause it to collapse.
- **Subsystems.** Insurgent systems may include subsystems. Within a movement, there may be logistics, intelligence, propaganda, recruitment, planning, and operational subsystems, among others. These are "systems within systems," and the thousands upon thousands of nested interactions of subsystems with the parent insurgency are key elements in its strength.
- **Boundary interactions.** These are the day-to-day events in the insurgency. They include incidents, attacks, popular support, territorial control, intelligence collection, information and media dominance, economic dominance, freedom of movement, and loss exchange ratios in combat. Because these are the physical manifestations of the insurgent system, they tend to receive the greatest attention from security forces—hence, most traditional means of attacking insurgencies focus on denying or disrupting boundary interactions. This is akin to treating the symptoms of an illness, and just as microbes develop drug resistance, so insurgents evolve and adapt to deal with these forms of attack.
- **Inputs.** These are the energy and matter the insurgency takes up from its environment. These include people (recruits, leaders, supporters, specialists) and materiel (ammunition, weapons, money, medical supplies). Grievances, ideology, religious belief, doctrine and tactics, techniques, and procedures are also inputs. Denying inputs is a method of reducing energy in the system, making it easier to suppress.
- **Outputs.** These are waste products or results that emerge from insurgent action. They include casualties, physical destruction, social and economic dislocation, new grievances, propaganda or

media coverage, and techniques that emerge as insurgents learn by experience. Choking off the outputs of an insurgent group may or may not affect that group but it may deny those outputs to other groups that would otherwise feed off them. Hence, at the "ecosystem" level, choking outputs can weaken an insurgency (see fig. 6.2).

Systems Dynamics in the Global Islamist Insurgency

As argued, the "War on Terrorism" can be understood as an effort to counter a global Islamist insurgency. In particular, the enemy syndicate appears to comprise an intricate, ramified web of dependency between

FIG 6.2   Model of an Insurgency as a Biological System

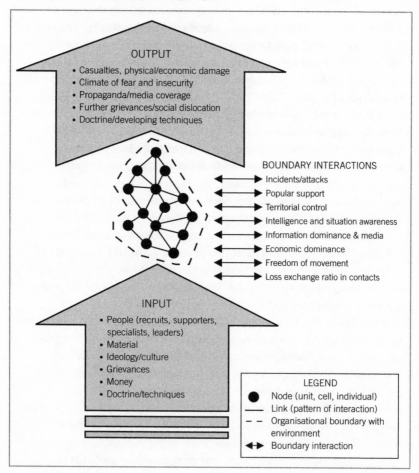

loosely allied insurgent and terrorist groups. This web—the network of links between individuals and cells in the jihad—is the most significant element in the insurgency: the actions they carry out are what the network *does* (its boundary interactions), not the network itself. Therefore (as the organic systems model of insurgency demonstrates), attacking the links, inputs, and outputs of the network may provide a more substantial payoff than attempting to eliminate individual nodes.

One insight arising from the systems model of insurgency is that the global jihad exhibits a series of nested interactions—systems within systems. For example, the global jihad comprises linked but interdependent jihads in Southeast Asia, the Middle East, and South/Central Asia, including the Caucasus. Each regional jihad, in turn, comprises linked but interdependent localized insurgencies—for example, the Middle Eastern jihad includes insurgencies in Palestine, Saudi Arabia, Iraq, and other nation-states. Each local insurgency is driven partly by local issues, partly by factors in the broader jihad. Regional and global players prey on, link, and exploit local actors in order to further their objectives. Each local insurgency comprises linked but interdependent insurgent movements—for example, the Iraqi insurgency comprises Kurdish, Sunni, Shia, Ba'athist, and tribal groups. Each insurgent movement, in turn, comprises linked but separate cells, units, factions, or local groups. For example, the Sunni insurgency in Iraq includes anti-Saddam Sunni nationalists, former regime loyalists, elements with links to the Muslim Brotherhood, tribal groups motivated by loyalty to local sheikhs, criminal elements, and foreign fighters linked to Al Qa'eda or Zarqawi. Many patterns within the jihad are repeated, on different scales, at several levels of analysis.

At each level of analysis—local, district, national, regional, global—there is emergence, as new characteristics and behaviors appear. Adaptation and evolution occur across and within all levels and regions. For example, some bomb-making techniques in Iraq appear to originate from Palestinian and Chechen groups, as well as homegrown Iraqi techniques. Methods used in Iraq have also proliferated to other regions and groups, through a body of jihadist doctrine and techniques distributed on the Internet and through electronic communication. Hence, members of the global jihad have a distinct tactical "style"—so while individual attacks may not be predictable, overall preferences and approaches are detectable.

The "foundation myth of al Qaeda [is] that a transnational body of Muslim militants can effectively wage holy war against the United States without having a Muslim state grant it safe harbor."[56] Since the destruction of its Taliban-sponsored safe haven in Afghanistan, the leaders of the global jihad have been putting this concept to the test, attempting to function as an insurgent pseudostate. Although Al Qa'eda does not use the term itself, in essence the global jihad represents a federated virtual state.[57] The notion of "parallel hierarchies" or "insurgent states" is central to classical counterinsurgency.[58] Indeed, Robert Thompson's influential view that a counterinsurgency is a "competition for government" with an insurgent "shadow-state" is based on this idea.[59] But in a globalized insurgency, the insurgents' parallel hierarchy is a *virtual* state: it controls no territory or population but exercises control over distributed systems that, taken together, represent many elements of traditional state power. It is also a *pseudo*-state: a false state, a governing entity that acts like a state but is not one in terms of legal or political legitimacy. Moreover, it is not a single hierarchy but a federated network of linked systems that functions as an "insurgent state" and competes with world governments. This is clear if we consider the global jihad using a national power model (see table 6.2).[60]

TABLE 6.2 A national power model of the Islamist virtual state

Element of national power`	Traditional Nation-state	Islamist virtual state
Geography	Exercises exclusive legal and administrative control over a definite geographical territory; is vulnerable to attacks on its territory.	Controls no territory but exists in the interstices of territories controlled by nation-states: tribal areas, failed states, unadministered areas. Exists in ungoverned or undergoverned space.
Resources	Exercises control or outright ownership over the natural resources within its territory, enables its citizens to access these resources, trades resources with other states, and exploits these resources to build economic and military power.	Controls no natural resources but exploits flows of international resources, by means of the international banking system, Islamic *hawala* banks, and charitable funds. Acts to affect the flow and trade of natural resources (e.g., oil).
Population	Derives strength from the size, composition, and skills base of the population (of all nations) within its territory and of its citizens throughout the world. Must protect its population.	Derives strength from the size, composition, and skills base of its adherents, regardless of where they reside. Must protect key nodes but has no requirement to protect an overall population.

Economic	Manages and develops a national economy that enables a standard of living for the population, funds government, finances military power, and supports trade relationships with other states. Is vulnerable to attacks on its economy.	Controls no national economy but accesses economic benefits through its adherents' wealth. Cannot guarantee economic benefits for its people but is free of the responsibility and vulnerability of having an economy.
Political	Seeks to maintain effective government through political unity, legitimate exercise of state power, and political institutions that maintain and enhance its stability.	Seeks to influence local, regional, and global politics through insurgent action. Has no requirement to govern a territory, but enforces political unity and coherence on its followers.
Military	Maintains regular armed forces to defend its territory and population and further its interests.	Maintains irregular forces to further its interests. Has little need to defend territory or population.
Psychological	Maintains the population's national will and morale, political resilience, national character, and integration. Acts to maximize the population's psychological determination in pursuit of the nation's objectives.	Maintains psychological morale, determination, and resilience through ideology based on (1) a specific interpretations of Islam, and (2) a geopolitical analysis of power relationships between the Islamic and non-Islamic worlds. Loses and gains adherents continually.
Informational	Maintains communications and informational presence on the national, regional, and global levels. Maximizes the effectiveness of its communications to further its interests.	Maintains informational presence through world media, internationalized communications, and the Internet. Uses informational power to further its propaganda aims.

* There are many models of national power. This is not the model taught in war colleges, but it is used here because it allows a fuller breakdown of relevant factors. For a fuller discussion of the model used, see D. Jablonsky, "National Power," *Parameters* (spring 1997): 34–54.
Source: David J. Kilcullen, 2003

The Islamist virtual state, like the insurgent shadow-state of classical counterinsurgency, engages in a "competition for government": it must be defeated through measures addressing all elements of national power. But unlike the traditional insurgent shadow-state, the Islamists ultimately cannot offer the material benefits of statehood—protection, stability, and economic prosperity—and thus cannot compete with nation-states for the long-term allegiance of uncommitted populations. Conversely, the Islamists are not subject to many restrictions that affect nation-states, giving them greater short-term tactical freedom of maneuver.

A Cold War analogy is appropriate. In classical counterinsurgency theory, competition for government is often depicted as a binary struggle between the insurgents and the government. As described, at the global level, there is no "world government," so many classical counterinsurgency measures do not apply. But that does not make the conflict unwinnable. During the Cold War, a fanatical ideology (Communism) aiming at world revolution was defeated by a diverse collection of states that all valued pluralism and liberty, despite individual differences. Competition for global domination between the Soviet Union and other communist actors on the one hand, and the Western democracies on the other, did not require a world government. But it did require leadership from the United States, and that leadership had to be calibrated in such a way as to preserve the long-term support of the rest of the world's democracies. Such leadership and support are equally necessary here.

In addition, as in most counterinsurgencies, it is critical to defeat the insurgency without radicalizing or alienating the population to the point that the security forces become recruiting agents for the insurgents. Hence a "battle of ideas" (in counterinsurgency terms, a struggle for the hearts and minds of the affected population) is central to the "War on Terrorism." Fortunately, liberal democracies have significant power in this area, though there is a need to coordinate this power more effectively to counteract the Islamist message.

The Role of Culture in Insurgent Dynamics

Cultures are common assumptions and norms about the nature of the world, how things are, and how things should be. Culture develops in all human groups: ethnic groups, organizations, and family, clan, or tribal structures. In terms of systems, cultures provide protocols: agreed patterns that enhance the efficiency of system interactions. Thus cultures form links, and important individuals, locations, and beliefs form cultural nodes in a system. Like other links, cultural links provide pathways along which energy flows within the insurgency.

In an insurgent ecosystem, numerous cultures are present. These include the national or ethnic culture of the country where the insurgency takes place, tribal or regional subcultures within it, urban and rural cultural structures, and—most important—the organizational cultures of insurgent movements and counterinsurgency forces. In globalized insurgency, all these cultures are still present, but there is also a cultural pattern relating to the overall jihad at the systemic level. So, in any jihad theatre where members of the global insurgency are present, the behavior of certain insurgent or terrorist groups will be conditioned by local cultural norms, whereas others will act according to cultural patterns established in the global jihad.*

This is a key source of conflict between insurgent groups—for example, local groups may disagree with methods adopted by "globalized" jihadists. The siege of School No. 1 at Beslan in September 2004 is a good example of this. Whereas some Chechen groups supported the attack, several local Chechen separatist groups also condemned it. Similarly, in 2002 the relationship between the Taliban in Afghanistan—a pseudoconventional force that fought using light-cavalry tactics—and Al Qa'eda came under strain due to disagreement over methods. By 2004 the original Taliban had undergone cultural evolution under the pressure of the Coalition's counterinsurgency operations, whereas Al Qa'eda had pulled back into a training and advisory role.[61] As a final example, when I was living with members of Negara Islam Indonesia in West Java in 1996 conducting fieldwork for a doctoral dissertation on insurgency, the group underwent a cultural shift. Some members joined JI (part of the global jihad) and took on a new cultural outlook. Others preferred a regional separatist approach based on their traditional allegiance to Darul Islam, a local guerrilla group active in the 1960s. This cultural shift resulted in intense disagreement and even bloodshed between former allies.[62]

As I will discuss later, security forces can use culture to develop leverage in insurgent theatres and disrupt insurgent systems. But this requires excellent linguistic and cultural competence.

---

* AUTHOR'S NOTE (2009): This set of ideas is presented in much greater detail in *The Accidental Guerrilla*. In addition to the examples given here, covering splits between locally-focused and globally-focused actors, the breakdown of the alliance between Sunni tribes and Al Qa'eda in Iraq, resulting in the lethal unraveling of tribe/insurgent relations, the Awakening and Sons of Iraq movements and the near-destruction of Al Qa'eda across much of western and central Iraq in 2007, further underlines this.

Adaptation and Evolution in Insurgent Groups

As noted, the most common method of attacking an insurgency is to target its boundary interactions or "symptoms." This *may* be effective but is unlikely to succeed unless combined with measures that address the overall insurgency at the systemic level. As discussed, boundary interaction attacks impose evolutionary pressure on the insurgents. Weak or unlucky cells and individuals are destroyed; but the insurgency learns and adapts to the challenge. At the systemic level, the overall insurgency becomes stronger.

One solution is "operational surprise," in which measures are introduced to which the insurgents cannot adapt in time to survive. Changing political strategies, altering tactical methods, or varying operational patterns are ways of seeking operational surprise. Surprise tends to be more effective than shock because it seizes the initiative, forcing insurgents to react to security forces.

To be effective, however, this method demands constant innovation in new measures (see fig. 6.3).

Another method is "operational shock," a maneuver concept that involves dislocating the insurgency at the systemic level, making it cease operating as a system so that components can be destroyed piecemeal. In practice, this is problematic because much insurgent infrastructure is hidden or invulnerable to military maneuver. Moreover, as noted, many modern insurgents are federations of loosely allied (even competing)

FIG 6.3   Effectiveness of Counterinsurgency Measures over Time

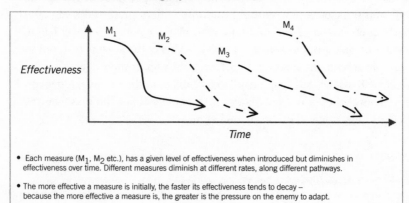

- Each measure (M_1, M_2 etc.), has a given level of effectiveness when introduced but diminishes in effectiveness over time. Different measures diminish at different rates, along different pathways.

- The more effective a measure is initially, the faster its effectiveness tends to decay – because the more effective a measure is, the greater is the pressure on the enemy to adapt.

local groups. Thus, insurgents are more resistant to operational shock than conventional military forces, which have sophisticated, integrated logistics, command and control, and communications systems and hierarchies that are closely interlocked can be readily attacked in such a way that damage to one part of the system disrupts another.

So insurgencies are not only complex systems, they are (like other organic systems) complex *adaptive* systems. They are relatively invulnerable to operational shock, so most conventional maneuvers (which use operational shock as a defeat mechanism) are ineffective. They are more vulnerable to surprise, but this demands continuous innovation: there will never be a single optimal solution. Indeed, the more effective a measure is, the faster it will be obsolete, because it will force the enemy to adapt more quickly. Ruth Margolies Beitler, analyzing the Palestinian intifada in 1995, argued that "the repression of a group's most effective tactic... will cause an increase in overall conflict activity.... Sanctions which can be effective at the outset of violence may lose their deterrent effect over time."[63] I find these conclusions intuitively correct, having watched insurgent groups adapt at first hand in East Timor and Bougainville.* The same conclusions are supported by current reporting from Iraq, and by substantial academic research.

Another insight is that in insurgent theatres, the most dangerous group is not necessarily the largest or best armed. Rather, the most adaptive groups are the most dangerous. For example, there are numerous insurgent and terrorist groups in the Philippines. But the largest groups may not be the most dangerous. Rather, groups with a high proportion of Arabic linguists, Internet communications, and personal connections to the Middle Eastern jihad may be better able to tap into the Islamist virtual state. These groups may prove most adaptable, hence most dangerous in the long term.

Critical Mass in Insurgencies

A key element in the systems dynamics of insurgencies—and another feature they share with other organic systems—is that given a sufficient, stable energy flow over time, these systems eventually become "self-sustaining." To borrow a term from nuclear physics, insurgent theatres given sufficient time and energy, can reach "critical mass."

When an insurgent theatre reaches critical mass, removing the initial cause of the insurgency will no longer cause it to wither. It has become

---

* AUTHOR'S NOTE (2009): And, since this chapter was first written, in Iraq, Afghanistan, and Pakistan.

self-sustaining, with sufficient energy and matter moving in the system (in the form of feedback loops such as revenge, economic dislocation, hatred, and violence) that it can continue to function without the initial stimulus. For example it has been argued that the premature disbandment of the Iraqi army by the Coalition Provisional Authority in Iraq created a large group of unemployed, trained soldiers with a grievance against the occupation and no future in an Iraq administered by the Coalition. This provided a key impetus to the development of the Iraqi insurgency. Arguably, however, it is now too late to go back and remedy this situation—the insurgency has become self-sustaining, and reemploying former soldiers will not make it go away. Similarly, in Northern Ireland the civil rights movement of 1968–69 was a key stimulus to the insurgency. But the issues raised by the civil rights movement have mostly been addressed, and even if all the original grievances that sparked the Troubles were remedied, it is now too late. The Irish insurgency reached critical mass in 1969, and has now become ingrained in the cultural and economic way of life of some sections in society.

In the global jihad, it is clear that the Middle Eastern and South Asian theatres reached critical mass some time ago. Insurgencies in these theatres cannot be resolved by simply addressing the grievances that gave rise to them. For example, the creation of the State of Israel, or the behavior of Israelis in the Palestinian territories, are often quoted as key grievances behind Islamist insurgency in the Middle East. But this theatre long ago reached a self-sustaining level. Removing Israel from the West Bank or complying with all Palestinian demands would not remove the insurgency. Likewise, the Chechen grievance—lack of self-government—was satisfied after the end of the First Chechen War in 1996. But this did not make the problem of Chechen-sponsored terrorism go away. Indeed, the Chechen insurgency had reached the self-sustaining level, where achievement of the objective of self-government merely caused the Chechen insurgents to seek fresh targets in European Russia.*

This does not mean that grievances are unimportant or should not be addressed—as shown, this is key to successful counterinsurgency. But

---

* AUTHOR'S NOTE (2009): This is not to suggest that resolving the Israel-Palestine conflict, or the issue of Caucasian separatism, is unimportant or is a low priority. It is merely to point out that resolving these issues will not in itself cause the current conflict to dissipate. There are good reasons—humanitarian, geopolitical, and economic—for the international community to make strenuous efforts to resolve these conflicts. But removing the casus belli for global terrorists is not one of them: at this point, the international takfiri movement has arguably reached critical mass and would continue to exist (albeit with less propaganda justification) even if every major jihadist grievance—Palestine, Chechnya, Kashmir, Afghanistan, Iraq—were resolved tomorrow.

the point here is that after a theatre has reached critical mass, addressing grievances will not solve the insurgency in itself.

Importantly, the Southeast Asian theatre of the global jihad has arguably not yet reached critical mass. There are legitimate Muslim grievances and issues, but they have not yet been so thoroughly compromised by association with terrorist groups or the terrorist agenda that they can no longer be effectively addressed. Similarly, jihad has not become a way of life in Southeast Asia, as it has for parts of the population in some other theatres of the jihad. Arguably, the Islamist insurgent system has recognized this, with Southeast Asia receiving a substantial proportion of Islamist funding, subversion, and organizational activity. Moreover, this theatre contains more Sunni Muslims than any other, dominates world trading and oil supply routes, and contains models of democratic responsible government in Muslim societies in Indonesia, Malaysia, and the Philippines that must be destroyed if the pan-Islamist caliphate model is to become dominant.

In particular, analysts are concerned about the situation in southern Thailand, which, although previously not seen as a major jihad front, has the potential to draw in substantial numbers of insurgents and significant terrorist activity.* The insurgency in Thailand seems to be gaining in energy and becoming a major grievance for some Southeast Asian Muslims. Should Thailand be allowed to develop into a major jihad front, the entire Southeast Asian theatre might quickly develop substantially more energy.[64]

All this means that the future of the global jihad may not be decided in the Middle East, even though that region is presently the most active theatre. If Southeast Asia is allowed to "go critical" as other theatres have already done, it is possible that the global jihad as an overall system may attain almost unstoppable momentum. Thus, Southeast Asia may represent the critical swing state that will be decisive in the future of the jihad.

---

* AUTHOR'S NOTE (2009): In chapter 4 of *The Accidental Guerrilla*, I examine both Indonesia and Thailand. In the event, Southeast Asia does not seem to have reached critical mass. This seems partly due to the extremely strong local motivation among groups like the Pattani United Liberation Organization (PULO), the southern Thai insurgents motivated more by Malay separatism than international jihad, and partly due to excellent community work, police and intelligence work, and restrained security policies by the Indonesian government and other Southeast Asian countries. The fact that Western attention has been focused heavily on Iraq and Afghanistan since 2001 may have been an important factor here: local governments themselves took the lead and sought local solutions, with only a low level of discreet, back-room support, almost entirely nonmilitary in nature, from the international community. Although JI, the Abu Sayyaf Group, PULO, and other organizations retain the ability to strike, and insurgencies are continuing in some parts of the region, Southeast Asia as a theatre of globalized insurgency seems to be in remission as of 2009.

Attack Methods in Counterinsurgency

Given the systems elements shown in figure 6.2, there is a finite number of ways to attack insurgencies. One can (**1**) attack nodes, (**2**) interdict links, (**3**) disrupt the boundary, (**4**) suppress boundary interactions, (**5**) choke off inputs, (**6**) deny outputs, or (**7**) use a combination of methods. Because of the adaptational dynamic, variety and continuous development of new methods are needed. Attacks that target a combination of elements simultaneously are likely to be more effective, since they give less opportunity for insurgents to adapt in response. A historical survey demonstrates that the majority of successful counterinsurgencies have used a variety of methods and that coordinated efforts against multiple elements in the insurgent system have indeed been the most effective. Table 6.3 summarizes historical data (indicating which of the aforementioned seven attack types were used in each counterinsurgency campaign).

As table 6.3 shows, successful counterinsurgency (at the strategic level) depends largely on generating an effective political solution, while tactical actions to counter an insurgency primarily serve the purpose of buying time for the political solution to be implemented. All the examples of successful counterinsurgency in table 6.3 attacked a wide range of elements in the insurgent system with a combination of measures. These counterinsurgencies also attacked links, disrupted subsystems, and sought to undermine the insurgency at the systemic level. However, in most examples, the counterinsurgency still had a heavy focus on attacking boundary interactions. The least effective examples were those in which counterinsurgents could not develop an effective political strategy, often because of interference by external actors who could not be neutralized (as in Vietnam, the Palestinian territories, and Northern Ireland). Under these circumstances, the best that the counterinsurgents could achieve was to contain the insurgency indefinitely.

Vietnam is worth examining in a little more detail, because of its continuing influence over the U.S. approach to insurgency.[65] One insight from this survey is that counterinsurgency in Vietnam was highly effective at the tactical level. Given the ultimate U.S. defeat in Vietnam, one might expect to see problems in the application of counterinsurgency in the war—poor coordination, a focus on nodes and links to the exclusion of other attack methods, or failure to prevent enemy adaptation. In fact, the opposite is true: counterinsurgency in Vietnam covered a wide range of methods, was well coordinated, and produced excellent overall results.

TABLE 6.3 Historical survey of attack methods used by counterinsurgencies

Insurgency	Counterinsurgency methods	Types of attack used	Comments
Malaya 1948–60	Resettlement program	3, 4, 5	Measures covered a good spread of methods. These were initially not well coordinated but improved dramatically with central coordination. Sociopolitical measures became effective once security measures began to "bite."
	Use of surrendered enemy personnel	1, 2	
	Special forces deep penetration patrols	1, 2, 3	
	Framework security operations	4, 5, 6	
	Key infrastructure protection	4	
	Hearts-and-minds program	5, 6	
	Political concessions to independence	5	
Darul Islam, Indonesia 1948–62	*Pagar betis* (civilian cordon operations)	2, 3, 4, 5, 6	Measures addressed most areas, with a preference for co-opting civil populations, harsh collective punishments, and decapitation strikes. Most successful in 1959–62 when integrated at theatre level.
	Village defense organisation	3, 4, 5	
	P4K (pacification) strategy	1, 2, 3, 4, 5	
	Civic action programs	5, 6	
	Decapitation strikes (against Darul Islam leaders)	1	
	Special forces deep penetration patrols	1, 2	
	Infrastructure/route security operations	2, 3, 4	
Vietnam 1959–73	Strategic hamlet program	3, 4, 5	Somewhat counterintuitively, Vietnam War methods appear to address the full spread of attack methods, with the actions (CORDS, combined action platoons, Montagnard operations) that addressed the most issues being most effective. Coordination initially poor but improved dramatically in 1968–72.
	Phoenix Program	1, 2	
	CORDS program	2, 3, 4, 5	
	Combined action platoons	3, 4, 5, 6	
	Search-and-destroy/sweep-and-clear operations	1, 2	
	Interdiction of supply routes (Ho Chi Minh Trail, Rung Sat, Mekong Delta)	2, 5	
	Sanctuary denial operations (DMZ, Cambodia)	5	
	Montagnard strike force operations	1, 2, 3, 4, 5	
	Pacification operations	3, 4, 5, 6	
	Winning Hearts and Minds	5, 6	

Insurgency	Counterinsurgency methods	Types of attack used	Comments
Palestinian (Al Aqsa) intifada (2001– present)	Decapitation strikes (targeted killings)	1	Measures cover a full spread of options, with a preference for attacks on nodes and links rather than territorial control, civic action, or hearts and minds. Measures appear well coordinated.
	Palestinian territories security barrier	3, 4, 5, 6	
	Settlement Demolition/ resettlement	3, 4, 5	
	Restrictions on Palestinian leaders' movements	1, 2	
	Incursions into refugee camps	1, 2, 3, 4, 5	
	Border control operations	4, 5	
	Route, infrastructure, and key point security	2, 3, 4	
Northern Ireland (1969– present)	Framework security operations	3, 4, 5, 6	Measures cover the full range, with a preference for denying the boundary interactions, penetrating and disrupting links, and political concessions to undermine the insurgent cause.
	Province reaction force	1, 2, 4	
	Intelligence-led covert operations	1, 2, 3, 4	
	Political concessions	5	
	Key infrastructure and route security	2, 3, 4	
	Border control operations	4, 5	
	Use of informants and locally raised forces	1, 2, 3, 4	

Ironically, by winning the counterinsurgency in South Vietnam the United States provoked a crossborder invasion from North Vietnam after the failure of the 1968 Tet Offensive all but destroyed the indigenous southern insurgent element of the Viet Cong. Thus, the very success of counterinsurgency measures provoked a wider war.[66] Because of a loss of political will, resulting from the length of time taken to adapt to the environment and casualties sustained in the earlier phases of the war, U.S. forces were unavailable to meet this invasion because they had been withdrawn.[67]

Jeffrey Record and W. Andrew Tyrell have pointed out that the differences between Vietnam and Iraq far outweigh the similarities (though their analysis considers Iraq only from the standpoint of classical, single-country counterinsurgency).[68] Nonetheless, at the tactical level, measures from Vietnam—combined action platoons, the Civil Operations and Rural Development Support (CORDS) program, the use of locally raised irregular forces under U.S. leadership, Accelerated Pacification and the Strategic Hamlet Program—may have potential in Iraq, provided the conditions of globalized insurgency are factored in. The conditions that allowed North Vietnam to invade the South (a superpower sponsor, sanctuary areas, ethnic similarity, historical legitimacy, and multiple covert infiltration routes) do not apply in Iraq. There is no neighboring state—not even Iran—for whom these conditions apply. It follows that methods from Vietnam may succeed in Iraq, and the United States needs to make a priority of denying neighboring states the motivation, means, and opportunity to invade or infiltrate Iraq. It also follows that the greatest threat to victory in Iraq would be a loss of political will in the United States, followed by premature withdrawal leaving Iraq unable to stand alone.

Another insight is that effective counterinsurgency demands a tailored systems analysis of the specific situation: not the application of templated techniques from other theatres. As I have shown elsewhere, a key Indonesian failing in the counterinsurgency in East Timor was the tendency to apply techniques from fighting Islamic insurgents in West Java to the radically different terrain and threat picture of East Timor. This tendency to "template" created unforeseen consequences that ultimately cost the Indonesians the province of East Timor.[69]

Similarly, some operators in Iraq have been wary of providing development assistance to the population for fear that money and supplies would percolate to the insurgents. This view is based on a set of assumptions, originating in Vietnam, about the economic relationship between the population and the insurgents. In Vietnam, the insurgents preyed on local populations for funds and supplies to enable the insurgency. Thus, any support given to the population had to be controlled to prevent the insurgents benefiting from it. In Iraq, the situation is exactly the reverse: the insurgents are lavishly provided with funds from Saddam-era sources or external backers. Conversely, the population is impoverished and economically vulnerable. Reliable sources estimate that 70–75 percent of insurgent attacks in Iraq are economically motivated.[70] Insurgents pay the population to conduct attacks, and the population is vulnerable to this approach because it is impoverished. Thus, far from helping the insurgents, a more lavish distribution of funds *reduces* the guerrillas' leverage. Tailored systems analysis is thus essential to ensure that templated techniques from earlier eras are not misapplied.

The next section applies the systems analysis of insurgency to propose a strategy for the "War on Terrorism."

PART 4: THE STRATEGY OF DISAGGREGATION

> *The shooting side of this business is only 25 percent of the trouble;*
> *the other 75 percent is getting the people of this country behind*
> *us.... The answer lies not in pouring more troops into the jungle,*
> *but in the hearts and minds of the people.*
> —General Sir Gerald Templer, High Commissioner and Director of
> Operations, Malaya (1952)

The Problem of Strategy

Despite the publication in mid-2002 of the *National Security Strategy of the United States of America*, the U.S. strategy for the overall "War on Terrorism" remains vaguely understood. Indeed, at several closed-door meetings with senior military personnel, analysts, and intelligence officials in October 2004, individuals seriously questioned whether in fact the United States actually *had* a coherent overall strategy for this war, and if so, what it was.[71] In part, this vagueness results from the application of a terrorism paradigm to what is essentially a counterinsurgency, as discussed above. But there are other reasons for this.

Despite the lack of clarity in some U.S. statements about this war, analysis of U.S. actions so far indicates a de facto strategy of "aggregation"—lumping together all terrorism, all rogue or failed states, and all strategic competitors who might potentially oppose U.S. objectives in the war. This de facto strategy creates several problems.

Jeffrey Record argues that

the administration has postulated a multiplicity of enemies, including rogue states, weapons of mass destruction (WMD) proliferators, terrorist organizations, and terrorism itself. It has also... conflated them as a general, undifferentiated threat. In so doing, the administration has arguably subordinated strategic clarity to the moral clarity it seeks in foreign policy and may have set the United States on a path of open-ended and unnecessary conflict with states and nonstate entities that pose no direct or imminent threat to the United States.[72]

In essence, aggregation runs the risk of creating new enemies and of fighting enemies simultaneously who could have been fought sequentially—thus posing sustainability problems.[73] A strategy of aggregation tends naturally to the logical outcome of a war against all terrorists or—far worse—all Muslims simultaneously. This creates enormous potential for overstretch, exhaustion of popular will, and ultimate failure.*

Moreover, such a strategy undermines U.S. legitimacy (and thus, as we have seen, its self-appointed role as global counterterrorism Supremo). This is because such a strategy tends to link obviously disparate conflicts, thus giving the appearance that the United States is using this war as an excuse to settle old scores. Similarly, such a strategy causes the United States to support morally dubious regimes and (by creating suspicion as to U.S. motives) undermines opportunities for common cause with other democracies—notably the Europeans.

On the basis of the preceding analysis of the global jihad and the organic systems nature of globalized insurgency, this section offers an alternative—indeed, a diametrically opposed—strategy for the "War on Terrorism": disaggregation.

The Strategy of Disaggregation

As described, dozens of local movements, grievances, and issues have been aggregated (through regional and global actors) into a global jihad against the West. These regional and global players prey on, link, and exploit local actors and issues that are preexisting. What makes the jihad so dangerous is its global nature. Without the "series of nested interactions" this chapter has described or the ability to aggregate dozens

---

* AUTHOR'S NOTE (2009): Shortly after this paper was first published, Usama bin Laden made a public statement on Al Qa'eda strategy that echoed this strategic approach. Speaking on al-Jazeera television in a video message, bin Laden said: "All that we have mentioned has made it easy to provoke and bait this Administration. All we have to do is to send two mujahideen to the furthest point East to raise a cloth on which is written al-Qaeda, in order to make the generals race there to cause America to suffer human, economic and political losses without achieving for it anything of note ... so we are continuing this policy of bleeding America to the point of bankruptcy. Allah willing and nothing is too great for Allah." Usama bin Laden, statement of November 2004, quoted in Kilcullen, *The Accidental Guerrilla*, p. 29.

of conflicts into a broad movement, the global jihad ceases to exist. It becomes simply a series of disparate local conflicts that are capable of being solved by nation-states and can be addressed at the regional or national level without interference from global enemies such as Al Qa'eda.

A strategy of disaggregation would seek to dismantle, or break up, the links that allow the jihad to function as a global entity. In this strategy, victory does not demand that we pacify every insurgent theatre from the Philippines to Chechnya. It only demands that we identify, and neutralize, those elements in each theatre that link to the global jihad. For example, Chechen separatism predates the involvement of Islamists in the Caucasus. Disaggregation does not demand an immediate resolution to the Chechen insurgency; rather, it demands that we deny the Chechen jihad its links to the global movement and then support Russia in addressing Chechen separatism. Similarly, disaggregation does not demand that we resolve the centuries-old Moro separatist issue in the Philippines. It only requires that we marginalize groups like the Abu Sayyaf Group that link into the global jihad and help the Philippines resolve its conflict with groups like the Moro National Liberation Front, who—although Islamic separatists—are seeking regional self-government, not endless global jihad.

Communal and sectarian conflicts at the local level are the driving force behind almost all the grievances that jihadist groups exploit. Therefore, a key element in a strategy of disaggregation is to address—at the local level—the prevention and (if it is too late for prevention) the amelioration of local communal conflicts. These can no longer be regarded as local, parochial, or limited problems. Rather, they provide the fuel on which the global jihad runs.

A strategy of disaggregation would therefore focus on:

- Interdicting links between Islamist theatres of operation within the global insurgency
- Denying regional and global actors the ability to link and exploit local actors
- Interdicting flows of information, personnel, finance, and technology (including weapons of mass destruction technology) between and within jihad theatres
- Denying sanctuary areas (including failed and failing states, and states that support terrorism) within theatres

- Isolating Islamists from local populations, through theatre-specific measures to win hearts and minds, counter Islamist propaganda, create alternative institutions, and remove the drivers for popular support to insurgents
- Disrupting inputs (personnel, money, and information) from the sources of Islamism in the greater Middle East to dispersed jihad theatres worldwide
- Preventing or ameliorating local communal and sectarian conflicts that create the grievances on which jihadist systems can prey

Thus, although dozens of local insurgencies contribute to the global jihad, victory under a disaggregation strategy does not demand the destruction of all local insurgents. Rather (systems analysis indicates), counterinsurgency at the systemic level is a matter of delinking local issues from the global insurgent system as much as it is about dealing with local insurgents themselves.

In practical terms, disaggregation does not provide a template of counterinsurgency measures that are universally applicable. As described above, such a template probably does not exist, and if it did, the adaptational dynamic in insurgency would render it rapidly obsolete. Instead, much like containment during the Cold War, a strategy of disaggregation means different things at different times or in different theatres but provides a unifying strategic conception for a protracted global confrontation.

Nevertheless, several practical insights arise through applying this strategic conception to the analysis of the jihad and the organic systems nature of insurgency. The first key insight is a theatre-level operational concept for counterinsurgency.

Operational Concept

Complex systems analysis shows that active fighters are only the "tip of the iceberg" in insurgent systems and that counterinsurgency must therefore address the whole system in a coordinated fashion. It also demonstrates that because the elements of insurgency are preexisting but the pattern of interaction is new, victory consists not in eliminating these elements but rather in returning them to a "normal" mode of interaction. That is, if insurgency resides in the pattern of relationships, victory consists in rearranging this pattern into a stable and peaceful "system state." Merely destroying elements without changing patterns of interaction may be counterproductive. This gives rise to the following operational concept:

The aim in counterinsurgency is to return the parent society to a stable, peaceful mode of interaction—on terms favorable to the government.

The caveat ("terms favorable to the government") is key because in at least some campaigns, the insurgent aim is also to return parent society to normality, provided certain conditions or demands are met. Therefore, the counterinsurgent objective includes an assessment of the postconflict societal order we seek: it is not simply a matter of crushing the insurgents. As insurgency is a political, social, and military problem, military measures alone cannot succeed in this aim. Rather, the role of military forces is to dominate the environment and reduce the energy in the insurgency, taking it "off the boil" so as to allow other elements of national power to become effective. Thus, military force alone can only contain and disrupt insurgent systems—but this is an essential first step in allowing other nonmilitary measures to succeed.

Defining "normality" is essential in this context. Different societies exhibit different normal, chronic levels of armed violence.[74] Victory does not demand that we reduce violence to zero or establish peace and prosperity in absolute terms. It only demands that we return the system to what is normal—for that society, in that region, in this period in history—so that the society can reestablish normal preinsurgency patterns of interaction.

This operational concept does not preclude change in societal order: for example, although the British won the Malayan Emergency, the people of Malaya still gained independence. The British defined victory as resistance to Communist takeover and transition to a self-governing democratic state rather than retention of Malaya as a colony in the British Empire. However, such societal change had to be achieved through peaceful, constitutional means. By contrast, the Dutch in Indonesia in 1945–49 sought to retain the Netherlands East Indies as a colonial possession—their definition of victory precluded peaceful societal change and gave insurgents no constitutional path to redress their grievances.[75]

In a global insurgency, this operational concept requires that individual counterinsurgency campaigns be conducted so as to reduce the energy level in the global jihad. It also demands that legitimate Muslim aspirations be addressed to provide a constitutional path and that military forces adopt an enabling rather than a dominant role. Military force is still essential and will inevitably, from time to time, be applied in large-scale counterinsurgency-style tasks, not limited counterterrorist operations. Nonetheless, military force can only create preconditions for nonmilitary measures to succeed. Practical insights arising from this operational concept are as follows:

A Global "CORDS Program"

As I discussed in Part 1, the enemy in this war comprises a multifarious, intricately ramified web of dependencies that—like a tribal group or crime family—exists for its own sake. This network behaves more like a traditional Middle Eastern patronage network than a mass guerrilla movement. The jihad is what the network does; it is not the network itself.

As the organic systems model of insurgency shows, disrupting this network demands that we target the links (the web of dependencies itself) and the energy flows (inputs and outputs that pass between actors in the jihad) as the primary method of disrupting the system. An exclusive focus on attacking the boundary interactions of the system—that is, attempting to stop terrorist attacks or catch terrorists themselves—simply imposes an evolutionary dynamic that causes the insurgent system to develop better means of attack.

This concept of "delinking" is central to the disaggregation strategy. De-linking would result in actions to target the insurgent infrastructure that would resemble the unfairly maligned (but highly effective) Vietnam-era CORDS program. Contrary to popular mythology, this was largely a civilian aid and development program, supported by targeted military pacification operations and intelligence activity to disrupt the Viet Cong infrastructure. A global CORDS program (including the other key elements that formed part of the successful Vietnam CORDS system) would provide a useful starting point for considering how disaggregation would develop in practice.[76]

Common Strategic Understanding

As noted, the world system does not enable the existence of an effective global Supremo for counterinsurgency. But the role of a Supremo in classical counterinsurgency was to generate unity of effort. The same effect can be generated through a common strategic understanding, a common diagnosis of the problem, and common "best practice."

A first step toward a common understanding for the present campaign is to clearly articulate its nature. This allows governments to discuss the problem in common language, adopting local measures that become mutually reinforcing at the systemic level. To borrow a phrase from the environmental movement (another attempt to coordinate action on a diffuse organic problem by disparate governments), a common understanding would allow us to "think globally, act locally."

For political reasons, no government has acknowledged this campaign as a war against a global Islamist insurgency. This unwillingness to speak the enemy's name creates ambiguities and apparent policy contradictions. As a result, much of the world's population remains unconvinced of the seriousness of the Islamist threat, confused by the generic description of "terrorism," or suspicious of Washington's strategic agenda. Without popular support, no democracy can sustain protracted irregular warfare against a diffuse enemy—so convincing populations of the threat is critical. This demands vastly increased, nuanced, and effective strategic information operations: a nontrivial issue. Victory (as over the Comintern) will come through the democracies' ability to outbid and outlast the appeal of extremist ideology—military measures are merely holding actions in a protracted civilizational confrontation.

A Constitutional Path

As shown, a key counterinsurgency technique is to counter the grievances on which insurgent systems feed, denying energy to their recruiting and propaganda subsystems and ultimately marginalizing them as irrelevant to the population's aspirations. For example, in Malaya the British countered the Communist appeal to nationalism by setting a date for independence and commencing a transition to self-government. Over time, this marginalized the insurgents—people saw their grievances being peacefully addressed anyway, so why support the insurgency? Similarly, strong anti-Communist trade unions were a key development in the Cold War. These provided a "constitutional path" for workers seeking a better life and legitimized their aspirations, while delegitimizing the Communist revolutionary methods. Instead of a stark choice between revolution and poverty, trade unions gave workers a constitutional path—accessing justice through the labor movement without recourse to (or need for) extralegal means.

A constitutional path is needed, but lacking, to counter global jihad: most measures so far have been "all stick and no carrot." For Muslims in much of the world, there is no middle way: only a stark choice between jihad and acceptance of permanent second-class citizenship in a world order dominated by the West and infused with anti-Islamic values. For many self-respecting Muslims, the choice of jihad rather than surrender is both logical and honorable. So a constitutional path is critical—one that addresses Muslim aspirations without recourse to jihad, thus marginalizing Islamists and robbing insurgent systems of energy.

It would require a separate chapter to articulate such a path in detail. But in outline, key elements might include exporting the Malaysian and Turkish approaches to representative government in Muslim societies; addressing the role of women, education, and governance; and building effective representational bodies for the world's Muslims. Measures like the Middle East Free Trade Zone, the Broader Middle East and North Africa Initiative, and the United Nations' Arab Human Development Report represent moves in the right direction, but these ideas have so far been ineffectual for a range of reasons. Their limited funding and haphazard administration suggests an uncertain commitment on the part of the United States—implying the need for greater commitment to this aspect of the "War on Terrorism."[77]

Understanding the "System in Focus"

As shown, the global jihad is a series of nested interactions—insurgencies within insurgencies and networks within networks. So it is important to understand which is the "system in focus": an individual group, a localized insurgency, a regional jihad, or a global insurgency as a whole. Most analysis of Iraq treats the problem in terms of single-country classical counterinsurgency. That is, the "system in focus" for most analysts is the Iraqi theatre, and links to the broader Middle Eastern jihad or global insurgency are secondary. Lacking a complex systems perspective, some analysts appear to assume that the "system in focus" is all that exists, whereas (as shown) the true danger of individual jihad theatres is their aggregated effect at the systemic level as a global insurgency.

This is important because counterinsurgency must be conducted with an eye to its long-term systemic effects. Measures that are highly effective in one theatre may simply export problems to other regions or breed more insurgents for subsequent iterations of the insurgent cycle. For example, Western support for anti-Soviet mujahideen in Afghanistan in the 1980s made good sense if the system in focus was the Soviet-Afghan War alone. But the boost to Islamists arising from victory in Afghanistan proved highly dangerous at the systemic, long-term level. Likewise, counterinsurgency in Iraq must be evaluated in terms of global jihad, not just the Iraqi theatre.

Applying a strategy of disaggregation changes the system in focus. For example, activities such as theatre security cooperation (training teams working with regional military and police forces), along with military humanitarian aid and assistance programs, governance support operations, and military diplomacy have only a tenuous connection to classical counterterrorism actions. They are not part of a case-based approach to catching the perpetrators of terrorism. But they are key elements in an overall counterinsurgency strategy such as disaggregation, which seeks to deny sanctuary, disrupt networks, build the capabilities of regional neighbors, and interdict the links between key players in the global jihad. This implies a substantially different approach to the activities and control of attachés, training teams, and military aid missions under a theatre security cooperation approach than is currently the case.

The Insurgent Ecosystem

Another insight is that insurgencies are part of larger "insurgent ecosystems." In classical counterinsurgency, the ecosystem was the nation-state. In globalized insurgency, the ecosystem is all of world society. Therefore, liberal democracies are inside, not outside, the jihad ecosystem. We are part of the system of global jihad—we provide inputs that sustain the insurgency, we are affected by its boundary interactions and outputs, and we are actors in the broader environment.

This means that the adaptational dynamic ("survival of the fittest") also applies to us: we must adapt and evolve faster and better than the Islamists in order to survive. Our armies must be flexible, versatile, and agile, but adaptability goes far beyond the military sphere: our whole approach to counterinsurgency must be characterized by continual innovation.

It also means that methods that treat the enemy primarily as a target set—seeking to destroy key nodes and hoping this will unhinge the insurgency—cannot work. These approaches (typical of conventional war-fighting) address the insurgency's boundary interactions, links, and nodes but do not interdict inputs or outputs. Instead, we must focus on taking the insurgency off the boil by denying it energy, thus reducing the coherence and stability of Islamist movements and allowing nonmilitary measures (governance, development, the constitutional middle way identified earlier) to have an effect.

This means that a decapitation strategy aimed at eliminating key Islamist leaders will not work here. Decapitation has rarely succeeded in counterinsurgency, with good reason—efforts to kill or capture insurgent leaders inject energy into the system by generating grievances and causing disparate groups to coalesce (consider the unifying effect on Somali clans of U.S. efforts to capture Mohamed Farah Aided in Somalia). Moreover, although leaders are key nodes, their destruction would do little damage to the linked but separate groups in the global jihad. Rather, their martyrdom would inject energy into the system and allow a new class of leaders to emerge. System dynamics would also predict that because these new leaders would emerge at a time of great evolutionary pressure on the insurgency, processes of natural selection might well generate even more capable and adaptive leaders than at present.*

Tailored Systems Analysis

The need for detailed, situation-specific analysis of each counterinsurgency has been discussed. Systems analysis shows that there is no universally applicable template for counterinsurgency: on the contrary, the better a method is, the sooner it is out of date. So constant innovation is needed, and this must largely be generated "from the bottom up," by practitioners in day-to-day contact with the insurgents. Each local counterinsurgency must be based on a detailed, local analysis—allied to a systemic perspective on how each theatre affects the global jihad.

---

* AUTHOR'S NOTE (2009): In practice, as events have shown since this paper was first written, counter-network operations (using the F3EA model discussed earlier) have actually been highly effective in targeting midlevel operatives and local insurgent leaders. In retrospect, I believe I underestimated the value of this approach in disrupting and collapsing local-level insurgencies and in keeping senior Al Qa'eda leaders on the run, looking over their shoulders, and dealing with issues of day-to-day survival, thus giving them a bandwidth problem in terms of planning and carrying out attacks. New intelligence, targeting, and operational techniques combined with an extremely impressive process of adaptation and very significant technological innovations have contributed to this success. Nevertheless, as the same F3EA operations have shown, killing of the most senior insurgent leaders (for example, Abu Musab al-Zarqawi of Al Qa'eda in Iraq, or Nek Muhammad or Beitullah Mashud of the Pakistani Taliban) can take enormous resources and lots of time yet ultimately have little strategic effect on the performance of an insurgency. And this is the best-case outcome: collateral damage arising from decapitation strikes can also alienate populations, increase militancy, create blood feuds, and ultimately do more harm than good. Targeting the most senior leaders also removes the very leadership cadre of an insurgency with whom any end to a conflict will ultimately need to be negotiated and replaces them with younger, more militant, and sometimes more effective subordinates. Rather, targeting midlevel targets—planners, financiers, trainers, recruiters, cell leaders and so on—seems to be the most effective approach; it disrupts the insurgency's operations significantly and creates a sense of futility and potentially a willingness to negotiate in the minds of senior insurgent leaders but ultimately leaves those senior leaders alive and in position, precisely so that they can negotiate an end to their own movement on terms favorable to us. Thus the "manhunting" method has value, but as a tactical disruption tool more than as a strategic silver bullet.

This demands intelligence collection and analysis capability at the lowest possible tactical level. Local commanders must have the means to analyze and understand their own environment, diagnose key local system elements and the best means of attacking them, and communicate this understanding across the entire civil-military organization. Higher commanders must generate unity of effort through a common understanding of the campaign and broad situational awareness of the overall conflict.

Specific past techniques may still work—for example, combined action platoons working with Iraqi Civil Defense Corps irregulars may be highly useful in Iraq.* But such techniques must be applied with a full understanding of *why* they worked in the past, what specific conditions contribute to success, and how they can be applied in today's environment. We must also be prepared to discard techniques as soon as their effectiveness wanes, not clinging (for the sake of familiarity) to techniques to which the enemy has already adapted.

Cultural Capability

The final insight concerns culture. As we have seen, cultures—organizational, ethnic, national, religious, or tribal—provide protocols for system behavior. Cultures determine how each actor in an insurgent ecosystem perceives the actions of the others and generates unperceived cultural boundaries that limit each actor's freedom of action. Cultures may differ radically between areas within an insurgent theatre or among different groups in it. Culture imbues otherwise random or apparently senseless acts with meaning and subjective rationality. Hence, it may be impossible for counterinsurgent forces to perceive the true meaning of insurgent actions, or to influence populations and their perceptions without access to local culture. Many links, boundaries, and boundary interactions in insurgent systems—and virtually all the grievances and energies that circulate within them—are culturally determined. Culture is intimately connected with language, since humans use language to make sense of reality and communicate meaning. Therefore, in counterinsurgency, linguistic and cultural competence is a critical combat capability. It generates a permissive operating environment and enables access to cultural centers of gravity, situational awareness, and interaction with the population.

---

* AUTHOR'S NOTE (2009): Indeed, variations on this approach proved highly effective during the "Surge" in 2007 through the Sons of Anbar and later the Sons of Iraq program, which created highly effective local irregular security forces under coalition, and ultimately Iraqi government control and contributed to the near-destruction of Al Qaeda in Iraq.

This is true of both traditional and globalized counterinsurgency. But systems dynamics demonstrates that in globalized counterinsurgency, security forces must work at several cultural levels simultaneously. For example, forces in Iraq must understand local Iraqi culture, jihadist organizational culture, cultural pressure points for tribal and sectarian groups in the population, cultural triggers for opinion in neighboring countries, and the culture of foreign fighters in Iraq. They must also understand both the implications of actions within Iraq in culturally different theatres elsewhere and the overall systemic culture of the global jihad. Identifying cultural pressure points of this kind is critical in generating deterrence and influence against insurgents.[78]

Linguistic and cultural competence must exist at several levels within a counterinsurgent force:

- **Cultural awareness.** Everyone in the force, regardless of role, must have a high degree of cultural awareness. This demands basic language training, understanding of cultural norms and expectations, and—most important—understanding of how local populations and insurgents think. A recent U.S. Army proposal (*Every Soldier a Sensor*) explicitly recognizes that in counterinsurgency most actionable information and most key interactions with the population present themselves at the individual soldier level.[79] Systems dynamics predicts that progress in counterinsurgency will reflect the aggregated effects of thousands of nested individual interactions—experience "on the ground" by practitioners confirms this. Importantly, noncombat elements (truck drivers, medics, engineers) are as, if not more, important than combat forces in terms of their interactions with the population.
- **Cultural understanding.** Planners, intelligence personnel, civil-military operations teams, and those working with local security forces need higher levels of cultural understanding. This involves more advanced language capability and the ability to "fit in" with local groups and to perform effectively while immersed in local culture. Training teams or military advisers working with local forces must achieve this level of understanding, which covers much more than simple military issues.[80] The capabilities required are akin to those of Rudyard Kipling's Colonel Creighton—a deep knowledge of language, ethnography, geography, and history.[81] The U.S. military currently seeks this level of capability through the Foreign Area Officer system. Australian forces have traditionally relied on intensive linguistic, area, and cultural training for selected personnel;[82] but (rather

than maintaining a separate career stream) these personnel are mainstream officers whose knowledge permeates the wider force.*

- **Cultural leverage.** The highest level of cultural capability is the ability to use culture to generate leverage within an insurgent system. Commanders working with local community and government leaders need such capability. Personnel working in the intelligence and covert action fields and in key nation-building programs also need this knowledge. At this level, individuals are bilingual and bicultural and can exploit cultural norms and expectations to generate operational effects. The "political officers" of the north-west frontier of British India, Edward Lansdale's performance in the Philippines Insurgency of the 1950s, and T. E. Lawrence's operations with the Arab Revolt are examples of this capability. Indeed, Lawrence's comment that "Arabs could be swung on an idea as on a cord" reflects this level of cultural competence.[83] No professional army will ever be able to generate more than a small number of individuals with this capability, but only a small number are needed—provided they are developed and employed effectively. This is difficult within the culture of regular armies, and such officers are likely to be mavericks: "Renaissance men" in the mold of Lawrence, Orde Wingate, or Roger Trinquier.

Because of the processes of cultural evolution and adaptation identified earlier, cultural capability must be maintained in an up-to-date fashion, taking into account current developments in a given theatre. Regular refresher and continuation training for key personnel is essential.

Whatever the cultural capability of a deployed force, it will never be able to dispense with extensive partnership with, and reliance on, local populations and security forces. Only locals have the access to the population and deep understanding of a particular insurgency that is necessary to combat it.[84] Conversely, those who are directing efforts to counter the global insurgency must understand issues across the breadth of the jihad—so key personnel need cultural agility. As noted, there is a distinct jihadist

---

* AUTHOR'S NOTE (2009): Since this was written, through the initiative of dedicated personnel within the U.S. Department of Defense, we have seen the creation and fielding of "human terrain system" teams that provide cultural and area knowledge, insight and advice to military commanders. Despite the rather infelicitous name, these teams have proven highly effective in both Afghanistan and Iraq, contributing to the saving of hundreds, perhaps thousands, of local civilian and Coalition lives through a reduction in violence and improved ability for security forces to cooperate with local societies to protect them against insurgents and terrorists. My colleagues Montgomery McFate, Andrea Jackson, Patti Morrisey, and Steve Fondocaro played key roles in developing and fielding this innovative capability.

culture. Jihadists do not operate in a completely savage and random fashion. Indeed, there are very specific, self-imposed limitations on their operational and targeting methods. These cannot be discussed here, but understanding and exploiting these limitations is important in countering global insurgency. It should go without saying, but unfortunately does not, that every key operator in the "War on Terrorism" needs a comprehensive understanding of Islam, Islamist ideology, and Muslim culture. Achieving this would be an important step toward victory.

Measures of Effectiveness

For disaggregation to be a practical strategy, it requires measures of effectiveness: indicators that allow progress in this war to be tracked at the strategic, operational, and tactical levels and—most important—to provide an understanding of the key pressure points in the global jihad and the effect that disaggregation is having on these pressure points.

In classical counterinsurgency, measures of effectiveness have always been a topic of debate. For example, as early as 1965, Bernard Fall argued that the United States was applying the wrong measures of effectiveness to the war in Vietnam. Counterinsurgency effectiveness was measured in numbers of guerrillas killed and amount of territory controlled. But Fall showed that the number of village chiefs being assassinated, the rate of tax compliance in rural areas, and the take-up rate of civil assistance programs were actually far more accurate indicators of insurgent activity.[85]

Detailed, theatre-specific measures of effectiveness are needed for disaggregation in each theatre of the global jihad. These will vary from country to country and will change over time as the insurgency develops. Thus, developing indicators and deriving measures of effectiveness from them will be an ongoing effort for intelligence staffs. In general terms, however, measures of effectiveness are likely to relate to the following aspects of the jihad:

- **Economic activity.** At the tactical, operational, or strategic level, economic activity is an excellent indicator of progress in counterinsurgency. Spontaneous local trade, industry, and economic development (as distinct from economic aid) are only possible in an atmosphere of relative stability and security. Experience of Islamist insurgency in North Africa, the Middle East, and Southeast Asia has shown that a revival of local economic activity in a given area indicates a lessening of insurgent influence.[86] At the strategic level, a revival of free trade and industrial interdependence within a given region is a key measure of effectiveness.

- **Spontaneous intelligence.** Intelligence generated spontaneously from the population is a key indicator of population confidence in security forces and in the long-term viability of the counterinsurgency effort. As such, "walk-ins" or other unsolicited informants are a key indicator of progress. In Northern Ireland, Cyprus, and Malaya such spontaneous intelligence—often coupled with defection and surrender of insurgents—proved a reliable measure of effectiveness. Similarly, in the global jihad, an increase in "walk-ins," surrenders, defections, and spontaneous informants is a key indicator of progress.

- **Moderate Muslim voices.** The jihadist worldview is not the only or indeed the dominant outlook in the Islamic world. There are many millions of moderate Muslims, but at present many feel afraid to express their views. An increase in the willingness of moderate Muslims to speak out is a key measure of the effectiveness of disaggregation. In this context, "moderate" does not mean pro-Western. Rather, it means antijihadist. Moreover, what Muslims say to each other matters much more than what they say to the Western, secular world. Thus, measuring the extent of moderate Muslim influence requires careful analysis and understanding, but such moderate influence is a solid indicator of progress in countering global jihad.

- **Initiative.** The final measure of effectiveness relates to which side holds the initiative in the war. Arguably, the West currently holds the strategic initiative through its actions in Iraq and Afghanistan. But at the tactical level, the jihadists are currently initiating the majority of incidents. A shift in the balance of initiation—away from incidents initiated by insurgents and toward incidents initiated by security forces—is an excellent indicator of progress.

CONCLUSIONS

You must know everything you can about military power, and
you must also understand the limits of military power. You must
understand that few of the problems of our time have...been solved
by military power alone.
—John F. Kennedy (1961)

This chapter represents only a first tentative step toward rebuilding counterinsurgency theory into an effective tool for global counterinsurgency. Nevertheless, the analysis does demonstrate that a complex systems approach, that treats insurgencies as organic systems can produce new insights and practical recommendations for the "War on Terrorism." The need now is for an in-depth, extended study of current operations that reassesses them in the light of this model and produces specific policy options for government and the military.

If there is one key message that emerges from this study, it is that Western democracies *are* capable of winning the "War on Terrorism"— provided that "victory" is defined appropriately. Our Islamist enemies are neither inscrutable nor invincible; their methods have flaws that can be exploited; and global jihad cannot ultimately offer the world's Muslim population the security, prosperity, and social justice that can only come through good governance at the level of nation-states. Therefore, victory in the long term is both possible and likely. But there are enormous challenges on the way. As counterinsurgency practitioners, soldiers and intelligence operators must rebuild their mental model of this conflict, redesign their classical counterinsurgency and counterterrorism methods to meet the challenge of new conditions, and continually develop innovative and culturally effective approaches. Because Iraq is now the center of gravity, the key focus of the global jihad, Iraq is the place to start. But the process must go well beyond Iraq to ultimately transform our whole approach to countering the global Islamist insurgency.

NOTES

PREFACE

1. For historical studies that trace the origins of insurgency and counterinsurgency back into earliest antiquity, see Walter Laqueur, *Guerrilla Warfare: A Historical and Critical Study*; Robert Asprey, *War in the Shadows: The Guerrilla in History*; Robert Taber, *War of the Flea*, and John Ellis, *From the Barrel of a Gun: A History of Guerrilla, Revolutionary and Civil Warfare from the Romans to the Present*.

2. Meredith Reid Sarkees, "The Correlates of War Data on War: An Update to 1997," *Conflict Management and Peace Science* 18, 1 (2000): 123–144.

3. Version 3.0 of the Correlates of War Inter-State War dataset identifies interstate wars and their participants between 1816 and 1997. "To be classified as an inter-state war, at least two participants in sustained combat should qualify as members of the interstate system and there should be at least 1000 battle related fatalities among all of the system members involved. A state involved is regarded as a participant if it incurs a minimum of 100 fatalities *or* has 1000 armed personnel engaged in fighting." (http://correlatesofwar.org/)

INTRODUCTION

1. U.S. Army and U.S. Marine Corps, *Counterinsurgency*, FM 3-24/MCWP 3-33.5 (December 2006), 1–2.

2. Ibid.

3. David J. Morris, "The Big Suck," *Virginia Quarterly Review* (winter 2007): online at http://www.vqronline.org/articles/2007/winter/morris-jarhead-underground/.

4. For a detailed but brief description of this operations-intelligence fusion approach, see Michael T. Flynn, Rich Juergens, and Thomas L. Cantrell, "Employing ISR: SOF Best Practices," *Joint Force Quarterly*, iss. 50 (third quarter 2008): 56–61.

5. Ben Shepherd, *War in the Wild East: The German Army and Soviet Partisans* (Cambridge Mass.: Harvard University Press, 2004), 118–119.

6. Ibid.

7. Ibid.

8. Laqueur, quoted in Leonid Grenkevich, *The Soviet Partisan Movement, 1941–44* (London: Frank Cass, 1994), 111.

9. Mark Mazower, *Hitler's Empire: How the Nazis Ruled Europe* (New York: Penguin, 2008).

10. Robert M. Citino, personal communication, conversation at Military History Center, University of North Texas, 22 October 2009.

11. This definition of "center of gravity," echoing Clausewitz, paraphrases Department of Defense, *DoD Dictionary of Military and Associated Terms*, U.S. Joint Publication 1-02 Washington D.C.: 2008).

12. Roger Trinquier, *Modern Warfare: A French View of Counterinsurgency* (London: Pall Mall Press, 1964), online at http://carl.army.mil/resources/csi/trinquier/trinquier.asp.

13. T. E. Lawrence, "The Science of Guerrilla Warfare," in *Encyclopaedia Britannica*, 14th ed. (London, 1929), online at http://pegasus.cc.ucf.edu/~eshaw/lawrence.htm.

14. Erin M. Simpson, "Politics, Popular Support and the Paucity of Victory in Third-party Counterinsurgency Campaigns" (Ph.D. diss., Harvard University, forthcoming 2010).

15. "In war, a grand strategist, general or statesman, does not fix his final object at the destruction of the enemy, which is but a means of attaining it, but at establishing a condition from out of which a better peace can be evolved." J. F. C. Fuller, *The Generalship of Ulysses S. Grant* (London: J. Murray, 1929), 407.

INTRODUCTION TO "TWENTY-EIGHT ARTICLES"

1. Headquarters Department of the Army, *Counterinsurgency Operations*, Field Manual Interim 3-07, 22 October 2004. This interim field manual was the U.S. Army's first attempt to produce viable field doctrine for counterinsurgency, mainly focused on operations in Iraq. It was a heroic effort by a small group of officers, led by Lieutenant Colonel Jan Horvath, working quickly under difficult circumstances, to compile and adapt the lessons and observations of an earlier counterinsurgency era and get these lessons out to commanders who needed them in the field. Horvath and his team subsequently played a major role in the writing of FM 3–24 and in the production of joint service doctrine for counterinsurgency.

2. See Janine A. Davidson, *Lifting the Fog of Peace: How Americans Learned to Fight Modern War* (Ann Arbor: University of Michigan Press, forthcoming).

3. John A. Nagl, *Learning to Eat Soup with a Knife: Counterinsurgency Lessons from Malaya and Vietnam* (Chicago: University of Chicago Press, 2005).

4. Timothy T. Lupfer, *The Dynamics of Doctrine: The Changes in German Tactical Doctrine During the First World War*, Leavenworth Papers no. 4 (Leavenworth, Tex.: U.S. Army Command and General Staff College, 1981).

5. This group included Scott Cuomo, Brian Donlon, Dave Buffaloe, Andrew Exum, Travis Patriquin (tragically killed in December 2006 in Ramadi), and many others across all services.

6. Including H. R. McMaster in Iraq, John "Mick" Nicholson in Afghanistan, Robert M. Cassidy, John Nagl, Chris Cavoli, and William "Mac" McCallister.

7. Including but by no means limited to Bruce Hoffman, Bill Rosenau, Angel Rabasa, Alan Vick, Russell Glenn, and Steve Hosmer.

8. This point was made by Janine Davidson in "Aylwin-Foster Misunderstands Nagl's Army," *Military Review*, January 2006, online at http://findarticles.com/p/articles/mi_m0PBZ/is_1_86/ai_n16346168/?tag=content;col1.

9. Nigel Aylwin-Foster, "Changing the Army for Counterinsurgency Operations," *Military Review* (November–December 2005): 2–15.

10. John A. Nagl, personal communication (March 2006).

11. William S. Wallace, letter to the editor, *Military Review* (March 2006): online at http://www.highbeam.com/doc/1G1-145473379.html.

12. T. E. Lawrence, "Twenty-seven Articles," *Arab Bulletin* (20 August 1917); www.usma .edu/dmi/IWmsgs/The27ArticlesofT.E.Lawrence.pdf.

13. David Howarth, *Waterloo: A Near Run Thing* (Moreton-in-Marsh, Gloucestershire: Windrush Press, 1998), 93.

INTRODUCTION TO "GLOBALIZATION AND THE DEVELOPMENT OF INDONESIAN COUNTERINSURGENCY TACTICS"

1. David J. Kilcullen, "Globalisation and the Development of Indonesian Counterinsurgency Tactics," *Small Wars and Insurgencies* 17, 1 (March 2006): 44–64.

2. David J. Kilcullen, "Political Consequences of Military Operations in Indonesia 1945–99" (Ph.D. diss., University College, University of New South Wales, 2001); http://unsworks.unsw.edu.au/vital/access/manager/Repository/unsworks:3240.

3. Sebestyen L. Gorka presentation to International Special Operations Forces Week conference, Miami, 6 April 2008 (conference notes in the author's possession).

4. Jeffrey Record, *War Comes to Long An: Revolutionary Conflict in a Vietnamese Province* (Berkeley: University of California Press, 1973). Gerald Cannon Hickey, *Village in Viet Nam* (New Haven: Yale University Press, 1966). Karl D. Jackson, *Traditional Authority, Islam and Rebellion: A Study of Indonesian Political Behavior* (Berkeley: University of California Press, 1980).

5. For a study of the forward school of Australian strategy, see David J. Kilcullen, "Australian Statecraft: The Challenge of Aligning Policy with Strategic Culture," *Security Challenges* 3, 4 (November 2007): 45–65.

6. Ibid., 56.

3. GLOBALIZATION AND THE DEVELOPMENT OF INDONESIAN COUNTERINSURGENCY TACTICS

1. "Islamist" in this chapter refers to political movements (violent or nonviolent) that seek imposition of sharia law and the adoption of Islamic rather than secular governmental models.

2. This "victory" was the destruction of Darul Islam's armed wing and the defeat of its insurgent campaign. Darul Islam became an underground subversive movement that lay relatively dormant until the 1970s, but it has since given rise to the Jema'ah Islamiyah terrorist group and several insurgent groups in post-Suharto Indonesia.

3. David J. Kilcullen, "Political Consequences of Military Operations in Indonesia 1945–99" (Ph.D. diss., University College, University of New South Wales, 2001).

4. C. Robequain, *Malaya, Indonesia, Borneo and the Philippines* (London: Longmans, Green and Co., 1958).

5. The West Java case study area comprised the Bandung valley on the west, the Garut valley on the east, and the intervening portions of the Priangan highlands.

6. For the seminal fieldwork on this issue, conducted in the 1960s, see Karl D. Jackson, *Traditional Authority, Islam and Rebellion: A Study of Indonesian Political Behavior* (Berkeley: University of California Press, 1980).

7. P. M. H. Groen, "Dutch Armed Forces and the Decolonization of Indonesia: The Second Police Action (1948–49), A Pandora's Box," *War and Society* 4, 1 (1986).

8. See, for example, Netherlands Expeditionary Forces Intelligence Service Situation Map, Kaart Behorende bij Pol. Verslag, maand January 1949, archives of Sectie Militaire Geschiedenis, Koninklijk Landmachtstaf (Military History Section, Dutch Army General Staff), The Hague.

9. This incident is depicted in a diorama at the Musium Mandala Wangsit Siliwangi, Bandung.

10. N. Notosusanto, *The National Struggle and the Armed Forces in Indonesia*, 2nd ed. (Jakarta: Pusjarah ABRI, 1980).

11. Dinas Sejarah TNI-AD, *Penumpasan Pemberontakan DI/TII S. M. Kartusuwiryo Di Jawa Barat* (Jakarta: Dinas Sejad, 1985), 80 (my translation from the Indonesian).

12. A. Sjarifuddin, *Kisah Kartusuwirjo dan Menjerahannja* (Soerabaja: Penerbitan Grip, 1962), 17 (my translation from the original Indonesian).

13. A. H. Nasution, *Fundamentals of Guerilla Warfare and the Indonesian Defence System Past and Present*, 2nd ed. (Jakarta: Puspen AD, 1952).

14. D. S. Lev, *The Transition to Guided Democracy: Indonesian Politics 1957–59*, Modern Indonesia Project (Ithaca, N.Y.: Cornell University, 1966).

15. This campaign plan emerged from a document entitled "Rencana Pokok 2.1" [Outline plan 2.1], which was produced by a specially constituted team in the headquarters of the Siliwangi Division in Bandung in late 1958; Dinas Sejarah TNI-AD, *Penumpasan Pemberontakan DI/TII S. M. Kartusuwiryo Di Jawa Barat* (Jakarta: Dinas Sejad, 1985), 129.

16. Ibid. (my translation from the original Indonesian).

17. Netherlands Expeditionary Forces Intelligence Service methodology for analysis of guerrilla activity divided regions into "regularly administered," "contested," and "controlled by guerrilla groups [*strijdgroepen*]." For a detailed discussion of Netherlands Expeditionary Forces Intelligence Service methods see R. Boerhout, and S. Lindhout, *NEFIS en KNIL in Indonesië* (Ph.D. diss., University of Amsterdam, 1982).

18. Suhanda, interview by David Kilcullen, 12 December 1996, quoted in Kilcullen, "Political Consequences of Military Operations in Indonesia," 71.

19. The following description of *pagar betis* is based on interviews, fieldwork notes, and archival material gathered during the West Java case study. The method is discussed in outline in Jackson, *Traditional Authority*, and Dinas Sejarah, *Penumpasan*, as well as in numerous postoperational reports held in the archives of the Musium Mandala Wangsit Siliwangi, Bandung.

20. See Dinas Sejarah, *Penumpasan*; Dinas Sejarah, Daerah Militer, VI/Siliwangi, *Siliwangi dari Masa ke Masa* (Bandung: 1979); Imran, Amin *Sedjarah Perkembangan Angkatan Darat*, Jakarta, n.d. and Saleh As'ad Djamhari (1971) *Ichtisar Sedjarah Perdjuangan ABRI (1945– Sekarang)* (Pusjarah: ABRI, Jakarta).

21. Dinas Sejarah, 1979.

22. See detailed terrain studies in Kilcullen, "Political Consequences of Military Operations in Indonesia," 213.

23. For a detailed description of the Indonesian army's unconventional operations in the lead-up to invasion see J. Dunn, *East Timor: The Balibo Incident in Perspective*, Australian Centre for Independent Journalism (Sydney: University of Technology, 1995) and H. Subroto, *Saksi Mata Perjuangan Integrasi Timor Timur* (Jakarta: Pustaka Sinar Harapan, 1996).

24. A. Magalhães, Barbedo de *East Timor: Indonesian Occupation and Genocide* (Oporto: Oporto University, 1992).

25. Kilcullen, "Political Consequences of Military Operations in Indonesia," 113.

26. Ibid., 114.

27. For accounts of this period see James Dunn, *Timor: A People Betrayed* (Sydney, ABC Books, 1996) and Andrew McMillan, *Death in Dili* (Rydalmere NSW, Sceptre Books, 1992).

28. See my fieldnotes in Kilcullen, "Political Consequences of Military Operations in Indonesia," 146 and C. O. Schuster, *East Timor Militias: Overview and Assessment* (Hawaii: Virtual Information Center, Asia Pacific Center for Security Studies, 1999).

29. Kilcullen, "Political Consequences of Military Operations in Indonesia."

30. Dunn, *Timor*, 304.

31. Kilcullen, "Political Consequences of Military Operations in Indonesia," 119.

32. Consider the role of French forces in the decisive Yorktown, Campaign of 1781 during the American War of Independence and the cooperation of British expeditionary forces with Spanish irregulars in the Peninsula campaign.

33. For example Lord Byron, who died on campaign with Greek irregulars against the Ottomans.

34. Mao Tse-Tung, *On Guerrilla Warfare*, quoted in Azzam Ibrahim, "Conceptualisation of Guerrilla Warfare," *Small Wars & Insurgencies*, 15, no. 3 (2004), 118.

35. Senior Indonesian officer (who wishes to remain anonymous), personal communication, Jakarta, 30 January 2002.

INTRODUCTION TO "REFLECTIONS ON THE ENGAGEMENT AT MOTAAIN BRIDGE"

1. George C. Marshall, ed., *Infantry in Battle* (Washington D.C.: Infantry Journal Inc., 1939).

2. See David Kilcullen, *The Accidental Guerrilla* (New York: Oxford University Press, 2009), chap. 4.

4. REFLECTIONS ON THE ENGAGEMENT AT MOTAAIN BRIDGE

1. U.S. Joint Chiefs of Staff, *Doctrine for Joint Operations*, Joint Publication 3-0, Washington D.C., September 2006 defines a stability operation as "activities conducted... to maintain or reestablish a safe and secure environment, provide essential governmental services, emergency infrastructure reconstruction, and humanitarian relief" (xxi).

2. As of the initial time of writing in early 2000—the area is quiet as of 2009.

5. DEIOKES AND THE TALIBAN

1. Bernard B. Fall, "The Theory and Practice of Insurgency and Counterinsurgency," *Naval War College Review*, U.S. Naval War College, Newport Rhode Island, April 1965.

2. Ibid.

6. COUNTERING GLOBAL INSURGENCY

1. Francis Fukuyama, presentation to Brookings Institution forum, Washington, D.C., 14 May 2003 (summary available at www.brook.edu/dybdocroot/Comm/events/summary20030514.pdf).

2. "The first, the supreme, the most far-reaching act of judgement that the statesman and commander have to make is to establish... the kind of war on which they are embarking; neither mistaking it for, not trying to turn it into, something that is alien to its nature. This is the first of all strategic questions and the most comprehensive." Carl Von Clausewitz, *On War*, trans. Michael Howard and Peter Paret (Princeton: Princeton University Press, 1989), 88.

3. In this chapter, the term "Islamist" describes the extremist, radical form of political Islam practiced by some militant groups, as distinct from "Islamic," which describes the religion of Islam, or "Muslim," which describes those who follow the Islamic religion. In this chapter, the term is used to refer primarily to Al Qa'eda and its allies and affiliates.

4. World Islamic Front, "World Islamic Front Declaration of War against Jews and Crusaders," 23 February 1998, online at http://www.mideastweb.org/osamabinladen2.htm.

5. Muslims disagree over precisely who can issue a fatwa. It is generally agreed, however, that only an Islamic cleric can issue such a religious ruling, and only the legitimate ruler of a Muslim state can issue a call to jihad. In this sense, by issuing a call to jihad in the form of a fatwa, bin Laden was claiming both religious and temporal authority. For a detailed discussion of these issues see Bernard Lewis, *The Crisis of Islam: Holy War and Unholy*

Terror (London: Weidenfeld and Nicolson, 2003), xxv–xxvii and 138–140. See also Peter L. Bergen, *Holy War, Inc: Inside the Secret World of Osama bin Laden* (London: Weidenfeld and Nicolson, 2001).

6. See "The Operations Man: Ayman al-Zawahiri," *Estimate* 14, 17 (September 21, 2001): available online at http://www.theestimate.com/public/092101_profile.html.

7. Ayman al-Zawahiri, "Knights under the Prophet's Banner," *Al-Sharq al-Awsat* newspaper, English edition, 2 December 2001.

8. Lewis, *Crisis of Islam*, xvi.

9. Al-Zawahiri, "Knights under the Prophet's Banner," n.p.

10. See Zachary Abuza, *Muslims, Politics and Violence in Indonesia: An Emerging Islamist-Jihadist Nexus?* (Seattle: National Bureau of Asian Research, 2004). For a slightly different interpretation, see also International Crisis Group, *Jema'ah Islamiyah in Southeast Asia: Damaged but Still Dangerous*, ICG Asia Report no. 863 (Brussels: International Crisis Group, 26 August 2003).

11. See, for example, U.S. State Department, *Patterns of Global Terrorism 2003* (Washington, D.C.: U.S. Government Printing Office, 2004); and *Patterns of Global Terrorism 2004* (Washington, D.C.: U.S. Government Printing Office, 2005).

12. Quotation from http://siteinstitute.org/bin/articles.cgi?ID=publications9504&Category =publications&Subcategory=0.

13. See David Meir-Levi, 2004, "Connecting the South American Terror Dots," *Front Page*, 9 August 2004.

14. SITE Institute, *Developing Trends in Terrorist Strategy, Tactics, Targeting and Propaganda* (Washington D.C.: SITE Institute, September 2004); www.siteinstitute.org.

15. See M. Levitt, "Smeared in Blood, Hezbollah Fingerprints All over Globe," *Australian*, 9 June 2003, and Ely Karmon, *Fight on All Fronts: Hizballah, the War on Terror, and the War in Iraq* (Washington, D.C.: Washington Institute for Near East Policy, 2003).

16. SITE Institute, *Developing Trends*.

17. The five pillars of Islam are confession of faith, prayer, fasting, almsgiving, and pilgrimage.

18. For detailed discussion of the theorists mentioned, see Australian Government, *Transnational Terrorism: The Threat to Australia* (Canberra: Department of Foreign Affairs and Trade, 2004), 21–24.

19. The Qur'an is only read and studied in the original Arabic, and strict Islamic religious instruction worldwide is conducted in Arabic. Vernacular translations of the Qur'an are not considered to be genuine copies of it. Thus, Arabic language is fundamental in the Muslim worldview.

20. See Michael Vlahos, *Terror's Mask: Insurgency within Islam*, occasional chapter (Laurel, Md.: Johns Hopkins University Applied Physics Laboratory, 2002).

21. See U.S. Department of State, Overseas Security Advisory Council, July 2003: *Chechen Female Suicide Bombers*, online at www.homelandsecurityssi.com/.../ChechenFe-maleSuicideBombers.ppt.

22. Australian Government, *Transnational Terrorism*, 43, 94.

23. Sidney Jones, "Terrorism in Southeast Asia: Focus on Jema'ah Islamiyah," address to the Australian Institute for International Affairs, Canberra, 30 November 2004.

24. For a detailed open-source description of Al Qa'eda planning and operational methods see Bergen, *Holy War, Inc.* See also Rohan Gunaratna, *Inside Al Qa'eda* (New York: Columbia University Press, 2002); Jane Corbin, *The Base: Al-Qaeda and the Changing Face of Global Terror* (London: Pocket Books, 2003).

25. Jihad Unspun operates a web site at www.jihadunspun.com.

26. Personal communication, confidential source.

27. For a series of extracts from the captured Al Qa'ida military manual, *Military Studies in the Jihad against the Tyrants*, n.d., see the Federation of American Scientists web site at www.fas.org/irp/world/para/docs.

28. For a series of translated summaries of issues of *Al-Battar*, see http://www.siteinstitute.org/terroristpublications.html.

29. For a detailed discussion of Hezbollah's global reach see Karmon, *Fight on All Fronts*, and Levitt, "Smeared in Blood."

30. Bergen, *Holy War, Inc.*

31. See for example Noam Chomsky, *9–11* (New York: Seven Stories Press, 2001).

32. See David J. Kilcullen, "Political Consequences of Military Operations in Indonesia 1945–99" (Ph.D. diss., University College, University of New South Wales, 2001); and Karl D. Jackson, *Traditional Authority, Islam and Rebellion* (Berkeley: University of California Press, 1980).

33. I am indebted to Ehud Yaari for the term "a ramified web of dependency," which he applied to Hizbullah activities in the Palestinian territories. See Ehud Yaari, "Unit 1800," *Jerusalem Report*, 18 October 2004.

34. For a detailed discussion of this idea, see Vlahos, *Terror's Mask*, passim.

35. This definition and the definition of terrorism that follows were developed specifically for this chapter. Both were derived through synthesizing several definitions used in the Western intelligence and security communities.

36. See Thomas A. Marks, "Ideology of Insurgency: New Ethnic Focus or Old Cold War Distortions?" *Small Wars and Insurgencies* 15, 1 (spring 2004): 107.

37. By contrast, most state terrorism seeks to preserve a status quo and is thus not insurgent in aim.

38. As expressed in statements by Usama bin Laden, particularly World Islamic Front, "World Islamic Front Declaration of War against Jews and Crusaders." See also comments in Paul K. Davis and Brian Michael Jenkins, "A System Approach to Deterring and Influencing Terrorists," *Conflict Management and Peace Science* 21 (2004): 3–15.

39. Usama bin Laden, "Declaration of War against the Americans Occupying the Land of the Two Holy Places (Expel the Infidels from the Arab Peninsula)," 23 August 1996, statement released online; for an English translation see www.geocities.com/dcjarviks//Idler/vIIIn165.html.

40. Web sites like Jihad Unspun (www.jihadunspun.com) are good examples of this tactic.

41. Ajai Sahni, "Social Science and Contemporary Conflicts: The Challenge of Research on Terrorism" 2001, South Asia Terrorism Portal, http://www.satp.org/satporgtp/publication/faultlines/volume9/Article5.htm. See also F. Schorkopf, "Behavioural and Social Science Perspectives on Political Violence," in C. Walter, S. Vöneky, V. Röben, and F. Schorkopf, eds., *Terrorism as a Challenge for National and International Law: Security versus Liberty?* (Berlin: Springer Verlag, 2003), 3–22.

42. Vlahos, *Terror's Mask*.

43. Federation of Malaya, *The Conduct of Anti-terrorist Operations in Malaya*, 3rd ed. (Kuala Lumpur, 1958).

44. I am indebted for this insight to Colonel Jonathan Fighel, deputy director of the International Institute for Counter-Terrorism Policy.

45. On 10 December 2002, Spanish forces intercepted a North Korean ship smuggling Scud-C missiles to Yemen. Actions against North Korean missile technology exports have since been stepped up through the multinational Proliferation Security Initiative. See the State Department web site for this initiative at www.state.gov/t/np/c10390.htm.

46. See Bruce Hoffman, *Insurgency and Counterinsurgency in Iraq* (Santa Monica, Calif.: RAND, 2004), for a discussion of this concept in relation to counterinsurgency in Malaya and Cyprus.

47. See Robert Kagan, *Of Paradise and Power: America and Europe in the New World Order* (New York: Knopf, 2003), and *America and the World: The Crisis of Legitimacy*, Twenty-first Bonython Lecture, Sydney, 9 November 2004; available online at the Centre for Independent Studies, Sydney, www.cis.org.au.

48. For a detailed discussion of Tukhachevskii see David M. Glantz, *Soviet Military Operational Art: In Pursuit of Deep Battle* (London: Frank Cass, 1991). For a broader discussion of the influence of systems thinking on twentieth-century warfare see S. Naveh, *In Pursuit of Military Excellence: The Evolution of Operational Theory* (London: Frank Cass, 1997).

49. See H. R. McMaster, *Dereliction of Duty: Johnson, MacNamara, the Joint Chiefs of Staff, and the Lies That Led to Vietnam* (New York: Harper Perennial, 1998). See also J. D. Kelly and D. J. Kilcullen, "Effects Based Operations: A Critique," *Australian Army Journal* 2, 1 (June 2004): 89–97.

50. Reductionist, or Cartesian, analysis approaches complex problems by reducing them to their component parts, seeking to understand each part, and then reassembling the parts to produce an overall analytical result. The assumption is that the characteristics of the whole can be inferred from the characteristics of the parts, and valid deductions can be drawn about the whole by examining the parts. Military analysis methods—most notably what are known as the military appreciation process (the British commonwealth military planning methodology) and the tactical decision-making process (the U.S. version of the same methodology)—are highly Cartesian.

51. See R. G. Coyle and C. J. Millar, "A Methodology for Understanding Military Complexity: The Case of the Rhodesian Counter-insurgency Campaign," *Small Wars & Insurgencies* 7, 3 (winter 1996): 360–378. See also Michael Beech, *Observing Al Qaeda through the Lens of Complexity Theory* (Carlisle, Pa.: Center for Strategic Leadership, U.S. Army War College, 2004).

52. This definition is based on the definition proposed by the Princeton University cognitive sciences laboratory at http://www.cogsci.princeton.edu/cgi-bin/webwn?stage=1&word=system.

53. See the dictionary entry at www.changezone.co.uk/glossary/.

54. F. Capra, *The Web of Life: A New Scientific Understanding of Living Systems* (New York: Anchor, 1996), 95–99.

55. Tawhid Wa'l Jihad (Monotheism and Jihad), the group headed by Abu Musa al Zarqawi, pledged allegiance to Usama bin Laden on 17 October 2004 and changed its name to Tanzim Qaedat Al-Jihad Fi Bilad Al-Rafidayn (Organization of al-Qaeda for Jihad in the Land of the Two Rivers [i.e., Iraq]).

56. Marc Reuel Gerecht, "The Long, Hard Slog," in *On the Issues*, American Enterprise Institute for Public Policy Research, 14 November 2003, online at www.aei.org/include/pub_print.asp?pubID=19473.

57. I am indebted for this insight to Dr. Mike Brennan, scientific adviser to the Australian Army.

58. See David J. Kilcullen, "Political Consequences of Military Operations in Indonesia 1945–99" (Ph.D. diss., University College, University of New South Wales, 2001), for a discussion of this concept in relation to the Islamic insurgency Darul Islam, the forerunner of Jema'ah Islamiyah.

59. See, among other works, Robert Thompson, *Defeating Communist Insurgency: Lessons from Malaya and Vietnam* (London: Chatto and Windus, 1966).

60. For the idea of using a national power model to analyze the virtual Islamist state I am indebted to Colonel Don Freeman, director of combat development, Australian Army Headquarters Future Land Warfare Branch.

61. See Lester W. Grau, "Guerrillas, Terrorists and Intelligence Analysis," *Military Review* (July-August 2004): 42.

62. See Kilcullen, "Political Consquences of Military Operations in Indonesia," and "The Indonesian Approach to Counterinsurgency," *Journal of the Royal United Services Institution of Australia* 24 (December 2002): 85–94.

63. Ruth Margolies Beitler, "The Intifada: Palestinian Adaptation to Israeli Counterinsurgency Tactics," *Terrorism and Political Violence* 7, 2 (summer 1995): 69.

64. Sidney Jones, "Terrorism in Southeast Asia: Focus on Jema'ah Islamiyah," address to the Australian Institute for International Affairs, Canberra, 30 November 2004, presentation notes in the author's possession.

65. See Vlahos, *Terror's Mask*; see also Steven Metz, "Unlearning Counterinsurgency," *Strategic Studies Institute Newsletter*, November 2004, www.carlisle.army.mil/ssi/newsletter/oped.cfm.

66. For example, Record and Tyrell estimate that "by the early 1970s the war and US and South Vietnamese military and pacification initiatives had crippled (though not destroyed) the original insurgency in the South." Jeffrey Record and W. Andrew Tyrell, *Iraq and Vietnam: Differences, Similarities and Insights* (Carlisle, Pa.: Strategic Studies Institute, 2004), 6, 8.

67. Note that this analysis does not purport to be a comprehensive assessment of Vietnam, merely an evaluation of the relative effectiveness of counterinsurgency measures based on an organic systems analysis.

68. Record and Tyrell, *Iraq and Vietnam*.

69. Kilcullen, "Indonesian Approach to Counterinsurgency."

70. From a Coalition officer in Baghdad (who wishes to remain anonymous), personal communication, October 2004. Insurgents pay approximately US$250 for an attack on Coalition forces, $1,000 for disabling an armored vehicle, and US$25,000 for the capture of a female Coalition soldier. Meanwhile, criminal gangs kidnap Westerners and then auction them to the highest bidding jihad group.

71. Personal communication, in confidence.

72. Jeffrey Record, *Bounding the Global War on Terrorism* (Carlisle, Pa.: Strategic Studies Institute, 2003).

73. Record regards Iraq as a "detour" from attacking Al Qa'eda—a view that this chapter's analysis of systems dynamics in global Islamism does not support. Nevertheless, the general point is valid.

74. For example, when I commanded an infantry company on counterinsurgency operations in East Timor, the rules of engagement initially allowed "armed" civilians to be engaged with lethal force. But in the border region of East Timor, adult males in certain tribal groups always carry spears and large knives. "Normality" did not demand that these people be disarmed—this would have created dozens of firefights and alienated the population. Instead, the decision was made to engage only individuals carrying firearms, not edged weapons. Returning a system to "normality" demands a clear understanding of what is normal—for locals, not security forces.

75. See Kilcullen, "Political Consequences of Military Operations in Indonesia," for a more detailed discussion of Dutch counterinsurgency methods in Indonesia and the subsequent effect of these methods on Islamic insurgents during the Indonesian War of Independence, 1945–49.

76. For detailed discussion on the Phoenix Program and the broader CORDS system, see Steven Metz, *Counterinsurgency: Strategy and the Phoenix of American Capability* (Carlisle, Pa.: Strategic Studies Institute, 1995). See also B. R. Brewington, "Combined Action Platoons: A Strategy for Peace Enforcement" (1996), U.S. Marine Corps Small Wars Center

of Excellence, Quantico VA, available online at www.smallwars.quantico.usmc.mil/search/ Chapters/brewington.pdf; and S. Metz and R. Millen, *Insurgency and Counterinsurgency in the Twenty-first Century: Reconceptualizing Threat and Response* (Carlisle, Pa.: Strategic Studies Institute, 2004).

77. A. Billingsley, "The Native Scene," *Diplomat* (August–September 2004): 23.

78. See Paul K. Davis and Brian Michael Jenkins, "A Systems Approach to Deterring and Influencing Terrorists," *Conflict Management and Peace Science* 21 (2004): 3–15.

79. Association of the United States Army, *ES2: Every Soldier Is a Sensor*, discussion chapter, 10 August 2004.

80. This insight is based on my personal experience as an adviser with Indonesian special forces in 1994 and 1995. However, almost every military adviser, special forces team leader, and training team member whom I have debriefed has raised the same points.

81. Quoted in Hoffman, *Insurgency and Counterinsurgency in Iraq*. For greater detail see Rudyard Kipling, *Kim* (London: Macmillan, 1937), especially Chapter 7.

82. For example, my language course in 1993 included residential fieldwork in the target country, total immersion language training for twelve months, and detailed area studies on history, geography, archaeology, civilization, and military culture. This is the norm for Australian personnel undergoing intensive training in preparation for crosscultural tasks— but these are mainstream rather than specialist personnel.

83. T. E. Lawrence, *Seven Pillars of Wisdom* (London: Jonathan Cape, 1935), 42.

84. For example, in September 2004 I debriefed an intelligence officer who indicated that local Iraqi security forces' insights into the origins of foreign fighters revolutionized that officer's approach to this problem. Such local insights, combined with broader understanding of issues in the global jihad, give powerful synergies.

85. See B. Fall, "The Theory and Practice of Insurgency and Counterinsurgency," *Naval War College Review*, April 1965.

86. See Kilcullen, "Political Consequences of Military Operations in Indonesia," for a detailed description of this process in relation to the Darul Islam insurgency in Indonesia.

INDEX

propaganda links, 179–80
protective equipment, 141
psychology of combat, 144–45
public safety function, 66
purchase of positions, 64

Al Qa'eda
   in Americas, 170
   in Australasia, 171
   bin Laden's authority and, 168
   in Caucasus/European Russia, 172–73
   Comintern and, 185
   competitors/allies/clones of, 182
   doctrine/technique/procedure links and,
      180–81
   in East Africa, 172
   financial links and, 178
   global expansion of, 169
   in Iberian Peninsula/Maghreb, 171
   ideological links and, 175, 177
   local/regional/global players and, 181–82
   in Middle East, 171–72
   operational/planning links and, 179
   as patronage network, 183–84
   propaganda links and, 179–80
   pure intimidation and, 153
   in South/Central Asia, 173–74
   in Southeast Asia, 174
   two phase strategy of, 168
   war declaration by, 167–68
   in Western Europe, 170

RAND Corporation Insurgency Board, 21
rank, as nothing, 34
recognition examples, 102–3
Record, Jeffrey, 78, 211, 212–13
recruitment to desertion rate, 68
reductionist analysis, 193, 236n50
resilient full-spectrum control, 152–54
resources, lack of, 47, 47n17
respect for noncombatants, 4, 5
Romans, techniques of, 7
rule of law
   competitive control theory and, 154
   Taliban, 157–59
Russia, Islamist insurgency, 172–73

salafist, 166
Samarra mosque bombing, 18
school

counterinsurgency, 35n5
   languages, 80
Schoonmaker, Peter, 21
science of complexity, 193
2 RAR. *See* Second Battalion, Royal
      Australian Regiment
Second Battalion, Royal Australian
      Regiment (2 RAR)
   food and, 113
   intelligence picture regarding,
      114–16
   loads carried, personal, 112, 140
   mapping situation of, 116–18
   mission of, 110–12
   Motaain patrol group of, 114–16
   patrol master and, 114
   seizing of border area by, 111–13
   water consumption and, 113
security force indicators
   air/artillery support reliance, 71
   combined action operations, 70
   dismounted operations, 70–71
   driving behavior, 71
   duration of operation, 69
   escalation-of-fire/civilian casualties, 69
   ghost employees proportion, 68
   guilty to innocent detainees ratio, 67
   kill ratio, 66
   kills to wounds/captures ratio, 68
   location at start of firefight, 68–69
   night operations, 69–70
   pattern-setting/telegraphing of moves, 72
   possession of high ground at dawn, 72
   recruitment to desertion rate, 68
   small-unit operations, 70
   win/loss ratio, 67
seek early victories, 38–39, 38n10
self-organization, 195
senior officers
   conventional warfare and, 19
   LOOs and, 54
Sepp, Kalev, 23
setbacks, 39
shared diagnosis, 52–53
sharia law, 157–58, 231n1
Shepherd, Ben, 5–6
SIGACTS. *See* Significant Activities database
Sigit Yuwono
   joint statement with, 130–31
   negotiation with, 128–29